# THE
# **DECODED**
# COMPANY

and fast. We'll show you how any manager in any size organization can personalize each employee's experience, increase emotional engagement, speed up mastery of new skills, and maximize his entire team's potential.

You'll learn about three disruptive Decoded principles that will accelerate your management practice into the twenty-first century:

 **Technology as a Coach and Trainer:** Transform your existing technology into a coach that brings out the best in your people rather than a referee that just yells "offside!" Discover how the technologies that power Amazon, Netflix, Google, and eHarmony can be used to engage, motivate, and train your people.

 **Data as a Sixth Sense:** Learn how UPS, 37signals, Bank of America, and Whole Foods give their people decision-making superpowers by pairing instincts with analytics to gain a perspective that's grounded in data but tempered by experience.

 **Engineered Ecosystems:** Discover the simple culture secrets that brought feedback to Salesforce.com, poured the heart into Starbucks's rebirth, and drive Valve's incredible $3 billion in revenue.

Along the way you'll assess your Decoded score, assemble your Decoded toolbox that can be easily applied in your organization, and explore new metrics for measuring the technology of human accomplishment.

## See you inside!
## LEEROM, AARON, JAY, and RAHAF

# THE
# DECODED
# COMPANY

## Know Your Talent Better than
## You Know Your Customers

Leerom Segal,

Aaron Goldstein,

Jay Goldman,

and Rahaf Harfoush

PORTFOLIO / PENGUIN

PORTFOLIO / PENGUIN
Published by the Penguin Group
Penguin Group (USA) LLC
375 Hudson Street
New York, New York 10014

USA | Canada | UK | Ireland | Australia | New Zealand | India | South Africa | China
penguin.com
A Penguin Random House Company

First published by Portfolio / Penguin, a member of Penguin Group
(USA) LLC, 2014

LIBRARY OF CONGRESS CATALOGING-IN-PUBLICATION DATA
Segal, Leerom.
    The decoded company : know your talent better than you know
your customers / Leerom Segal, Aaron Goldstein, Jay Goldman,
and Rahaf Harfoush.
        pages cm
    Includes bibliographical references and index.
    ISBN 978-1-59184-714-4
  1. Organizational behavior.   2. Employees.   3. Corporations.
4. Big data.   I. Title.
    HD58.7.S435 2014
    658.3'14—dc23
    2013039082

Printed in the United States of America
10  9  8  7  6  5  4  3  2  1

Set in Gotham Book
Designed by Adrian Morris and Jaime Putorti

Leerom

My father, who made me into who I am today, and Peter Cordy, who has been a second father to me.


Aaron

For my loving families, both at home and at work.


Jay

For Bianca and Sophie. You make life worth Decoding.


Rahaf

To Jesse, my partner in crime and the pictures to my words.

# CONTENTS

# THE
# DECODED
# COMPANY

# INTRODUCTION

Dear Reader,

On behalf of my coauthors Aaron, Jay, and Rahaf, it's my pleasure to welcome you to *The Decoded Company.*

We're living in a time of accelerating change and increasing uncertainty in the workplace—just as much as (or even more than) we are in our personal lives. A global war for talent is already under way and we firmly believe that its victors, the companies that survive and thrive over the next decades, will be the ones that reject the status quo and redefine the very basics of their approach. To borrow from Einstein, today's problems cannot be solved with the same thinking that created them. The way we organize, communicate, train, and make decisions—the technology of management—is the very thinking that has created today's managerial challenges. Unbelievable advances in consumer technology have changed almost every facet of our lives over the last twenty years, and yet the rickety technology of management that most managers use today is older than they are.

*The Decoded Company* argues that the consumer technology revolution sparked by the Internet has only begun to invade the workplace. These advancements have come primarily in the form of user centered design, consumer devices brought into the workplace, and the adoption of cloud-based technologies. That said, the marketplace has largely missed what's at the heart of why companies like Facebook, Google, and Amazon have outperformed their counterparts. These companies have understood how to leverage data as a sixth sense, how to personalize their customers' experiences with that data, and how to completely embrace the open and participatory nature of the Web. We believe these ideas are universal and can be effectively leveraged by any company in any industry, with both their internal and external stakeholders.

*The Decoded Company* encourages organizations of any size to reject the notion that their people are interchangeable "resources" and to invest in systems and processes that are action oriented, people centered, disruptive, and sometimes radical. We believe that audacious and exponential ideas trump incremental thinking. You'll be provoked into making big bets based on real data, to experiment early and often, to systematically codify learnings, and to allow urgency to conquer your fears.

If you accept the challenge, the benefits of decoding your organization include increased agility and speed, evidence-based decision making, decreased bureaucracy, and the ability to predict problems before they occur. By creatively applying technology and data analysis to all of your internal processes you'll be able to understand and optimize systematically. Decoding delivers personalized training at the precise moment that it's required, resulting in increased consistency and performance in everything your organization does. The true advantage of decoding your company is for it to become a center of gravity, attracting and retaining the best talent your industry has to offer and unlocking crazy-high engagement from them.

# INTRODUCTION

*Decoded* is the right philosophy for you if you've read enough strategy books to know that you don't need a shiny new strategy but a better way to orchestrate your people's efforts and execution. We all have the same questions whenever we pick up a business management philosophy book: Will this be relevant to me? Can I apply these methods within my team? Will these ideas translate into my industry? Will it have a real material business impact?

We'd like to respond with a question of our own: Do you work with people?

If so, you probably have endless meetings that you wish you could avoid. What if you could respond efficiently to patterns instead of to exceptions? What if your meeting agenda was informed by evidence and the right information you need to make an effective decision?

You probably also find yourself buried in e-mail threads that get longer without solving any real issues, and certainly not with intelligent prioritization. Is e-mail your primary collaboration tool? What if you could get a dynamically prioritized list of goals and then capture, socialize, and reward the best ideas?

You probably suffer through some form of performance review that does nothing to improve performance. There are probably times when you wish you had some coaching or feedback but have to operate in a leadership void. How certain are you that your people are clear on their objectives? Do they have a daily feedback loop that they can see? How clear are you on yours? What if you could operate in a constant state of clarity that showed you what your people need and helped you deliver it right when they needed it most?

The solutions to these problems—the tools we will introduce throughout this book—become the basis of your center of gravity and enable you to attract, activate, and lead an incredible team.

That's the first step. Your next objective is to operate with speed and confidence. At its core, strategy is about moving resources toward opportunity and away from risk. Execution is about increasing predictability and consistency while minimizing risk. These were competing priorities in the data-poor world in which management technology was forged. Minimizing risk required structure, formalized processes, and policies that introduced and exploded bureaucracy. Maximizing opportunity requires autonomy to make evidence-based decisions and orchestrate teams with the agility to respond to rapid environmental changes.

We no longer live in a data-poor world, but we continue to use the management tools designed for one. If you're a manager, you're probably sensing that the world gets a little faster every day, and the degree of uncertainty is accelerating. The techniques and tools you're using to manage your people can barely keep up with the challenges you're now facing. The sad part is that we've solved this challenge in the consumer world. Amazon, for example, has developed an entire toolbox of clever ways to learn about you, adapt to your preferences, and separate you from your hard-earned dough. Why haven't we applied these learnings to the world of work?

This book is a chronicle of our obsession with a deceptively simple question: What if we understood our talent better than we understand our customers? Or to put it in a slightly different way: What if we learned to decode the real story that is embedded in the data trail that follows every person in our company and every project they work on? What if we put its messages to use—not to get the better of our talent but to empower the best from them, to make their jobs better, and to improve the performance of our whole organization?

The answer, it turns out, is radically transformative.

# INTRODUCTION

Based in part on our own experience building Klick Health over the last fifteen years, and in part on the early indicators and evidence we've found in the marketplace, this book is a manifesto for the Decoded movement. It lays out an argument that the key to sustainable competitive advantage is in creating a data-driven, talent-centric company culture. In the chapters that follow we'll explain what a Decoded Company is and how to create one, drawing on examples from our own business and many others across a wide range of industries.

## WHY SHOULD YOU LISTEN TO US?

While we're certainly not the first people to write about the ideas and trends that inform this book, we've lived them in a way that most management theorists haven't. For the past seventeen years, we've watched as Google, Amazon, Facebook, eBay, and others have disintermediated entire industries, fascinated by the consistent patterns that each of their trajectories reveals. At Klick we've been at the convergence point of a number of these trends, and we've learned how to apply them to our advantage. Our company and the people who work for it have prospered, but for us it's not just about the money. We are passionate—possibly even evangelical—about the Decoded Company because we believe that it points to a better way of life. More than a catchphrase, more than a tool kit, it is a whole ethos.

Seventeen years is a long time to have been tracking anything. Think back to 1997—What were you doing? Does it bear much relation to what you're doing today? For Aaron, our partner Peter Cordy, and me, 1997 marks the year that we chose freedom over a miserable corporate culture that we despised. The three of us were working for a big public company. The dot-com craziness was at its height and our bosses were obsessed with pleasing their institutional investors instead of mentoring their people. Decisions were made with zero concern or accountability for their impacts on people's lives. At the same time, we were flying blind with respect to our day-to-day performance. And so we left, choosing to build something that we could be truly passionate about. That something became Klick.

Klick is a nonstop experiment in reinventing the technology of human achievement, and it is now the world's largest independent digital health agency, a $100 million company with more than four hundred employees spread out across North America and the world. Klick provides digital marketing services (Web sites, apps, mobile, social media, etc.) to pharma and biotech companies that are reinventing the technology of human health, a perfect parallel to our own mission. We design and deploy tools that help our clients bring their message to an increasingly digital market, introducing their often lifesaving therapies and drugs to both patients and health-care professionals. We help them to recruit patients into clinical trials, to shape their market approach based on real data, to craft the channels through which their message is delivered, and to ensure that their patients achieve better outcomes through support programs. Our work touches every phase of a drug's life cycle, starting from clinical trials on through prelaunch and launch right through to our client's loss of patent exclusivity.

The advantages that come from being Decoded have set us on a very different and much steeper path than the rest of our industry (and than most companies in any industry). In our worst years we've grown 30 percent and in our best, 60 percent and more. The primary driver of our success is our crazy-high team loyalty and engagement. In an industry in which the voluntary attrition rate for privately held agencies is at mid-20 percent and 30 percent–plus for big agencies, ours is about 3 percent. Although many of our competitors (especially our undecoded ones) might find our track record enviable, we believe that our growth is just beginning.

## BEWARE BIG BROTHER

Any approach built on data will inevitably encounter a Big Brother reaction. In our seventeen-year history we have seen it many times as we've lived and breathed the Decoded philosophy. We've become very familiar with the rising implications of living in this new data abundant landscape. Privacy and surveillance issues are nothing to laugh about, and we've grappled with many of them. These concerns are important and deserve to be addressed head-on. The Decoded Company is one that has a thoughtful and transparent data policy that demonstrates an understanding of this new environment and knows to protect its employees. You'll learn about the Decoded data policy guidelines that you can use to ensure that you properly manage your data in a safe, trusted, and ethical way. We'll show you some examples of companies that are doing it right and of others that have committed some scary missteps.

## WHY NOW?

You're probably familiar with a quote from Henry Ford that dates back more than a century, to the last time the culture and theory of management were undergoing the kind of revolutionary changes that they are today. When asked how he was able to understand the needs of his market, Ford is reputed to have answered, "If I'd asked people what they wanted, they would have said a faster horse."

That's what almost all of the enterprise technology from the last thirty years amounts to: a faster horse. Consider e-mail. It's just a digital way to deliver a letter to your friend or a memo to a colleague. It might have more bells and whistles, but you can easily trace its lineage all the way back to the first intraoffice memo, with its carbon copies both blind and seen (BCCs and CCs). You can scale that concept all the way to the biggest, scariest enterprise resource planning (ERP) system, which has essentially digitized a whole bunch of offline processes, documents, spreadsheets, and other legacy business paraphernalia into electronic versions that are almost exactly the same as their paper equivalents.

Most of us in leadership roles spend our time tinkering with the "technology of management" when we should, as Gary Hamel so aptly put it, be reinventing the "technology of human accomplishment." *The Decoded Company* is a book about business management, but it's also about much more than that. It's about learning to see your environment through the lens of data rather than the prejudices, preconceptions, and perceived wisdom that they were teaching in business schools fifty years ago. It's about the importance of treating human beings as autonomous individuals rather than as standardized, replaceable cogs in a machine. It's about what business can be and should be—a data- and technology-driven field of incredible human accomplishment.

# THIS IS A MOVEMENT

If you're hoping to learn how to apply data so you can message, merchandise, or up sell more precisely, you're holding the wrong book. But if you're an empathetic and progressive leader who is eager to find effective ways to empower your people, keep reading. You'll learn how to make more informed decisions, execute faster, operate with less bureaucracy, drive higher engagement, and eliminate surprises.

If you've been searching for fantastic ways to keep your team motivated, then you're in luck.

*The Decoded Company* is much more than a book. First and foremost it's a tribute to the people who inspired us. We very much believe that we're standing on the shoulders of giants who have published their ideas, shared their stories, and deliberately engineered their corporate ecosystems. *The Decoded Company* is our attempt to weave those individual threads into a cohesive philosophy and movement. Though we won't spend a lot of time on theory and social analysis, we will provide reading lists for anyone who wants to dig into

 the why behind the how. Reading lists and recommendations are highlighted in the text with the icon at left and are available in a single list at decodedbook.com/reading-list.

Learning by doing is a very important part of our theory, so we've also provided a number of experiments that you can perform yourself. Each is called out in the text with the Experiment icon seen below. We hope that this book inspires you to adopt the same culture of experimentation that we have been pursuing and to share your

 results at decodedbook.com. We still have many more questions than answers; we'll be thrilled if you decide to join us in this shared adventure of inquiry and discovery.

## BEYOND THIS BOOK

The companion Web site (decodedbook.com) is full of additional resources that we invite you to explore, including videos, workbooks, experiments, a full description of our own case study, and a lively community of Decoded readers and practitioners.

## THANK YOU

We've struggled with all of the challenges outlined in this introduction, and we think we've come up with some radical solutions to help tackle them. It is my absolute pleasure to welcome you to *The Decoded Company*. We couldn't be more excited to share these ideas with you, and we hope they inspire you to revise everything you thought you knew about management. Aaron, Jay, Rahaf, and I are really looking forward to hearing about how much decoding has improved your people's morale and productivity, your company's bottom line, and your life. If solving these challenges for yourself is worth a few hours of your time (and we think it is!), read on.

Thank you for investing your time with us—we know how valuable it is. We promise to make it worth your while, and we guarantee that you'll walk away with at least one game-changing idea for your business. I would love to hear about it if you do, and I would doubly love to hear from you if you don't. Please reach out to me at leerom@decodedbook.com.

Here's to experimenting!

Leerom,

Aaron, Jay, and Rahaf

# CHAPTER 1: THE DECODED COMPANY

 Klick's evolution into a data-driven company was born out of our desire to be more efficient—and a deep hatred for e-mail.

It began with a small decision that was made more than seventeen years ago, when Klick was just a few employees and everyone was sitting within an arm's length from one another. Leerom, Aaron, and their cofounder, Peter Cordy, have been friends for more than twenty years; they trusted each other and could practically complete each other's sentences.

The first few employees to join were easy to integrate through communication channels such as e-mail, but as the company grew, the increasingly complex client projects were generating e-mails that were tens of pages long and distributed to dozens of recipients, who were forwarding them to still more people, resulting in a cacophony of miscommunication and unnecessary mistakes. Cue the deep hatred.

Like many businesses, we needed a better way to manage the information that was floating around inside the company and to apply it in a useful way. We were surrounded by data that we weren't using. Taking inspiration from tech support systems, Aaron implemented a simple ticketing system that tracked each individually assigned task—the prototype of the system we would come to call Genome.

And then he banned internal e-mail.

To be more accurate, he instructed the entire delivery organization to disregard any task assignment given via e-mail. This forced client-facing teams to create tickets in order to get anything completed by the organization. In and of itself, it didn't seem that monumental at the time. Ticketing systems were already a fairly well-known way of tracking requests and work orders.

In the process, though, we stumbled across a powerful insight. As Genome started to collect vast amounts of data, we realized that we could use it to gain new understandings of how our company was running. We could see the number of tickets that were created by a specific department or a particular individual, and we could see the average time it took to close a type of task. We could identify whom any task was assigned to, when it was opened, and the informal comments that surrounded it. But that was only the beginning.

The really big breakthrough was when we realized that the information we were amassing allowed us to read our teams' digital body language. We could identify the patterns of behavior that led to success and those that led to problems—and by catching those potential problems early, we could correct them with a relatively small change of course. (For a much deeper look into Genome, check out decodedbook.com/genome.)

We are not the first or the only data-centric company. As recounted in the book and the movie *Moneyball,* for example, baseball general manager Billy Beane used sabermetrics, a form of data-driven analytics, to lead the undervalued Oakland Athletics to a play-off series victory in the American League Division Series in 2006. In 2007, Tom Davenport published *Competing on Analytics*, which explained how companies like Amazon, Barclays, and Capital One were using sophisticated statistical analysis to understand their customers and make better decisions. In 2008, United Parcel Service (UPS), a 105-year-old company, rolled out its algorithm-powered juggernaut, ORION, to help its fleet drivers reduce their carbon footprint by optimizing their daily routes. By 2010, authors like Tim Ferriss were really hitting their stride in showing us how we could use data to hack our own bodies.[1]

In 2011, analytics and data science jobs accounted for a quite remarkable 0.1 percent of all job listings at LinkedIn, up from less than 0.01 percent just a decade before.[2] (The year-over-year growth of profiles with data science as a skill is up 46 percent in 2013.[3]) Google's People Analytics team has also been very active, sharing their early results in public forums. Finally, in 2012, author Charles Duhigg showed readers of *The New York Times Magazine* how the retail giant Target had gotten so good at analyzing our purchasing behavior that it could predict the products we would buy before we even knew we would need them.

We have now firmly transitioned to the next phase of our technological evolution: the data era. We have gotten exceedingly good at tracking margins, inventory, turnover rates, financial performance, and customer preferences, and many of us are learning to compete on those and other metrics. This book isn't about any of those things.

 **Reading List:** For a list of books about Big Data see http://decodedbook.com/bigdata

What we discovered after building Genome was the next stage of data evolution: data superpowers. Data superpowers are less like Superman's and more like the X-Men's Professor Xavier or Spider-Man's—the ability to know things that aren't directly observable through your five senses. They're what Leerom calls a data-powered sixth sense, giving everyone in your organization an awareness of the entire organization well beyond their immediate realm.

For example, a car insurance company generates personalized policies for customers by using vehicle telemetry data to understand each driver's unique habits. An online dating site uses the data it culls from extensive surveys to measure the compatibility between potential love matches. A government agency uses analytics to track down tax evaders and identify instances of fraud. Data has become one of the most valuable resources we have for uncovering insights about our motivations and behavior. But every one of those examples is about the use of data for external (e.g., customer-facing) purposes. What happens when you turn those algorithms around and look inside your own company? The result is extraordinary insight into your talent that reveals the keys to breakthrough performance. In searching for a name to call these insightful organizations, we turned to the science of the human genome. Decoding our genome has given us radical insight into what makes our bodies work. Decoded Companies likewise decode themselves to gain equally radical insight into what makes their people work.

Before we go any further, it's important to explain what we mean by "company." We're often asked if an entrepreneur with a handful of employees can be Decoded, if a manager of a small team within a big corporation can apply these tools, or if they can be used with entire divisions or across giant multinationals. The answer to all of the above is a resounding *yes*. Being Decoded doesn't require a sizable team, companywide buy-in, C-suite sign-off, or a massive budget (though all of those things would obviously help). Some of these tools will apply more to your scenario than others, which is why we have an awesome community at de codedbook.com to help you figure out how to adapt them.

The Decoded Company is an organization of any size that rejects the notion that its people are interchangeable resources. It invests in the systems and processes that enable it to understand its people better than it understands its customers and is characterized by increased agility and speed, evidence-based decision making, decreased bureaucracy, and the ability to predict problems before they occur. It creatively applies technology and data analysis to all of its internal processes in order to decode, understand, and optimize. It delivers personalized training at the precise moment it's required and benefits from increased consistency and performance in everything it does. The true decoded advantage is to become a center of gravity for talent, attracting and retaining the best people your industry has to offer, and unlocking crazy-high engagement from them. Decoded Companies become top performers, reshaping their markets and industries.

If you were to write the exact opposite of the paragraph above, you would be describing most businesses today. It's not that everything they do is wrong; it's that they exist in a pre-Decoded state. All of them will be faced with a decision over the next decade: adapt or die. That may sound overly dramatic, but the bottom line is that every industry, no matter how slowly it adopts technology or how hard it resists the change, is in a global battle to attract the best talent it can find—top performers who understand the power of technology and can leverage it more effectively. Decoded Companies are talent magnets. They are destined to win.

The good news is that we don't have to tell you that—the fact that you've bought this book shows that you are already onboard.

The bad news is that you can't become a Decoded Company overnight.

You certainly can't do it until you learn to cultivate a healthy disregard for the status quo. Over the course of your career you've been told many things about how to manage and lead your team. Most of them were true at some point, but they no longer apply in today's world. First and foremost, a Decoded Company bases its decisions on data, not on the dogmatic management principles that were propounded in the last century. By doing exactly that, Klick has enjoyed a fifteen-year ascent while most of our industry has contracted and/ or assumed massive debt loads to stay afloat. Our internal corporate slogan—The Relentless Pursuit of Awesome—is our approach and it inoculates us against the evil inherent in good enough.

## THE DECODED MODEL

All the theory in the world isn't going to help you solve your real-world problems. We'll encourage you to embrace three Decoded principles and support you with tools to implement them. Our approach can be applied in any work setting, regardless of how big or small your team is or the culture of your company. As you'll soon learn, we've developed a custom, dedicated software system that we call Genome to put them into practice at Klick. Look out for the icon at right for suggestions of off-the-shelf products that will allow you to achieve the same goals.

 ## Principle 1: Technology as a Coach and Trainer

Imagine you understood your people and their skill sets well enough that you could transform the role of technology within your organization from a referee into a coach. Instead of yelling "offside!" after something happened, you could predictively anticipate the issue with an early detection system and instead use these moments as the best opportunity to coach and inspire. If it was this team member's first time trying to accomplish something, you could leverage that teachable moment in order to deliver a small learning intervention that's precisely timed and adapted to their individual learning style. Decoded organizations personalize everything that happens internally by knowing more about their talent than about their customers. By knowing enough about your people, you'll be able to dynamically adjust processes and provide information precisely when people need it. We'll encourage you to depart from any one-size-fits-all solution, process, or policy to an alternative that is much more efficient, pleasant, and productive.

 ## Principle 2: Data as a Sixth Sense

The second principle is all about using the data-rich environment that surrounds us to inform our intuition and make better decisions. In other words, it's about using data as a sixth sense. We'll teach you how to instrument your team or organization to capture ambient data and then to analyze it to identify patterns of behavior that can help you predict outcomes. Take, for example, the best World War II pilot in a Bell P-59 Airacomet, the first jet fighter flown by the United States, and pit him against an average modern pilot in an F-22 Raptor: The World War II pilot loses every time. Aside from differences in speed, maneuverability, and weapons, the Raptor augments the pilot with a heads-up display that feeds real-time data and situational awareness to him. He can make smarter decisions much faster and handle situations that his colleagues from seventy years ago couldn't even dream of. This is one of the tightest man-machine bonds and an excellent example of the power of informed intuition. Now consider that the vast majority of the management practices we use today predate World War II. Our technology has advanced at least as much as the differences between the P-59 and the F-22, and yet our approach to arming our people with data has trailed behind. Informed intuition is the heads-up display that can give you—and your people—that edge.

## Principle 3: Engineered Ecosystems

Finally, the third principle is our ability to use data to foster a particular set of behaviors within our organization—it's a deliberate step to building better corporate environments. This principle is driven by the new digital social norms, such as transparency, connectedness, and community, that are at the core of everything on the Web. We've entered an era of conversations in which influence is attained based on merit rather than on the size of an advertising budget. The same thing is happening inside your company whether you realize it or not. Many have written about the connected enterprise, but with engineered ecosystems we challenge leaders to understand the role that technology has in shaping culture and breaking down preconceived ideas about how control is shared. It will inspire you to think critically about empowerment and orchestration. It will challenge you to ignore dogmas and get creative with a systematic approach to solving problems, one experiment at a time.

## This Is a Model That Works

The Decoded advantage helps you leverage the knowledge that exists in your company right now to create a work environment that is not just running more smoothly, with fewer bottlenecks and less bureaucratic inertia, but is insanely engaging—one that motivates your people to do their best and soundly outperform the competition. We've used this model at Klick to keep us from firing a valuable member of our team even though his project went hugely overbudget. Whole Foods used it to radically restructure its teams and give it a trust-filled environment that delivers true autonomy. At the extreme radical end, Valve Software applied the Decoded model to completely flatten its entire $3 billion company. You'll learn about all of these case studies in later chapters.

# DECODING TRENDS

We are at an unprecedented convergence point in the emerging technology of what Gary Hamel—recently ranked by *The Wall Street Journal* as one of the world's most influential business thinkers and dubbed "the world's leading expert on business strategy" by *Fortune* magazine—calls "human accomplishment," one that provides us with a unique opportunity to move from antiquated and obsolete management philosophies to a data-driven, talent-centric approach.[4]

In order to truly understand the Decoded principles, we have identified three trends—informed intuition; personalize everything; and the connected enterprise—which have laid the groundwork necessary for our model to become possible. They are a combination of emerging online norms, increases in mobile and Web penetration, and the availability of an abundance of data that has changed the way consumers interact with organizations.

To successfully apply the Decoded principles, we need to understand these trends fully. They are born out of technology— smartphones, massive databases, scalable cloud architectures, and fast processors. They live in the social consumer Web, in the devices in our pockets, and on our Internet-connected TVs. They are new to our world, having emerged only within the last decade (and matured only within the last five years), and yet their impact on our day-to-day existence is already more significant than almost any other technology in history.

None of these trends existed when the vast majority of the management philosophies we follow were created. Gary Hamel considers management to be one of humanity's most important inventions, but one that suffers from a significant problem. "Most of the fundamental breakthroughs in management were made decades ago," he writes. "Workflow design, project management, variance analysis, budgeting, financial reporting, performance appraisals and a host of other notable inventions trace their origins back to the early years of the twentieth century. Truth is," he continues, "much of what passes for 'modern' management was invented by individuals who were born in the middle of the nineteenth century." And yet we still continue to follow them today, struggling to apply their anachronistic approaches to our modern workplaces.

 **Reading list:** *The Future of Management* by Gary Hamel, with Bill Breen

The will to change has been there for some time, but the technology that was needed to truly evolve into the data era did not yet exist. It is the convergence of our three trends that has finally paved the way for the emergence of the Decoded Company— driven by data, powered by personalization, and built on an engineered ecosystem.

# 1. INFORMED INTUITION

We live in a data-rich world. The cost of data storage and processing is going down exponentially every year. This enables us to instrument our organizations to capture ambient data, which is any data that can be sensed without the bias or overhead of self-reporting. Ambient data includes everything from patterns of communication between employees and customers to activity in the office to use of your intranet and more—for example, we drank 61,392 cups of coffee across our company last year, as ambiently measured by our network of coffee machines. The more we understand the dynamics of the most granular data points in our enterprises, the more reliably we can predict outcomes and reduce surprises. By tracking everything from basic patterns of behavior to individual experience, we're able to decode long-term patterns that separate signal from noise. This allows us to create predictive models that automatically flag potentially dangerous situations.

One of management's most vexing problems is how to learn from history and avoid repeating the same mistakes. This becomes more important as organizations scale in size. A company that scientifically correlates its mistakes with patterns in its historical data can literally codify that learning into algorithms that sound an alarm when those same patterns recur.

Mistake avoidance is not the only challenge that keeps us up at night. Many of us are struggling to create systems that ensure that talent is fully engaged at every level in the organization. There's a wealth of great literature out there on the topic, including Dan Pink's *Drive*, which describes how people seek purpose, mastery, and autonomy in their work. Pink's insights are part of the foundation that *The Decoded Company* is built on, and you can count us as fans of his thinking. But we go a step further and show how these ideals can actually be achieved through quantifiable data-driven approaches.

**Reading list:** *Drive* by Daniel H. Pink

Though data can't necessarily ensure purpose, we believe it can be leveraged to accelerate mastery and increase autonomy while at the same time reducing risk. In support of mastery, we can quantify the parts of every individual's experience that are felt, such as feedback, challenge, change, learning, and opportunity. To increase autonomy we can make use of tools that watch our blind spots, freeing our people from the tyranny of one-size-fits-all policies and processes that simply slow them down. It's this shift that has enabled us to develop and use what we call informed intuition, in which your systems analyze data to monitor your blind spots and to look for patterns that match lessons learned, literally codified into your company's operating system. At Klick we accomplish this with Genome, the powerful system that we described at the beginning of this chapter.

## 2. PERSONALIZE EVERYTHING

One of the things we take for granted is the degree to which our communications with companies are personalized and relevant to our interests. Whether we're reading a promotional e-mail from Amazon or thinking about watching a movie that Netflix suggested, their recommendations are shaped by our past purchases and are thus uniquely curated for us. When we log into Facebook, our newsfeed is driven by whose profile we last viewed, who we frequently communicate with, and the type of content we typically engage with. In every aspect of our personal lives, whether we're viewing videos on YouTube, reading news on Flipboard, using shopping and dating sites, or listening to music services such as Spotify and Pandora, intelligent algorithms are consuming data, learning our preferences, and shaping our experiences.

That's sadly not true in our workplaces, where we're subjected to one-size-fits-all policies and processes in everything we do. Why? Processes and bureaucracy protect organizations from risk. When a professionally managed organization makes a mistake, it carries out a postmortem, determines where in the process it could have caught the error, and then adds a control to prevent that mistake from recurring. It probably also updates its training materials, communicates the change, and trains appropriately. That might seem like a reasonable process to you (especially if you work in an organization that isn't Decoded), but we think it's like slow death by heart disease. All those proliferating processes build up like plaque in an artery, causing the organization to get slower and slower, until it eventually stops completely. We're going to show you how to clean that plaque right out and install organizational stents when required. If Decoded Companies are dogmatic about one thing, it's the rejection of one-size-fits-all anything. The truth is that one size fits none.

One of our favorite quotes on complexity comes from Antoine de Saint-Exupéry, author of *Le Petit Prince*, who said: "Perfection is achieved, not when there is nothing more to add, but when there is nothing left to take away." Our ability to deliver personalized services has empowered organizations to free themselves from the restrictive referee that terrorizes their teams and shift to an approach we call Technology as a Coach and Trainer. This powerful tool helps identify teachable moments, the best possible time to deliver a learning intervention.

# 3. THE CONNECTED ENTERPRISE

This is an exciting time to be a consumer. Companies are more accountable to their customers because the Web amplifies the opinions of any individual. Gone are the days of one-way broadcast marketing; we've entered an era of conversations. Influence is attained based on merit and is more powerful than any advertising budget. We have become what you might call the connected society, joined at the hip (or, more accurately, at the smartphone in the hip pocket), constantly networked to our friends and family, and expectant that those connections will provide a constant stream of useful content and data. Our everyday tasks—from errands to choosing a restaurant to sharing photos—are made easier by our connection to the network.

Unfortunately, it's not nearly as exciting a time to be an employee. Although we strive for a work-plus-life balance, the latter part of that equation is far more connected than the former. IT systems are increasingly converging with consumer systems, as fewer and fewer of us are willing to put up with terrible enterprise software.

That said, we believe that those same principles of openness, transparency, and connectedness are destined to transform our business culture no less radically than they have our consumer culture, leading from the connected society to the connected enterprise. The changes that we've seen in the consumer Web and in consumer technologies have already begun to make their way into the business setting and will continue to do so with increasing force, requiring us to rethink the structure and culture of our companies just as much as we've had to reevaluate what it means in our personal lives.

Culture is classically defined as the customs, arts, social institutions, and achievements of a set of people. The term gets misused all the time in corporate settings, especially among tech start-ups. Shanley Kane, writing on exactly this topic, said:

> Culture is not about the furniture in your office. It is not about how much time you have to spend on feel-good projects. It is not about catered food, expensive social outings, internal chat tools, your ability to travel all over the world, or your never-ending self-congratulation.
>
> Culture is about power dynamics, unspoken priorities and beliefs, mythologies, conflicts, enforcement of social norms, creation of in/out groups and distribution of wealth and control inside companies. Culture is usually ugly. It is as much about the inevitable brokenness and dysfunction of teams as it is about their accomplishments. Culture is exceedingly difficult to talk about honestly.[5]

Decoded Companies view their investments in their culture (of time as well as money) as some of their most critical expenditures. This leads to Engineered Ecosystems: very deliberately and intentionally designed cultures.

We're not the only ones who believe this, as you'll see later in the book. The connected enterprise is a reality for many people today, which you'll discover through a number of compelling case studies and stories.

## ALWAYS IN BETA

At its heart, a Decoded Company is an ongoing experiment. We practice this at Klick by following a "question everything" approach, building our culture on the belief that we should never stop relentlessly pursuing the ideal of a perfect business, even though we know we will never actually attain it. Each experiment has the potential to bring us one step closer to that state.

Experimentation requires risk taking, which means that you have to encourage your people to constantly push limits and test established practices. They have to feel secure enough to fail. All of this comes back to becoming a center of gravity for the best and brightest: Hire damn smart people, really trust them, empower them to take risks, and what they deliver will blow you away.

Empowering risk taking means removing obstacles. Decoded Companies often have an inverted leadership model in which the employees closest to the customers make the key decisions while managers are seen as facilitators and orchestrators (it's no accident that Leerom refers to himself as Klick's chief exception officer). Being a master orchestrator means fighting constantly against our natural bias toward complexity. Dharmesh Shah, CTO and cofounder of HubSpot (you'll hear more about them later), says, "Ironically, adding complexity is easy and maintaining simplicity is hard." Left unchecked, this tendency will turn even the most basic process into a massive standard operating procedure that will eventually grind down your people's will to live (if not their actual life force, then definitely their will to continue to be employed by your company). It will also inevitably lead to one-size-fits-all policies that feed into one-size-fits-all training that feeds a one-size-fits-all culture.

Your data will tell you what needs to be taken away. A Decoded Company has made the significant commitment to instrumenting everything it does, thereby creating its data superpower. It has data coursing through its veins. It has educated and trained its people to be data literate, so that they can interpret it and make the right decisions based on it.

Genome allows Klick to scale quickly while minimizing risk. By putting the right information in front of the right person at the right time, we ensure that they can make the right decision based on the right priorities. The knowledge of what's right comes from our carefully engineered culture.

The path is not easy and it's not short, but it does lead to significant riches. An October 2012 Economist Intelligence Unit survey of 530 senior executives from North America, Asia Pacific, Western Europe, and Latin America, across a broad range of industries, found that companies that rate themselves substantially ahead of their peers in their use of data are three times more likely to rate themselves as substantially ahead of their peers in financial performance.[6] We found many similar weak signals—early, quiet indicators audible only slightly above the noise—across a wide range of companies and industries wherever we saw the early adoption of big data, people analytics, or intentional cultures. We've shared a whole alphabet of examples in these pages, from Amazon to Zappos and nearly everything in between. If you're ready to start down this path yourself, read on.

# CHAPTER 2: TECHNOLOGY AS A COACH

- How did the conversion of alarm clock factories for the war effort nearly cost us the war? Where are you making similar trade-offs that are nearly destroying your company?

- What's the cure for *annual reviewitis*—the most despised of all HR-inflicted policies?

- What is the connection between HubSpot's running out of whiteboard space and its inability to use most enterprise software? The answer might reshape how you think about your organization's structure.

- Why is the soft stuff so hard? How can you quantify mojo? And what does all that have to do with selling shoes?

- How different would your education have been if your textbooks had been customized to your unique learning style?

- What would drive someone to turn down a half-million-dollar cash bonus to stay in a job, and what does that tell us about the global talent market?

- Why did GE start offering its employees a choice between Mac OS and Windows? You might be surprised to learn that the answer has nothing to do with productivity.

Wars are won for many reasons: the accuracy of defense intelligence; the heroism of soldiers; the sophistication of advanced military technology; and, of course, the functionality of citizens' alarm clocks. Believe it or not, at one point in American history one of the nation's critical success factors was that little piece of effective, albeit annoying, technology.

The production of most consumer goods ground to a halt in America during the spring of 1942 as factories were converted for war work, and the use of materials such as metal and rubber for nonmilitary purposes was heavily restricted. This created shortages of many everyday items, such as garden tools, razor blades, bedsprings, and both small and large appliances. By July of that year the ban had grown to include alarm clocks. They just weren't considered important enough to justify the diversion of precious resources from wartime production.

In war and peace they say that half the battle is showing up, but that's really hard to do if you're still in bed. By the time 1944 had rolled around, alarm clocks were notoriously difficult to find, and employees with critical roles in the war effort were showing up late for work. The most oft-given excuse? Lack of a good alarm clock. By November of that year, chronic absenteeism had gotten so bad that employers successfully lobbied the government to allow alarm clocks to be manufactured again.[1] Ever since, our little war hero has played a critical if unsung role in our daily routines—and today it's inspiring us to pay new attention to an often unarticulated human need, by looking at it through the lens of data.

# TECHNOLOGY AS A COACH

How many times have you been jolted awake by an alarm clock in the middle of a really great dream? This jarring and disorienting event leaves many people groggy and irritable for the rest of the day. It's not the alarm clock's fault—don't shoot the messenger— but a case of bad timing. Our sleep naturally cycles between light sleep, deep sleep, and the dream state known as REM sleep (rapid eye movement, a flickering of your eyes back and forth).

If your alarm happens to go off during one of the deeper phases, it can negatively affect your mood, productivity, and alertness. The alarm clock might have been revamped on the outside, with digital displays that project the time on the ceiling, but at its core it still performs its primary function in the same way that it did during World War II. It doesn't know you or your habits, and so it applies its standard *wake the hell up!* protocol for you in the same manner that it would for anyone else. It's a prime example of technology used as a referee. It tells you when you're out of line, and that's it.

But what if technology acted as a coach instead?

Think back to the personalize everything trend. We'll explain how that applies to talent in a moment, but let's start with how it can apply to something as lowly as the venerable alarm clock. A company called Zeo produced a high-tech product called the Personal Sleep Manager (PSM) to solve this abrupt waking issue with hyperpersonalization (before they unfortunately went out of business). You wear a somewhat dorky-looking headband to bed that monitors your brain waves and communicates with a base station alarm clock. Instead of setting it to go off at a definite time, users identify a thirty-minute window during which they'd like to be awakened (e.g., no earlier than 7:00 A.M. and no later than 7:30 A.M.). The device then uses the data it collects to identify the best possible moment in your sleep cycle to rouse you. The PSM was like a personal coach that used technology to help you achieve better sleep performance. Its legacy lives on in other sleep trackers, such as Jawbone's UP System, which will wake you up at the best time based on your body's natural sleep cycle.

There are a number of less accurate sleep sensors on the market too, from apps such as Sleep Cycle, which uses your phone's accelerometer to measure tossing and turning, to wearable sensors such as the Fitbit. Jay has experimented with a number of them and learned that he has a roughly three-hour sleep cycle, meaning that he feels most rested when he sleeps in multiples of three hours. Although three hours of sleep leaves him feeling tired, counterintuitively, he feels better than he would have after four and a half hours of sleep, which leaves him groggy and grumpy.

 **Try this now!** This is a great place to start collecting ambient data if you're curious about the Quantified Self movement. You can get started tonight by searching your phone's app store for "sleep." (We'll cover the Quantified Self in more detail in chapter 6.)

Where customization once meant offering alarm clocks of different colors, sizes, and shapes, technology now enables them to include features that are intended to be unique to your individual circumstances; they are driven by analytics and embedded into the DNA of the clock user's experience.

Data can give us a lot of context that we might otherwise overlook. In 1942, it would have been inconceivable to anyone except maybe a highly imaginative science-fiction writer that the standardized bell and clock would ever come to assume so much importance for the war effort, or that so much cutting-edge technology would be put to use waking us up today. Because our resources (particularly of time) are limited, we're constantly forced to prioritize. Personalized alarm clocks hardly feel like the world's squeakiest wheels when so many other things around us need grease. Until we have the proper data, that is. Aside from helping to win world wars, smart alarm clocks can serve a possibly more important role in our own individual health and welfare.

Research into circadian cycles and sleep deprivation is revealing the role that sleep plays above and beyond just making us feel rested. Recent research by University of Surrey sleep expert Professor Derk-Jan Dijk found that insufficient sleep affects more than seven hundred genes, causing some of them to dampen their activity and others to become extra-active.[2] The affected genes are associated with the body clock cycle, metabolism, and immune and stress responses. Other UK scientists, from University College, London, and Cardiff Metropolitan University, have found a significant linear association between sleep duration and telomere length, particularly for men.[3] Telomeres are short regions of repetitive nucleotides at the end of our chromosomes whose job appears to be protecting the chromosome from deteriorating or unraveling over time. It's generally believed that they play a significant role in the aging process, helping to avoid mutations in the gene copying process. Longer telomeres are thought to be better, so shortening due to lack of sleep is significant.

Way above the cellular level, we've all experienced one of those sleepy, zombielike days when we can't get anything done. At the individual level we simply write them off. Now think of the economic impact that all of those days across all of your people are having. For a company of Klick's size, losing one day a year for each of our employees is about $500,000 in lost revenue. Investment into alarm clock R&D seems like a much sounder proposition now. We just didn't have the data to understand it before.

## TECHNOLOGY AS A COACH

Technology as a coach is the use of data and systems to transform your technology from a referee shouting "offside!" to a coach who provides real-time guidance and recommendations to help your people avoid behavior patterns that have proven problematic in the past. A referee enforces rules; a coach helps your team win. Technology as a coach allows your organization to radically accelerate execution and manage risk without drowning in bureaucracy.

A recent ESPN readership survey chose John Wooden, the legendary UCLA basketball coach who won ten NCAA championships in a twelve-year run, as their top coach of all time.[4] It's rare that sports fans agree so strongly on any Top Ten list, but Wooden was the number one choice of more than 4,000 of the 15,131 votes submitted. One of their readers summed his choice up perfectly:

> There can be no other choice but John Wooden. While his 10 championships speak for themselves, what says more about Wooden than any other fact is his admitted absence of "coaching" during a game. He always had his teams prepared well ahead of time. Unlike today, where players call timeouts they don't have, Wooden's players were so grounded in the fundamentals that not only would such an error be inconceivable, but it did not even need to be mentioned in the huddle!

Wooden's first year at UCLA demonstrates what a good coach can do: The team went from a 12-13 win/loss record the year before to Pacific Coast Conference (PCC) Southern Division champions, with a 22-7 record. Along with his seven books on coaching and leadership, Wooden gave us his Pyramid of Success, which is as applicable off the court as it is on it.

 **Reading list:** *Coach Wooden's Pyramid of Success Playbook: Applying the Pyramid of Success to Your Life* by John Wooden and Jay Carty[5]

Coach Wooden's thoughts on the topic of success expertly sum up our approach to coaching. Here are a few of our favorite quotes:

- "Success is peace of mind which is a direct result of self-satisfaction in knowing you made the effort to become the best of which you are capable."

- "Failure is not fatal but failure to change might be."

- "Ability is a poor man's wealth."

- "It's the little details that are vital. Little things make big things happen."

- "Don't measure yourself by what you have accomplished, but by what you should have accomplished with your ability."

- "Don't let what you cannot do interfere with what you can do."

- "Never mistake activity for achievement."

- "Be quick, but don't hurry."

- "Be prepared and be honest."

- "If you don't have time to do it right, when will you have time to do it over?"

- "A coach is someone who can give you correction without causing resentment."

So the question becomes: How do we Woodenize software? How do we transform eReferees into eCoaches? How do we take decades of enterprise software design that is stubbornly based on enforcing business rules and transform it into an intelligent, dynamic, performance-enhancing agent of success? If you've read this far, you probably already know that the answer lies in data.

Let's take a look at a story that very deliciously demonstrates the frustration we encounter when dealing with a system that uses technology as a referee. Like most airline loyalty systems, Air Canada's Aeroplan allows its members to create a profile and specify their meal choice. Jay is a vegetarian who eats dairy and eggs, so he was thrilled to discover that their system actually includes a "lacto-ovo-vegetarian" option. Unfortunately, it also includes a rule that says a custom meal must be ordered at least eighteen hours before a flight. Given that Klick's headquarters is located in Toronto, there are few choices other than Air Canada for regular service to the places where our clients are located. The nature of our business means we often have to change our travel plans within a few hours of departure, but the Aeroplan referee has been coded to prioritize customers' food over their schedules.

Someone—probably a business analyst—decided that late schedule changes should be rejected if they meant that Air Canada couldn't deliver an Aeroplan member's preferred meal choice. Although Jay appreciates their slavish dedication to culinary excellence, he ultimately had to remove his dietary preference setting so he could do his job.

Air Canada could have solved the problem by building a manual override into the system, allowing passengers to fly when they need to even if that meant not getting their special food. But they didn't, and now Jay can't eat the food on most of his Air Canada flights because most of it contains meat. This is classic referee behavior. The system is yelling "offside!" because a rule is being broken instead of questioning the validity of the rule itself—a feeling many of us have had while trying to slog through some pointless task imposed by our company's ERP system.

## PERSONALIZE EVERYTHING

The evolution of the Web as a social platform has given organizations their most powerful tool yet to drive their segmentation efforts into the realm of hyperpersonalization.

The Internet makes it easy for anyone to create content—content that can easily be mined for information. Every day more than 300 million photos are uploaded onto Facebook, and users generate an average of 3.2 billion likes and comments.[6] Twitter has more than 465 million active account holders who send an average of 175 million tweets a day.[7] Two new members join the professional social network LinkedIn every second, and in 2011 the site recorded 4.2 billion professionally related searches.[8] Forty-eight hours of video are uploaded onto YouTube every minute, and the site gets two billion views a day.[9]

Web 2.0 brought us the conversational Web we know and love, and mobile enabled us to access it from our pockets. For Rahaf, it was her work with the Technology Pioneers program at the World Economic Forum in Geneva that showed her how the brightest start-ups were taking advantage of this data-rich environment.

She observed companies that were leveraging this new world in ways their predecessors couldn't even imagine. They understood that each piece of content we produce contains information and metadata about us: what we think; what we know; what we like; and the mobile layers of geolocation and social connections, which add where we are now; where we were; and who we're with. By becoming content producers we have also become data powerhouses, churning out gigabytes of information that act as digital bread crumbs, a trail of valuable data nuggets that we leave behind. That led Rahaf to realize that even if we're not actively producing content, we're always producing data. Her digital footprint includes her Web history, her IP address, her search history, and all the other bits that she's collected during her online travels.

Consumer-focused marketers have long used demographic buckets to segment their target audience by gender, age, marital status, socioeconomic level, geography, etc. But with all this rich ambient data, the even more powerful tool of behavioral targeting can now be used. Think of demographic targeting as a one-size-fits-most approach to marketing: It forces us to assume that everyone of the same age and gender who lives in the same zip code and has red hair is the same person (at least for the purposes of marketing to them), because we've lacked the data we'd need to do otherwise. In addition, we make all kinds of assumptions about their needs and motivations that are not actually connected to their demographics, though they are often a reasonable proxy for them (or, at least, the most reasonable proxy we've had).

Behavioral targeting, in contrast, ignores demographics in favor of the actual behaviors of a potential buyer. Consider, for example, when Rahaf was looking to purchase a new kayak as a Christmas gift for her husband. Rahaf lives in Paris—nowhere near water—and shows none of the demographic markers that match a kayaker, so she wouldn't pop up as a target for traditional marketers. But her digital body language—her searches on Google for information about kayaks, her views of kayak dealers' Web sites for deals, her reading reviews in *Kayak Monthly*, etc.—would quickly give her away as a prime target for a Christmas kayak campaign. We no longer need to categorize ourselves or our potential customers under broad umbrellas such as gender or socioeconomic level. Instead, we all exist on a continuum where each unique individual can find their place, and products are designed or optimized specifically for them.

## FROM SEGMENTATION TO HYPERPERSONALIZATION

*"There is no such thing as the perfect Pepsi, there are only perfect Pepsis!"*

That was the eureka moment for Howard Moskowitz, an American psychophysicist who was hired by Pepsi in the 1970s to find the perfect level of sweetness for the company's new diet soda. After months of focus groups, taste tests, and surveys, Moskowitz realized that the key to Pepsi's success would be a *variety* of products.

His unconventional results were met with skepticism until he was able to apply his theory to another, seemingly unrelated, market: spaghetti sauce.

As documented by Malcolm Gladwell in his book *What the Dog Saw*, Moskowitz was brought in by Campbell's to find out why its Prego spaghetti sauce wasn't gaining any traction in a market dominated by their main competitor, Ragu. Just as with Pepsi, Campbell's had been trying to perfect Prego, making it the ideal sauce. Instead, based on the data he collected, Moskowitz pushed Campbell's to create different sauce offerings. "Moskowitz learned that more people's preferences fell into one of three broad groups: plain, spicy, and extra chunky, and of those three the last was the most important," Gladwell wrote. "Why? Because at the time there was no extra-chunky spaghetti sauce in the supermarket. Over the next decade, the new category proved to be worth hundreds of millions of dollars to Prego."

During his 2004 TED talk on the same subject, Gladwell joked about a phrase that Moskowitz had been fond of saying: *The mind does not know what the tongue wants.* It's a variation on the sentiment expressed by Henry Ford in the introduction: Though Campbell's had conducted focus groups and surveys, consumers had been unable to articulate their desire for chunky sauce, just as Ford's horse and buggy riders were unable to express a desire for automobiles. It was the various data points that Moskowitz had collected, a combination of self-reported and ambient data, that enabled him to identify the various segmentation groups that led Campbell's to an unserved market worth $600 million. Moskowitz's findings would kick-start the practice of consumer segmentation, as companies raced to understand what people want.

Consumers today have the ability to customize nearly every

aspect of their lives. They can wake up refreshed and ready to tackle their day, thanks to their trusty Sleep Cycle app. They can drink a custom-made blend of coffee (customcoffees.com) as they read their customized Flipboard magazine. They can get dressed in custom-made clothes they ordered online (indochino.com for him, eShakti.com for her) and put on a custom-made pair of shoes (shoesofprey.com). They can commute into work listening to a custom-made radio station.

Everything is getting the mass personalization treatment, from sneakers to ice cream. Nike's highly successful NIKEiD is a service that enables customers to personalize their shoes.[10] From picking out the materials to choosing the colors, customers can create a Nike shoe that reflects their own unique personality. Since its launch in 1999, the service has continued to evolve, and in some stores it even includes special stations where customers can touch and feel the various fabrics and get guidance from trained designers to ensure a great final product. In 2009, NIKEiD got the mobile treatment, which allows its customers an even greater level of flexibility, as well as PHOTOiD, an application that enables a customer to transfer the color palette from any photo onto the shoes they want to customize.

On the food end of the spectrum, eCreamery is an ice-cream maker that allows customers to create and name their own flavors of ice cream online.[11] Chocomize does the same thing but for chocolate bars. Customers can select from three delicious Belgian chocolate bases, and choose from more than one hundred different toppings to create their own flavor.[12]

One of the most promising fields of data science is adaptive learning: using data to create algorithms that learn from a user's behavior and adapt accordingly. Sites like Pandora, Rdio, and

Spotify offer listeners the ability to create their own radio station. Users have to select a few songs to get started, and the sites will analyze the song's similarities to identify what they like, and then continue to suggest other songs and new artists it thinks they will also like. Users can specify whether they like or dislike the suggestions and the sites learn from the feedback and fine-tune their recommendations. As of their IPO in 2012, Pandora had more than 80 million users.[13] That's 80 million unique radio stations, each of them applying data-driven insights to deliver a great musical experience.

Much like the Moskowitz spaghetti sauce experiments, all of these sites recognize that people don't always know what they want. Each of them has sections featuring the most popular selections, enticing consumers with things that they might not have even known they wanted. Marshmallow and candy corn dark chocolate anyone?

Even educators are taking note. Classrooms have long been plagued with outdated textbooks. While a step toward keeping classroom resources current, electronic textbooks are just another example of faster horses. Translating text from a page to a screen and adding some interactive elements is an incremental innovation when what we need is a radical transformation of the whole classroom experience, something that will put an end to one-size-fits-all teaching.

Knewton, an adaptive learning technology company, is aiming to do just that. The New York–based start-up is helping publishers, schools, and other organizations deliver personalized educational content to their students. We all know that people learn things differently. Knewton analyzes thousands of data points, such as concepts, difficulty levels, institutions, and media formats. Its platform takes into account the order of the subjects the students are learning, how they're being given the questions (text versus video), the format of their answers (multiple choice versus fill in the blank), the length of time it takes them to complete each learning module, and even the time of day when they're most receptive to learning. Then it uses an algorithm to generate a customized interactive textbook that is individually optimized for each student. Knewton offers a service to teachers too. Since its platform is used in 190 countries, the data it collects from millions of students around the world gives it insights into global learning trends that can help teachers improve their lesson plans.

 If you're part of an education organization, you need to have a vision for how you will take advantage of big data. Wait too long and you'll wake up to find that your competitors (and the instructors that use them) have left you behind with new capabilities and insights that seem almost magical. —Jose Ferreira, CEO, Knewton[14]

## MEASURING THE SHOULDERS OF CONSUMER GIANTS

The examples below are of companies that have gathered the available data and applied it externally to derive more meaningful consumer insights. Though operating in different sectors, each of these tech companies has invested effort to really understand and master the potential uses of their respective channels. They are worth billions of dollars and have disrupted entire industries because they've learned to read their consumers' social graphs with increasing precision and create a genuinely individualized experience. Whether their business model ultimately delivers books, videos, news, music, or romantic partners, these companies are able to personalize everything.

- **Amazon** realized it could beat its competitors by changing its focus from warehousing and fulfillment to a radical new use of data. It expends considerable effort decoding consumers' purchasing preferences to generate personalized recommendations, giving each customer an online storefront that's populated with products that reflect their interests.

- **Netflix** destroyed Blockbuster by using data to generate highly accurate personal viewing recommendations combined with a hassle-free online ordering system. No more wandering around aimlessly at the video store. Instead, Netflix members enjoy a selection of queued-up recommendations that the data says they're sure to enjoy, any of them available with the click of a button. In 2009, after three years of submissions, the company signaled its seriousness about data and algorithms by awarding a $1 million Netflix Prize to team BellKor's Pragmatic Chaos; using their algorithm, Netflix realized a 10.6 percent improvement over its own Cinematch recommendation engine.[15] "Accurately predicting the movies Netflix members will love is a key component of our service," said Neil Hunt, chief product officer.

- **Google** has deployed social results algorithms that deliver personally relevant content alongside its traditional search engine results. Instead of results generated solely by its PageRank algorithm, users find results based on their own search history behavior and information that is pulled from their own social networks, generating a unique experience with every search.

- **eHarmony** uses data to apply some rigor to its analog competitor: the blind date. Instead of being at the mercy of whatever stranger your best friend or your mother thinks would be a good match for you, you fill out a hefty survey that enables eHarmony's computers to analyze some five hundred variables. To date (pun intended) the site has more than 33 million members. According to a recent Harris Interactive poll, 542 eHarmony members get married in the United States each day.[16]

- **Apple and Samsung** build mobile devices, such as the iPhone and Galaxy, that consumers can customize in a variety of ways. Whether they're creating unique ring tones or using personal photos as a wallpaper, it's amazing how two people can have the same device but very different ways of using it.

Amazon is interesting beyond just its ability to make personalized recommendations. As far back as the early 2000s, Jeff Bezos was making an investment in using its consumer-facing technologies to decode and optimize for his team. We had a chance to chat with Buster Benson, who will make a reappearance in the Quantified Self section, about his time at Amazon in 2002–2003.[17] Buster was part of a team of three people (along with Andy Harbick and Eric Campbell) known as Bezos's Personal Programmers that was tasked with applying technology about connecting people, sharing info, keeping people informed, and using services architectures internally within the company. They gave everyone a blog, built an ideas tool, and created an event calendar, in order to solicit information from the right people and to pass it on to others when they needed it. That dedication to turning their technology around and focusing it internally makes them one of the earliest Decoded Companies.

All the companies listed above exist at the nexus of some powerful tools, including a deep understanding of their customers' need states, the capabilities of the technologies and channels they're using, the ability to define and map their desired outcomes, and a mastery of ambient, real-time data to personalize their customers' experience and drive critical business decisions.

What's true for the consumer Web will eventually become true for the workplace. Decoded Companies are working to make that a reality today.

 **Try this now!** Compare screen shots of the home screen of your smart devices with those of members of your team, your friends, or your family. What similarities can you see? What are the differences?

## THE RECALIBRATION OF EMPLOYEE EXPECTATIONS

Our daily online experiences as consumers are changing our expectations for the technology systems we interact with at work. We have come to expect the speed and immediacy of Google, the connectedness of Facebook, and the beautiful interface of Flipboard from our corporate systems, and we are usually sadly disappointed. As these consumer services continue to improve our lives, the gaps between what employees need and what they are getting are becoming more and more evident. According to a recent study, over a quarter of employees said they regularly downloaded and used noncorporate applications at work that help them work better.[18]

The differences between corporate and consumer-focused systems have never been clearer. Workplace systems are built around business needs, processes, and metrics and are almost always designed and purchased by people who won't be forced to actually use them. Consumer technologies, on the other hand, are built on user desires: They are intelligent, well designed, useful, and personalized, and they deliver what the user wants, when they want it. Simply put, they provide a better experience. This is due to the Darwinian nature of consumer natural selection: We use the consumer technologies that appeal to us, not the ones that are forced on us.

As you will see later in this chapter, your workforce is using many of these technologies on the job already, with or without your consent. From time-tracking software to online collaborative project-management tools, employee-driven technological innovation is becoming increasingly common in businesses across all industries.

## THE HUMAN AGE: TALENT

Though they use these advanced technologies to deconstruct consumer preferences, most enterprises have failed to apply the same practices internally. At home the Internet has radically improved and personalized how we connect, shop, travel, learn, and have fun. At work, we're slaves to legacy systems and decades-old closed thinking. This massive disconnect has created lower engagement, loyalty, and performance.

Why is this important? Why should we care about employees' expectations, especially when the global economy is in trouble and they should be grateful for the jobs they have?

Simple answer: because that assumption is wrong.

For companies like Google, Facebook, and Apple, talent retention is a major strategic priority. According to former TechCrunch editor Michael Arrington, these companies are willing to go to extraordinary lengths to keep their talent. Arrington wrote in 2010 that "one recent Googler, we've confirmed, was recently offered a counter offer he couldn't refuse (except he did). He was offered a 15% raise on his $150,000 mid level developer salary, quadruple the stock benefits and . . . wait for it . . . a $500,000 cash bonus to stay for a year. He took the Facebook offer anyway."[19]

Despite the global economic downturn and the prevalence of high unemployment levels across many different sectors, talent shortages are rampant, according to a 2013 Manpower survey. The study reveals that 39 percent of U.S. employers are having difficulty filling jobs (35 percent globally).[20] Economic difficulties have pushed employers to continue to perform with limited resources, and the result has been an emphasis on the importance of having the right talent in place in order to perform within this resource-constrained landscape. "Talent," the Manpower report continued, "is becoming the key competitive differentiator, and countries and companies with access to the right talent are positioning themselves to succeed in the rapidly changing world of work." Manpower describes this new professional environment as the "human age," in which finding and keeping the right talent is a critical strategic priority.

Those with the right skill sets are in high demand; they have been empowered to choose the employers that best suit their needs. The case of the Googler who turned down half a million dollars makes an important point about motivation: It isn't just about the money. In fact, companies that rely solely on financial incentives might actually be having a detrimental impact on their best talent's performance. Dan Pink, the author of *Drive* and *Free Agent Nation,* has written about the intrinsic factors that drive a person to be motivated: autonomy (our desire to be self-directed); mastery (the joy that comes from getting better at a task); and purpose (our desire to contribute toward something meaningful). His research has shown that financial incentives only work for largely mechanical tasks. When a task requires any creative or strategic thought, the use of a financial motivator often results in decreased output from the highest performers.[21]

The high-order significance of purpose, mastery, and autonomy would be impossible to refute. But can they be measured? Our answer is a resounding yes. How people feel about their work can definitely be microcalibrated. How people feel about the high-order goals of purpose, mastery, and autonomy is a function of their daily opportunities for change, challenge, learning, feedback, etc. This is where data unleashes a whole new set of opportunities, as these data points can be quantified and ultimately leveraged to shape your people's experiences.

As Decoded Companies well know, their talent is their most important asset and differentiator. Most CEOs, even of non-Decoded Companies, rate talent attraction and retention as the biggest challenges facing their organizations, especially with the projected labor shortage in North America. And yet, despite the looming crisis, it seems that they are investing the lion's share of their economic resources in developing new markets and attracting new customers instead of in developing the tools that would enable them to better understand their own labor force.

Most companies intuitively grasp that data is the key to strategic business decisions: the better they understand their customers, the better they can serve them. And yet, that same intuitive understanding has yet to penetrate most workplaces. If data can unlock such potential externally with customers, imagine what it could unleash if we applied that same strategic and analytic focus to our own people. The insights we would glean would impact everything from recruitment and retention to incentive programs, operations, process efficiencies, and more.

This is why we consider the principles of Technology as a Coach and Trainer (see the next chapter), powered by personalizing everything, to be such critical aspects of the foundations of Decoded Companies. Just as consumers have responded with high enthusiasm to the hyperpersonalization movement, employees are sending organizations the same message: It's time to start using some of these new data-driven tools to make the workplace more efficient, more personalized, and more fun.

## THE RULE OF 5 DEGREES

Being surprised by "constructive" feedback that's two quarters old is a very familiar occurrence for almost everyone who has been exposed to inefficient, un-fun workplaces. For many sad reasons that we'll dig into below, this is the standard operating procedure for most companies: very infrequent performance conversations, usually tied to compensation reviews, that provide unactionable feedback months after it would have been useful. We think of this as the Rule of 5 Degrees—if you start out 5 degrees off course, you will wind up completely missing your mark.

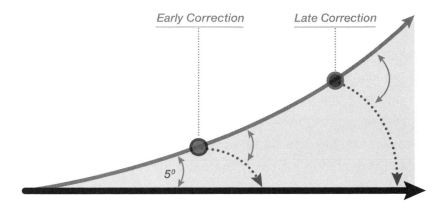

*The Rule of 5 Degrees: a small course correction at the start of a journey is much easier than a large correction later.*

Very early and very slight course corrections are much less disruptive than infrequent and massive ones. At its best it's the difference between feedback (you did something wrong a while ago) and feed forward (based on past data and patterns, it looks like you might be about to do something wrong).

"Companies don't set goals on a frequency that's high enough," explains Dan Martell, CEO of Clarity.fm, a Silicon Valley start-up that connects start-ups with seasoned entrepreneurs. "Some goals should be tracked on a daily or weekly basis, not annually—especially performance."[22]

Traditional annual performance reviews assume that the goals you identified at the beginning of the year are going to still be relevant twelve months later. Goals are often identified without a clear understanding of market realities, leading many people to blindly guess and set the bar too high or too low. Goals should be challenging enough to be motivating; if they are impossible, they'll discourage you from even trying to better yourself.

Almost every company gets annual reviews wrong. This has been a constant theme in Leerom's leadership of Klick. He feels strongly that sticking to an annual cycle just because that's the way other companies have always done it makes no sense at all. The reality is that goals need more fluidity to remain relevant and motivating. Annual planning made sense once upon a time, but today's goals need to be renegotiated whenever needed. Plus, continual feedback is critical. The more iterative you get in your feedback, the better. Agility requires you to be able to adjust targets quickly and continue to move forward.

Annual reviews (or even quarterly reports) provide the same static, infrequent, and rearward-facing perspective as annual physicals; they don't account for the dynamic complexity that encompasses most businesses.

Annual performance reviews have been a staple of human resource talent management strategies since there have been human resources talent management strategies to write about. They have been the major deciding factors in determining promotions, bonuses, and ongoing development. They're linked to the hard truth that you get what you measure. They reduce agility by focusing employees on achieving the goals set during their last review, limiting their ability to compensate for any unforeseen variables. They are backward looking, dissecting mistakes and reviewing behaviors long after the fact. For many employees an annual review is the first time they hear about issues or skills their managers want them to address. They are often colored by recency bias—the looming influence of more recent events over more distant

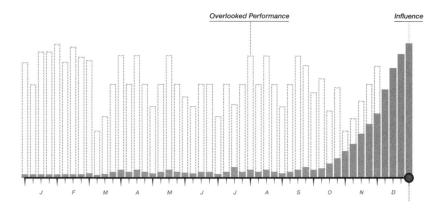

*The recency effect in performance reviews: The influence of recent performance (good or bad) is much stronger than all of the overlooked performance that preceded it. An employee could have excelled from January to October and then hit a roadblock. Their December annual review will be bad even though ten twelfths of their year was awesome.*

ones—instead of providing a comprehensive look at the year as a whole.

At Clarity, the entrepreneur coaching service mentioned at the start of this section, Dan Martell's seven employees use a dashboard tracking thirty-five data points that breaks their growth target down to a weekly figure, helping them stay on track (you'll read more about this later). A red/yellow/green system highlights any potential issues that come up. All employees see the same dashboard, but they can augment it with data reports that are customized specifically to their individual responsibilities.

Martell often meets with surprised reactions when he explains that his very small company has such a sophisticated infrastructure. The system has more than paid for itself by rewarding his people with deeper engagement and better compensation, as well as increasing their performance. Martell gives his employees weekly performance bonuses, a technique he finds highly effective. "Most people are really intelligent, and they want to know how the game is played and how they can score. They want to do their job," he says. "Then they get into big companies and their managers or CEO doesn't tell them what the rules are, or what they can do to be really successful in their roles." He shook his head. "At Clarity, we measure every metric on a weekly basis and that gives us fifty-two opportunities to adjust and be flexible, so we can meet our goals."

 ## THE WEEKLY ONE-ON-ONE

At Klick, performance reviews are grounded in a weekly one-on-one coaching session between an employee and their manager. These sessions are generally twenty minutes long and consist of a review of the employee's goals as well as a snapshot of the status of their projects. The weekly structure provides Genome with a series of data points that can be very useful in identifying trends in an employee's performance. This objectively gathered data enables managers to give highly relevant and personalized feedback.

Behind the scenes, Genome is constantly running thousands to tens of thousands of queries. Thanks to a data warehouse filled with years of historical data, the platform knows the average time it takes to complete various types of tasks and projects for each discipline, type of project, and individual. It can tell when a pattern of behavior is outside those norms. It knows what the parameters of a healthy project look like and can identify if an individual is acting outside of those boundaries. It also knows what that person's previous experience is and past reviews were, and it uses a multitude of other inputs to evaluate their current against their past performance and forecast goals. Once it runs the queries, there are three possible outcomes:

1. If the results indicate that everything is running within appropriate norms, it is green-lit and nothing is flagged.

2. If there is something outside the norms, then Genome either flags it as a concern (you're going to miss an upcoming deadline!) or offers some kudos (you're under budget!).

3. Genome will also offer suggestions based on similar cases that it has encountered previously.

These reports provide managers with a wealth of information, giving them a comprehensive overview of every team member's performance. By then applying their own insights, they can coach their team to ensure that productivity remains within the desired ranges.

These coaching sessions are important for several reasons.

First, no matter how talented someone is, they are bound to make mistakes. Most companies handle this by conducting postmortems, tediously backtracking to discover where a project went offtrack, then adding new steps to their processes to prevent the same thing from happening again (assuming the people carrying out the processes take the time to read the three-hundred-page manual). All in all, it's a recipe for paralysis. You can avoid it by using an adaptive system like GeneSequencer, Genome's project management tool, which codifies all of its project-level learning in order to minimize risks. The weekly reviews do the same thing at the individual level, enabling managers to be forward looking and to use the data they have at hand to flag any potential risks or issues before they happen.

Second, and as we'll discuss in greater depth in the next

chapter, data can help inform your intuition. Intuition is also known as "gut feel," a process through which we attain direct knowledge or cognition without a rational train of thought leading to it. Thanks to the reduced costs of cloud storage and increased computing ability, we can run thousands of queries simultaneously, enabling us to check and model scenarios while monitoring a multitude of data streams and checking progress, deliverables, and budgets in a meaningful way. The output from all of that can be delivered to your team as a constant stream, keeping them informed so they won't need to track it down. All of that information collects in the backs of their heads, giving them the context and data they need to make better gut-feel decisions when they need to do so. Additionally, any issues are flagged early on: Catching them at the 5-degree point prevents massive mistakes later. Because these assessments and interventions are evidence-based, trust and rapport are enhanced rather than degraded.

Third, not every manager is well skilled, especially when it comes to evaluating their employees. Unlike a self-reported 360 tool, which gathers feedback from all of the internal and external stakeholders who surround and interact with the employee and is filled with biased information, data-driven reviews paint a much more objective picture of performance. Ticket statistics, likes, comments, and other Genome tools incorporating data from colleagues and collaborators are seamlessly combined into a unified report. By correcting managers' biases, Genome has your employees' backs.

Fourth, because the weekly reports are linked to the ticket database and GeneSequencer (among other tools), Genome will remind you if something needs to be done and will pester you until that task is completed. Unlike human managers (and spouses), tools don't get upset if they have to remind you twenty-five times to do something, freeing your relationship from the burden and frustration of nagging (and your review from the impact that that can have).

Finally, having regular dialogue between managers and employees built in makes it a part of their weekly routine and removes the stress that often comes with these types of conversations, linked as they so often are to bonuses and promotions. Weekly reviews are much more informal than full-blown performance reviews and, thanks to Genome, they provide employees with regular, quantifiable feedback that is balanced and constructive. (It's worth noting that the combined results of those weekly reviews may ladder up to an annual performance review in order to assess compensation and promotion, if required.) The general concept here is to make every manager as good as your best manager by building their practices into simple tools that everyone can use.

Martell believes that the exercise of weekly reporting will force companies to instrument their systems to accommodate the new pace. "Instead of taking two weeks to reconcile something, forcing yourself to do it weekly will mean you have to make changes to the process to make it more agile," he says. "More agility is always a good thing. It will help companies respond better and faster to a changing environment."

## THE DAWN OF THE CUSTOMIZED DASHBOARDS

Having everyone focused on the same goal has a rather obvious benefit that many companies unfortunately miss. Gengo, a Japanese start-up that offers fast and reliable translation services through a global network of verified translators, provides a perfect example.

In 2012, Gengo translated more than forty million words in over thirty languages for customers all over the world. Clients submit their translation requests into the Web-based Gengo system, which generates a quote that's sent out to the company's network of pretested translators. Less than twenty-eight minutes after the order is placed, 95 percent of jobs are picked up. Once the translation is completed, the client can review the document, add comments, request corrections (if necessary), and then, when they are happy with the final product, collect their document.

As a relatively small company—about forty employees—Gengo relies heavily on its decentralized network of more than seventy-five hundred translators who are located throughout the world. In the absence of face-to-face meetings, it's all the more important that the lines of communication be kept clear.

Gengo projects its dashboards on large screens inside its office so that everyone can see the numbers that are driving business decisions. Rahaf had a chance to chat with Gengo's CEO, Robert Laing, who explained why they are so important to him.[23] He is so convinced of their power that Gengo will be releasing a dashboard for the company's decentralized network of translators, so that they too can achieve the same level of insights into their behavior and alter their productivity positively.

"If you put a goal up on a screen in front of everyone, it becomes much more top of mind for people and gets everyone on the same page," he explained during our chat. "We're about to launch a new dashboard for our translators so they can see their own data and how they compare with others on quality, completion time, or ratings from customers. We're making that data available to them so they can see which metrics we're using and to encourage them to improve their own performance." Additionally, sharing data visually helps people understand things faster. "Visual reporting allows you to communicate quite complex data in a few instants, which means more people in the company understand things, and spend less time wondering."[24]

When we asked if he had made any mistakes with the implementation of this type of technology, Laing admitted that at one point he had overwhelmed the dashboard with too much data. After the release of the internal dashboard in 2009, a new, more complex system was introduced with more inputs and metrics. "All the queries were optimized, all the numbers were perfect, all the numbers were there. You could filter by language pair and level and time period and everything," he recalled. "But sadly there was too much data, not enough visual interpretation, and it took too long to load." So Gengo ended up scrapping it and combining its own custom charts with off-the-shelf dashboard tools. He's thrilled with the results. "It's so much faster, more agile, and more satisfying."

 **Reading list:** *The 4 Disciplines of Execution: Achieving Your Wildly Important Goals* by Chris McChesney and Sean Covey. Excellent, flexible data-driven framework for getting teams focused on a shared goal.

## DATA-DRIVEN DRIVING

Changing gears, so to speak, let's say you're a driver for UPS. You have an hour and a half left before your shift ends and you still have twelve packages to deliver. Your challenge is to find the shortest route that takes rush-hour traffic, the higher priority of premium packages, the construction zone up ahead, and a slew of other variables into account. Knowing that customer satisfaction and mile optimizations are both measures of your performance, should you try to shave a few miles off your regular route or deliver a high-priority package early?

What would you do? In the past you would have used your experience as a driver and your knowledge of local conditions to make a call based on your instincts. This time, thanks to the analytics team at UPS, you have a technical resource that can help make that call for you.

Meet UPS's On-Road Integrated Optimization and Navigation, or simply, ORION. The platform is the brainchild of Jack Levis, UPS's director of process management, and it uses so many algorithms—nearly eighty pages of math formulas—that Levis describes it as "something Einstein would have on his blackboard."

ORION harnesses its analytical genius to plan routes better than any mere mortal ever could. The platform was developed in-house and uses a variety of data streams, including map data, customer information, business protocols, and work rules to calculate the most streamlined and efficient delivery route.[25]

Levis had the idea in 2000 and worked on it for nearly a decade before the first test implementation occurred in 2008. UPS is planning on fully rolling out the system over the next five years, giving frontline supervisors and fifty-five thousand drivers access to a sophisticated decision-making platform that is estimated to have already saved UPS thirty-five million miles a year.[26]

One of the biggest misconceptions about data-driven decision making is the idea that it's far removed from your industry or role. Many people think of data as something technical that only accountants, warehouses, data scientists, or the latest slew of tech start-ups need to worry about. They don't recognize the strategic connection between information collection and decision making. They don't see how data can help increase their own performance.

This skepticism was in evidence during UPS's first rollout of ORION. In hindsight, Levis admits that he bears some of the blame for that. "We'd go in the morning and say, here's your planned number of miles," he recalled. Telling a driver with years of experience that an algorithm knew how to plan a route better than he did struck them as more than a little dismissive.

Levis's team decided to change approaches and tackle the drivers' resistance head-on by issuing a challenge. Drivers were encouraged to try to "beat the computer" by combining ORION's suggestions with their own. One driver who used ORION's suggestions subtracted thirty miles from his daily route.[27] By framing the challenge in easy-to-understand terms—decreasing miles means increasing profitability—they helped frontline staff understand how the variables they put into the system impacted results, creating strategic opportunities.

This is important, because the skills needed to understand and analyze data to some degree are creeping into nearly every job description, making analytical training a top priority. It's not enough just to know how to carry out a series of commands to generate some numbers; you have to understand the underlying factors that generated those numbers—and why they matter. According to Levis, it's the difference between "moving from mathematics that happens to work mathematically, to mathematics that works the way that people actually do."[28]

Beyond that, data-smart devices like ORION can help integrate policies that would be too difficult for drivers to remember and implement individually. For example, after analyzing the vast amount of data gathered from drivers around the world, UPS's sustainability team realized that left turns increased the company's carbon foot-print because of the gas trucks wasted and the emissions they created while waiting for traffic lights to change. Scott Wicker, UPS's chief sustainability officer, revealed in a recent interview that by using their analytical technology to map routes that avoid left turns, the company had saved ninety-eight million minutes of idling time in 2011 alone.[29] ORION's mile-reducing feature created a savings of nine million gallons of fuel, which would net you a cool $32 million at the neighborhood pump (though presumably UPS buys in bulk).

We'll revisit UPS in a few of the later chapters. As for the question that we opened this section with—whether to reduce your miles or deliver a package early—the answer is clear: You should trust your informed intuition. ORION will take everything happening at that exact moment into account before it tells you which choice to make. So instead of just tapping into the knowledge of one driver (you), you can tap into the knowledge of every driver, every combination of routes, and a wealth of other data streams, taking the guesswork out of a decision that will generate happier customers and stronger performance ratings.

 ## GENOME DASHBOARDS

Our knowledge workers are a lot like UPS drivers. Although they spend their days shepherding virtual bits between destinations rather than driving physical boxes around, they still face many of the same prioritization and optimization challenges. One of the most important tools we use at Klick is our Genome-powered dynamic dashboard. Employees use it on a daily basis to help them prioritize their time, based on an ever-changing set of priorities. Each employee and their manager can define anything as a goal as long as it can be tracked using Genome's available data repertoire. Genome then does so and displays the values in real time, taking into account milestones, deadlines, and goals. The platform balances all of these priorities and then displays the most essential goals and tasks that need to be completed at that time. Each employee's goals are therefore constantly being updated based on current information, and each employee knows that their dashboard will show them the right information at the exact point in time when they can act on it.

As an example, let's consider a product manager who reports to Jay as part of the Klick Labs team. Product management is a fairly new role at Klick, since we're primarily a professional services company, so this is a particularly good example of where the system adapts and iterates quickly. Genome's dynamic dashboards enable Jay to easily and quickly set goals for his Labs team. During a weekly review or ad hoc conversation, Jay can use Genome's powerful query builder to pull up virtually any data about the past and current performance of the entire company. He can zoom in to a particular data point with a member of his team (e.g., on-time delivery of scheduled product releases) and then right click to set a goal and timeline for achieving it. Genome will add that goal to the employee's dashboard and provide live trending information, so that he or she can monitor their progress on an ongoing basis.

This ability to measure performance in real time provides a foresight superpower that's unheard of in most organizations; it keeps the team forward looking and focused on goals rather than backward looking and focused on assigning blame.

Instead of a list of nice-to-haves that remains frozen in time all year round, Genome's list is always changing, reflecting the fluidity of the real world. It doesn't assume that the goals you identified for yourself in January will still be your most important goals in August.

Even if you work in an industry where goals tend to remain relatively consistent throughout the year, a dashboard is useful for ensuring that everything is being prioritized at the right time as well. Additionally, dashboards can ensure that there are no surprises at a quarterly or annual review—we can track our progress daily to make sure that we remain on track to meet those goals head-on.

## CUSTOMIZED HUMAN RESOURCES

*Today you are YOU, that is truer than true. There is no one alive who is Youer than You.*
    *—Dr. Seuss*

*Life isn't about finding yourself, life is about creating yourself.*
    *—George Bernard Shaw*

*There isn't another in the whole wide world who can do the things you do because you are special—special.*
    *—Barney the Dinosaur*

*Let's find a solution just for you.*
    *—No HR person, ever*

Growing up we are told that we're all beautiful, unique snowflakes, blessed with exclusive talents and abilities. That message persists through our early school years, but then it's slowly beaten out of us until we get thrown into the workforce and discover the world of one-size-fits-all policies. It's not that the people who designed these approaches were necessarily sadists, or even particularly evil, but rather that the policies and processes come from a data- and technology-poor era in which personalization simply didn't scale. There are many competent and passionate human resource professionals who are frustrated at their inability to transcend a system that puts people last.

This typical approach to human resources management is symptomatic of a much larger disconnect between the management theory they still teach in business school and the age of Decoded Companies. We are heavily invested in turning our Decoded organizations into centers of gravity for talent based on the belief that our people come before our customers and that our customers come before our profits. This inverted model is carefully designed to attract the best and smartest people in our industries and optimized to engage and retain them. Compare that with the traditional principles of management, which Gary Hamel labels as Management 1.0. They go all the way back to the Industrial Revolution and treat people with the same consideration as the machines in a factory: They are regarded as interchangeable units whose output is standardized and who can easily be replaced once they are depleted.

Before anyone accuses us of beating up on the HR department (Hey now! Some of our best friends are in HR!), this approach made sense a hundred years ago, when most businesses were focused on agriculture or manufacturing, and Human Resources departments represented the organization's best effort to manage risks. Lacking any mechanisms for large-scale data collection, process, or analysis, personalization was not to be thought of. Instead they imposed a standardized set of policies and mandatory compliance training. People were sorted into predetermined boxes in an effort to minimize organizational risks and liabilities and maximize efficiency and revenues. They lived in a data-poor world; their systems made do with what they had.

With the rise of a data-abundant economy and a talent-centric marketplace, this archaic management philosophy has become worse than useless. In fact, it detracts from organizations' abilities to succeed.

Which brings us to one of the other major function of Human Resources: managing force reductions. Cutting the workforce is often a company's first approach to managing costs, partly because it's the fastest way to show a big difference in operations and make shareholders happy. In 2010, *Bloomberg BusinessWeek* reported that U.S. Labor Department data showed that 2009's big gains in the S&P 500 were happening precisely as U.S. nonfarm payrolls were declining by five million jobs. Although correlation is not causation, it's hard to imagine that such significant trends are not related.

"Downsizing has been a pervasive managerial practice for the past three decades. Over the years, a firm's standard response to finding itself in financial difficulty was to reduce its workforce," said Franco Gandolfi, professor of management and director of the MBA and Executive MBA programs at Virginia's Regent University School of Business & Leadership.[30]

> While there is ample evidence suggesting that downsizing activities rarely return the widely anticipated benefits, there is also a sobering understanding that downsized firms are forced to deal with the human, social, and societal aftereffects of downsizing, also known as secondary

consequences. While workforce reductions cannot always be avoided, there are compelling reasons why downsizing-related layoffs must nonetheless be seen as a managerial tool of absolute last resort.

The very term "human resources," in our opinion, is horribly offensive. People aren't machines or pawns that can be moved around on a chessboard. This approach is an extension of the hierarchical command-and-control structures from military strategy. (In chapter 5 we'll show you how well that's working out for the army.) When it's difficult or impossible to acquire data and communicate it swiftly across a whole organization, the most efficient way to get something done is to have someone at the top pulling all the strings. From generals on the field to managers in the boardroom, the principles have remained the same: a top-down, do-as-I-say mentality that has simply become outdated.

Decoded Companies don't want to control their people; they want to unleash them.

## QUANTIFYING THE SOFT STUFF

Human Resources departments have been gathering the data from traditional performance reviews and other metrics for decades and using it as an integral part of their tool kit. Referred to as "hard human resource management," these types of metrics often assess employees as depreciating assets, much like buildings or machinery, that incur a lot of costs.

From an accounting perspective they are expenses—salary

costs, insurance costs, etc.—that take a bite from the bottom line. The amount of data HR generates can be mesmerizing, but don't be fooled! It's not the right type of information at all.

The emerging alternative has been dubbed "soft HR management," and it takes a more humane approach, treating employees as an essential component of competitive advantage. The HR department's focus is thus shifted to concentrate on the needs of individual employees by identifying where they can make the best contributions within the business. The soft approach was always considered a nice-to-have, but perks, training services, and coaching were always the first items to be cut during lean times. Soft metrics tend toward self-reported qualitative data that's difficult—if not impossible—to analyze at any kind of scale. Tying them to results is difficult, especially in a world measured by generally accepted accounting principles (GAAP). The result is that expenditures on soft items have traditionally been viewed as costs rather than as investments.

When we collect ambient data it allows us to quantify those gray areas and gives us a transparent look at what's happening within our organizations. This unlocks the ability to deliver customized training, processes, and policies to employees but also requires a significantly new approach to human resources. Luckily for you, dear reader, we've got one, which we'll share in a moment. But first, a brief aside on happiness.

## DELIVERING HAPPINESS—NOW AT WORK!

Confucius reportedly said, "Choose a job you love and you will never have to work a day in your life." We might add that jobs you love are almost always the ones that make you happy. Who better to speak on happiness in the workplace than Tony Hsieh, CEO of Zappos, bestselling author, and master happiness scientist.

 **Reading list:** *Delivering Happiness: A Path to Profits, Passion, and Purpose* by Tony Hsieh

Tony cofounded a company called LinkExchange in 1996, which grew to become a link network that reached over half of all Internet-enabled households every month at its peak. He loved working at the company when it was young and small and mostly made up of his friends, but the culture slowly eroded as it grew and hired from the outside. Eventually he hated the experience and says that it was difficult to get out of bed in the morning to go to work at his own company. They sold it to Microsoft in 1998 for $250 million shortly after hiring their hundredth employee.

Much like Leerom and Aaron's postacquisition experience, which led to the founding of Klick and the formation of many of our cultural touchstones, Tony's formative experience at LinkExchange was critical in his later development of the Zappos culture. He now says, about his new company: "Our number one priority is company culture. Our whole belief is that if you get the culture right, most of the other stuff like delivering great customer service or building a long-term enduring brand will just happen naturally on its own."[31] Sound familiar? That thinking has driven Zappos to over $2 billion in annual revenue and contributed significantly to its November 2009 acquisition by Amazon for a reported $1.2 billion.

Tony's bestselling 2010 book led directly to the formation of Delivering Happiness LLC, an organization dedicated to creating lasting happiness in companies, communities, and cities around the world. Zappos appears from the outside to be a shoe e-commerce play, but it's really an experimental lab for perfecting the science of happiness. Delivering Happiness at Work, the culture-consulting team within Delivering Happiness, took more than fifteen years of research into happiness from leading institutions like Harvard, combined it with lessons learned at Zappos, and now uses it to help other companies engineer their ecosystems and cultures. Through consulting, coaching, workshops, and their unique happiness at work survey tool they lead clients through a five-step process.

1. Ask why you should make work happy: Understand the science, ROI model, and Zappos success.

2. Measure and plan your journey through the happiness at work survey.

3. Align, define, and launch through executive workshops and consulting.

4. Live your culture by coaching your internal coaches to spread the word.

5. Celebrate! Look, listen, and evolve by retaking the happiness at work survey, capturing your company in a Zappos-style culture book, and joining the broader Delivering Happiness at Work global community.

We had the chance to sit down with the very aptly named Sunny Grosso, culture and brand boss for Delivering Happiness at Work, for a conversation all about quantifying the soft stuff.[32] "The soft stuff is the hard stuff," she told us when sharing some of Delivering Happiness's core philosophy. "Getting the soft stuff right is what we're all about."

The happiness at work survey is their primary tool for measurement. It can be done individually or as an organization; the people who work at Delivering Happiness complete it quarterly, though most organizations opt for semiannually. Jay completed the individual study and was excited to find out that he ranks a 7.7 for happiness at work. His "happiness landscape" (the immediate, interactive, and highly visual results presentation from the study) helped to put that in context, providing scores for his home, work, job, relationships at work, organization, and social impact.

 **Try this now!** Individuals can use the happiness ROI calculator and the happiness at work survey tool for free at https://app.happinessatworksurvey.com

Sunny explained that the four parts of the survey (personal, work environment, actual job, and feelings and emotions at work) help to quantify four key areas: progress, control, connectedness, and higher purpose. These align well with Dan Pink's ideas about mastery, autonomy, and purpose from *Drive*, as well as speaking to the value of connectedness that we'll see in the Data as a Sixth Sense and Engineered Ecosystem chapters.

We asked Sunny about the importance of connections between people. She shared that Zappos has always put a big emphasis on what they call personal emotional connection (PEC), going so far as to create specific programs to increase it. Employees, for example, are given an extra fifteen minutes before their lunch break to write thank-you cards to their customers or to send them flowers. There are no rules around these connection creators, and they aren't abused (a consistent theme when you design trust into your systems and policies). Sunny elaborated on why this is so critical: "Transparency is like a tsunami. People can see what happens inside your organization through your Web site and the interactions they have with your people. You need to get your culture right, so that they see a true picture and choose to do business with you." That's the real value of quantifying the soft stuff.

## THE CONCIERGE: A NEW MODEL FOR HUMAN CAPITAL MANAGEMENT

As noted earlier, the cost of delivering bespoke policies and training was simply too high to be feasible until the convergence of data, personalization, and social tools as covered in this book. In the data-poor world in which the discipline of HR came of age, the only reasonable approach was to attempt to make everything "fair" by grouping employees into buckets, usually based on role and seniority, and then applying the same one-size-fits-all policies to everyone in them.

Unfortunately, this quest for fairness, while well intended, has turned out to be fundamentally unfair: When you create a policy that standardizes how people are evaluated and rewarded, it ends up being a straitjacket. More important, it "levels the playing field," making your worst performers appear better and your best performers appear worse. Like all demographics-based approaches, it assumes that everyone in the same bucket is motivated by the same things and ignores their unique histories and personalities.

One of this book's leitmotivs is a question: What would happen if we used data to understand our talent the same way we use it to understand our customers? Now we'd like to add another question: What if we treated our talent as well as we treat our best customers? Although there are certain assumptions inherent in those questions—namely that you invest both in understanding your customers and in treating them well—we believe that this represents a very significant shift, and that it's applicable to virtually any organization of any size.

 At Klick we struggled with this idea during our earliest years, when we were still a small, owner-managed company. Decisions around who got promoted and who didn't were based on Leerom's and Aaron's opinions about who they thought could handle the challenges. The decisions were made on a case-by-case basis, using a small variety of inputs. The introduction of competency models—standardized job descriptions and clear development plans that outlined an individual's progression through the ranks of the organization—ended up solving one set of issues while creating another. On the one hand, standardized roles made it easier for Klick to identify gaps in the workforce and guide recruiting. On the other hand, there were several instances where the people who checked all the necessary boxes for the job requirements ended up not being the right people for the job. This was one of our first indicators that we weren't identifying or measuring the right attributes to determine who would be a good fit for a particular role, and it sparked our ongoing experimentation with new models for managing our people.

Over time, as our company has expanded many times over, doubling and redoubling in size, we came to see Human Resources as a support function for the strategic development of talent. We eliminated the traditional HR department and replaced it with what we call a *Concierge Service*, whose mission is to continually deliver the best possible products and services to our staff. This department is able to respond to specific requests based not on general policies but rather on the unique needs of individuals and the value they deliver to the organization. Its role is built on a system that runs on the principles of merit rather than seniority.

Generally, we recruit people into the Concierge team who have three to five years of experience in training and development, career counseling, corporate communications, performance reviews, and/or metrics/key performance indicators. Most important, though, we look for individuals who are self-starters, who excel at motivating people, and who love experimenting with new ways to increase the cultural cohesiveness of our organization.

Our concierges are there to help managers when they identify a unique need and to work with them to come up with a customized solution. They are our resident people experts and are measured themselves primarily on employee engagement metrics. Once a quarter we ask individuals to identify on a scale of one to ten how much they love working at Klick. The quarter's results are benchmarked against historical data, and any significant deviations are immediately investigated. For example, if one employee constantly rates their work experience as an eight and suddenly it drops to a five, the Concierge team will analyze that data to identify the reason for the drop. Maybe it was a complex project, a demanding client, or a new manager, all of which can be easily addressed if caught early enough. We often get asked about whether or not people will respond honestly to these types of questions, and the answer is: It depends on your culture. If you have a culture that values talent above all else, people will feel that and want to participate in maintaining a happy and positive environment. These self-reported numbers are also just one data point—a change in satisfaction is often accompanied by a host of other behaviors that can be easily picked up on by an astute manager with the right tools.

For example, at Klick, in addition to this self-reported data, we also rely on ambient data that tracks whether an individual has been at work for above average hours by looking at the times they badge in and out of the building. We combine this with more accurate predictors of employee happiness, such as the retention level and number of promotions across the company and the activity level on Genome's social features—the number of posts, dialogues, likes, etc., that are happening on the internal network.

Our concierges' objective is to turn Klick into a center of gravity that attracts and retains the best and most engaged talent. We believe this should be the objective of every Human Resources department—and that they should be evaluated on how well they are increasing the learning and engagement of the workforce.

 **Privacy:** Announcing that we collect badge data always gets us the same reaction: "Isn't that a little too Big Brother?" In chapter 4 we will go into more detail about our decoded data principles, where we'll show you how to evaluate your data policy to make sure it addresses privacy concerns. For now, know that Klick is completely transparent about the data it collects, and that transparency is applied companywide, meaning that everyone can see everyone else's data. Everyone at Klick understands that all companies with badge-swipe capabilities collect and measure data; Klick just happens to be very open about it. Finally, Klick's culture is the key to why employees don't consider this a breach of privacy: People are never reprimanded or evaluated on when they arrive or leave the office.

# ENGAGEMENT THROUGH SPHERE OF INFLUENCE AND PERSONALIZED POLICIES

Our concierges' abilities to use data to identify each individual's contribution and deliver customized solutions goes against the traditional outlook, which assumes that each person in the same role creates the same value within an organization. Thanks to Genome's ability to track each individual's project contributions, we can see the number of billable hours that each individual generates for themselves or for their team, a critical success factor for any professional services business. This figure helps the concierges develop an objective understanding of each individual's revenue-generating value and makes it easier to deliver services personalized for them at an appropriate scale. Concierges are empowered to make decisions based on what's best for both the business and its employees. There are no strict one-size-fits-all policies but general guidelines that can be adapted to suit each individual's needs.

HubSpot, a Cambridge-based marketing automation company, was founded in June 2006 by Brian Halligan and Dharmesh Shah. We had the chance to chat with Brian and Andrew Quinn, their director of training and development, about a variety of topics, including their influence-mapping project.[33]

Brian never wanted HubSpot to follow a traditional management hierarchy. He designated one of its meeting room whiteboards as its official influence map when it moved into its current offices, using it to understand the flow of power and influence among their people. The map helped HubSpot answer questions such as:

- Who are the power brokers in the organization?

- Who gets stuff done?

- Who drives change and innovation?

- Who has the most sway over the organization?

Traditional org charts answer none of those questions (though they are useful for figuring out who you should ask for a raise). Hierarchical reporting relationships rarely define the flow of true influence, which follows a more matrixed model.

HubSpot's map ran on an honor system. Each employee would write their name into a free spot on the board when they started. They'd add black lines to reflect their reporting relationships, erasing and redrawing them as their role changed over time. More important, they'd add blue lines whenever they felt that someone had had a repeated influence on them or the work they were doing. Andrew, for example, had a lot of blue lines coming into his spot, because he runs training and development for the whole company and was an early influence on most new hires.

The board was a huge success for HubSpot during its early years. In classic get-what-you-measure fashion, the board drove HubSpotters to go out of their way to meet new people and collaborate across org chart black lines in order to accumulate more highly valued blue lines. The board was ultimately a victim of its own success, though, helping to grow the company to the point where the whiteboard could no longer hold all the relationships (and the meeting room was needed for office space!). The influence map was so important to Brian and Dharmesh that they've resisted rolling out most collaboration and ERP systems because they're too hierarchy-based. They're still looking for a digital influence map to this day. We'll have more to say about HubSpot in chapter 5.

 **Try this now!** This is a simple exercise you can do with your team on a whiteboard or even just a sheet of paper. Compare your organizational chart with the map of the people who influence each other the most on your team that you create. What does the map look like? Are you surprised by the findings?

Understanding and mapping influence enables a company to accommodate the needs of its most important assets: its talent. One of Klick's application developers had been with us for about a year when he approached the Concierge team with a challenge. His wife was attending graduate school 230 miles away. After their first child was born, he wanted to spend more time with his family. Thanks to Genome, the Concierge team could see how much value he had brought to the company; they knew how important it was that they keep him happy. So they crafted a custom telecommuting solution that allowed him to spend some weeks in Klick's offices and some working from home. At his desk in his home office is a screen attached to a webcam and a microphone, which allows him to be digitally present at Klick. He's taken to leaving the webcam running all day so that people feel comfortable just popping in to say hello, much as they would if he were physically present. Thanks to Genome, his team is always aware of what he's working on, ensuring transparency and accountability and forestalling the stigma that colleagues sometimes attach to remote workers.[34] This has proven so effective that we now have live video portals between all our offices.

This is just one example of how data can drive personalized

services and policies. A traditional company with a no-remote-work policy might have simply said no and lost out on all the value that that person brings to his job. For more examples of personalized policies, check out decodedbook.com/tech-as-a-coach.

# CUSTOMIZED RECRUITING

We believe that talent is the most important asset within today's organizations, which means that recruiting talent is one of the most essential roles. Recruiting can be a hit-or-miss process; a balancing act between experience and cultural fit is often required (we like to say that it's 100 percent skill and 100 percent cultural fit—and yes, we know that's 200 percent). At Klick, we trust our people to help us identify the rock stars we want to work for us. Instead of working with traditional recruiters, Klick uses its data-centric culture to identify high-value targets. The Concierge team is constantly analyzing online data from sources such as LinkedIn to identify people who have the appropriate skill sets to fill a role. By overlaying that data on Genome's own information, the concierges can see if any of Klick's employees have previously worked with any of the potential candidates. On a weekly basis, appropriate staff are asked to rate their desire of working with one former colleague or another. Candidates who are consistently ranked highly by several people go to the top of the list and get scouted. Our data has shown that the people who are hired through this method consistently outperform those recruited through traditional means.

Instead of relying on just one person's judgment (e.g., the concierge or HR professional), this data-centric approach to recruiting benefits from the experiences and insights of the whole company, adding another level of scrutiny and vetting to our hiring process and dramatically increasing the odds of hiring someone who will get along well with the rest of the team. Hiring people who are well rated has a positive impact on the morale of existing staff, because they know that their input is valued and that their new colleagues will be people they work with well. This method also increases the likelihood that the person who ends up being hired will share the same values and drivers that will help them thrive at Klick.

## RECRUITING, BYOD, AND THE CONSUMERIZATION OF ENTERPRISE IT

Any company that adopts a people-first belief system understands the importance of finding and hiring the right people. We've been basically doubling our team every year for the past few years; we are constantly in a hiring state and always on the lookout for really good people. You have to be a company that top talent wants to work at in order to win the war for top talent; this means that we are constantly tweaking our environment and culture to make sure that we stay (at least) one step ahead of our competitors in delivering the kinds of things that employees want. It might not seem obvious at first, but IT policies can be a major factor in this.

One of the ways that some companies are responding to changing consumer expectations is by allowing their employees a wider scope of choice and control over their workplace technology. Bring your own device (BYOD) sounds like an IT policy, but for companies like GE, the freedom to pick the type of technology you use at work is a large part of their recruitment and retention strategy.[35]

Under a pilot project introduced in early 2011, some GE employees had the option of choosing Apple's Mac notebooks or desktops over Windows PCs. The pilot was built on a successful rollout of iPhones that began in 2008, when ten thousand employees chose to make the switch from BlackBerry. Greg Simpson, GE's chief technology officer, said that recruits often ask whether GE supports Macs and iOS devices as a way of asking "Is it a contemporary company or not?" Providing such support was "a recruiting-positive thing" for GE, he added.

In 2010, IBM introduced an official BYOD policy, which allowed employees to use their own smartphones and tablet devices to access company e-mails, servers, and databases.[36] IBM's chief information officer, Jeanette Horan, says the program "really is about supporting employees in the way they want to work. They will find the most appropriate tool to get their job done. I want to make sure I can enable them to do that, but in a way that safeguards the integrity of our business." The recognition that employees have the power to drive decision making in the C-suite of the world's largest companies is a powerful example of the consumerization of corporate IT. As noted above, it can have big benefits for recruiting and retention, but it's not without its potential issues. The policy has created real challenges for Jeanette Horan and her five-thousand-strong team.

Horan said that many IBM staffers were "blissfully unaware" of the security risks posed by many of the apps that they download on their devices for fun. An internal staff survey revealed several practices that could put the company's intellectual property (IP) at risk. By using their devices to create unsecured Wi-Fi hot spots to forward work e-mails to their Gmail accounts, Horan and her team discovered, there were myriad ways that confidential information could be inadvertently released to the public.

Now IBM configures each personal device to enable remote

wiping in case an employee misplaces their phone or it is stolen. Horan's team has created twelve "personas" that outline specific-use cases for what employees can and can't do with their personal devices. She has even introduced new software that encrypts information sent on IBM's networks.

As new applications and devices are introduced, IBM must constantly review and update their BYOD practices. In 2012, Horan's team banned the use of the cloud storage device Dropbox, which employees were using as an easier alternative to IBM's private servers. Employees were creating their own personal Dropbox accounts, making it impossible for IBM to track or control access to proprietary information, especially if an employee's contract was terminated. In addition, IBM has banned the use of iCloud, Apple's rival cloud storage service, and disabled Siri, the voice-activated personal assistant available on the iPhone 4s and higher, for fear that the voice queries could reveal sensitive information, since they are uploaded to Apple's servers. Even a seemingly innocuous question about finding a lunch spot near a certain location could show a trend of increased visits to a specific client's site if looked at across a lot of users. These challenges will only grow as workplace technology becomes increasingly consumerized.

And there can be no doubt that it will. In a 2011 Accenture Survey, 45 percent of respondents indicated that their personal consumer devices were more useful than the tools and applications provided by their IT departments. The study, which surveyed four thousand employees in sixteen countries, found that 27 percent of respondents were willing to pay for their own devices to use at work because of the improvement in productivity and job satisfaction.[37] "Employees are surprisingly willing to pay in order to use the technologies they love at work," said Jeanne Harris, executive research fellow and senior executive at the Accenture Institute for High Performance. "As a result, they are going to use them, with or without their company's approval." Using the latest technology is a big priority for talent. A third Accenture study revealed that 88 percent of executives surveyed believed that employee use of consumer technology can improve job satisfaction.

That third study also revealed that for the most part companies are addressing the issues that arise on an ad hoc, case-by-case basis (e.g., Should employees be allowed to have personal blogs? Can employees store information on iPads?). Only 27 percent of the executives stated that they were beginning to look at the consumerization of the workplace in a broader, more holistically strategic way.

# LIPSTICK ON A PIG

Not all companies are willing to tackle these changes as directly as IBM has. As the social Web continues to focus on beautifully designed, easy-to-use platforms and services, there are some in the enterprise space who are trying to embrace the aesthetic shifts without recognizing the underlying behavioral shifts that are driving them. Though some designer-led tech start-ups place the user experience at the core of their offerings, many legacy-burdened enterprise-focused companies are trying to compete with these socially integrated, seamless experiences by applying a glossy sheen of design without adding any actual improvements in functionality— the equivalent of slapping a new coat of paint on a crumbling house.

Workday, a software-as-a-service (SaaS) company that provides human resources, payroll, and financial management solutions, is one example. The interface looks glossy, which puts it a leap ahead of its competitors, most of which are still designing software that looks and feels like the mainframe era. But at an underlying level, there's not much else about Workday that is different. It is in many ways a natural evolution of PeopleSoft, where Workday's founders got their start. Henry Ford would call it a faster horse; we would say that evolution rather than revolution has produced a faster clipboard. Pursuing an aesthetic adaptation without taking the data-centric trends that are shaping consumer behaviors into account is one of the fastest ways we can think of to redundancy. Employees know what a good experience feels like, and they aren't going to be fooled by impostors.

Smart companies that want the decoded advantage are looking beyond the surface to the cores of their businesses, especially when it comes to empowering and retaining talent. As we've seen, employees are eager for technologies that make their job easier, and they are willing to pay for it. They want a technological experience that's easy to use and incorporates the norms they have become accustomed to: collaboration, speed, and transparency. Decoded companies are embracing these trends and using them not just to reshape their markets but to empower their talent to create products and services that set new standards.

## TECHNOLOGY AS A COACH IN ACTION: GENESEQUENCER

Instrumenting your HR department, training and development, and policies are all great first steps. Don't stop there! How awesome would it be to have an intelligent, predictive, helpful data-driven coach with you every step of the way when you are completing a process? (Answer: very.) Klick has just that in GeneSequencer, a feature of Genome that uses ambient data and personalization to ensure a smooth work flow.

Although most people rarely think of it in these terms, organizations should be focused on the idea of accelerating tenure. Attracting the best people by creating a center of gravity is just the beginning of a process that can span years of training and development. Every team leader, manager, and CEO obsesses about how to make all of their people as good as their best people, which usually means turning them into experts. Malcolm Gladwell quoted neurologist Daniel Levitin on the ten-thousand-hour rule in his book *Outliers:*

> "The emerging picture . . . is that ten thousand hours of practice is required to achieve the level of mastery associated with being a world-class expert—in anything," writes the neurologist Daniel Levitin.[38]

If world-class experts are defined by the amount of time they've invested in developing their skill, then the challenge is to accelerate the process. Decreasing the ten thousand hours to five thousand would create a very significant gain in productivity. At Klick, we're somewhat obsessed with the challenge of accelerating tenure; it is at the heart of many of our ongoing experiments.

Tenure acceleration has a direct bearing on project management. The ability to deliver a given work unit on time and on budget turns on the expertise and experience of the team that is working on it. Although project management is particularly important for professional services firms, it transcends the boundaries of our business model and industry. And most of the methodologies that exist to optimize it fail.

From lean operations to Six Sigma, project management philosophies all suffer from a key weakness. All of them are backward looking and inefficient when it comes to optimization methodology. A company starts with an idea for a particular work stream, someone makes a mistake, and management reacts by adding a new step to the process to manage this risk and stop it from happening again. Think of the original process as a nice, clean artery through which the blood streams smoothly and rapidly. Each addition is like so much plaque collecting on its walls. The work stream gets slower and slower until it eventually stops and you have a bureaucratic heart attack.

Bureaucracy is not necessarily evil in and of itself. But it puts processes before people; it assumes that workers are standard products and that everyone involved in a process has the same level of experience and savvy as everyone else. We believe that the best way to optimize a process is to have a better understanding of the people who are involved in it, whose collective experience levels will be far more predictive of high-quality output than any process itself. Organizations that don't want to restrict their top performers with cumbersome processes but at the same time want to minimize the errors being made by more junior talent have to do a complicated balancing act.

In Klick world the answer is GeneSequencer, a Genome feature that uses data and analytics to help project managers stay on track—and to provide team members with appropriate support when they need it. GeneSequencer is preloaded with descriptions of many of the types of projects completed at Klick. It provides a detailed, customized checklist for any project type and, drawing on a compilation of what Leerom calls "every mistake we've ever made," a list of special considerations to be aware of. In essence, it leverages all of Klick's collective experiences and failures in order to avoid repeating them, while providing a supportive structure for employees who are trying out something for the first time.

We can already hear your objections. A tool that generates checklists for people? How is that innovative or customized? The difference is in Genome's use of ambient data to give each checklist a unique and personalized twist. Since Genome knows the entire project history of every individual in the company, it can generate a checklist and items to watch out for that takes each project manager's experience into account. A project manager who is running a particular type of project for the first time will receive a much more comprehensive checklist than someone who has completed this type of project several times in the past. Genome watches your back, ensuring that you're aware of all the best and worst practices of everyone who has done the same project before you, helping you stay on top of the process.

For the newcomer, Genome does several things automatically to help ensure a smooth execution. First it alerts the PM's team and their boss to let them know that this is the first time their colleague is running this type of project. Genome automatically pairs the PM with a more experienced "buddy" who will be a source of support during their first run. Second, if the project requires certain training, Genome will alert the PM at the appropriate moment in the project's timeline that they should take an online mini–training session. Finally, Genome increases the documentation, providing an exhaustive checklist that clearly outlines all the steps that need to be taken, as well as a list of risks and potential pitfalls to avoid. Leerom and Aaron recognized that a project is the most at risk when someone is running it for the first time. By turning that risk into an ideal time for a training intervention (what we call a *teachable moment*—see the next chapter for details), GeneSe-quencer maximizes the chances for success.

Note that some items will be generated for every PM's list, and others will be included only on those of beginners. This approach manages work flow without adding more bureaucracy. Genome will react differently every time that same PM is faced with that same type of project, generating successively less and less rigorous lists. The key is that the system dials processes up or down to meet the individual's needs rather than forcing the individual to conform to a one-size-fits-all process.

Once a task is repeated enough times it becomes a habit—something whose execution is so automatic we don't even need to think about it. Genome's approach capitalizes on our brain's natural mechanisms. In his book *The Power of Habit*, author Charles Duhigg writes about the ingrained process that causes our brains to create a habit. There are essentially three main components. It starts off with a cue, such as the blare of the morning alarm. This triggers your brain to start the associated routine: You shuffle out of bed and head downstairs. That, in turn, generates the final and best part: the reward we receive when we take our first sip of coffee and the jolt of caffeine kicks in and helps us become completely awake.[39]

 **Reading list:** *The Power of Habit* by Charles Duhigg

Once a habit like this has formed we crave the endorphins that are released with getting that reward. A former smoker who used to take a cigarette break every afternoon at 3:00 P.M. will still find himself struggling with his urge to light up around that time, despite the fact that the addictive effects of nicotine are eliminated one hundred hours after the smoker's last cigarette. Often it's not the drug withdrawal that drives people to smoke but the craving for the pleasure they'd learned to anticipate at a particular time of the day.

This cycle is called a habit loop. Companies have used their understanding of this psychological mechanism to influence consumer behavior for decades. Duhigg tells the story of Claude Hopkins, the Pepsodent toothpaste marketing genius who in the 1900s co-opted the habit loops of millions of Americans by transforming the feel of film on their teeth into a cue that could only be rewarded by the minty tingle of Pepsodent.

Genome uses data to create cues and deliver rewards, using checklists and other resources to establish behavioral routines that will help PMs be accurate and efficient. Once those routines have been established, Genome can step back and let the brain's natural tendencies take over, getting out of the way and letting the staff do its job.

By collecting internal data on the scale that Klick does we are continually drawing on the accumulated sum of every employee's experiences, mistakes, and lessons learned. This enables us to reduce the risk associated with taking on increasingly larger projects while maintaining the autonomy and flexibility that motivates our top performers to help the company retain its agility. Leerom feels that the alternative is that you keep learning, keep doing postmortems, and keep adding to the processes. We've talked about the plaque that builds up in the organization's arteries before—the end result is that one day you wake up and you're a massive, inefficient company losing ground to your more nimble competitors (good luck with that!). Our efficiency has steadily increased since we rolled out GeneSequencer, and we've seen an obvious and measurable revenue and profit increase.

 ## EVOLVE OR DIE

Decoded Companies are flexible in identifying stress points and nimble in quickly finding solutions, which helps them stay ahead of their competition. Such agility would be impossible without a culture that not only values the strengths, insights, and experience of employees but also provides a trusted place for open dialogue to take place. Decoded Companies can't afford to stand on ceremony.

When Aaron noticed a dip in the number of people who were tracking their hours, he logged on to Chatter, Genome's micro-blogging platform, and wrote a post about it.

> At the core of our business, we charge our clients for our time. This means that for every individual in a billable role, there is a baseline amount of revenue that must be billed out in order to maintain our financial ratios. The simplest way to achieve this is for every single individual to properly bill their time.

Aaron suspected that the emphasis on tracking time might not have been accurately communicated to employees who had recently joined Klick's team and wanted to make sure that this trend was reversed.

> The data is used to inform our decisions around when to hire, our rate card targets, how much to charge for deliverables,

and who is going above and beyond. Tracking time does not necessarily mean we will get the client to pay for all of it, but we do need know exactly how much value we're giving away (or investing), so that we can make better estimates next time.

After his post was published, a conversation immediately started in the Chatter comments. One staff member was quick to point out, "Always having an appropriate place to bill the time is the biggest problem. I know in my case, the time involved to beg someone for the proper ticket often isn't worth it." This seemed to resonate with other Klick staff, who agreed. "I've been struggling with this problem for a while now," another wrote.

As Aaron read through the comments he quickly realized the real issue: People weren't failing to track their time because they didn't want to or because they didn't understand the importance of doing so. Rather, there appeared to be a gap in the process that was getting in the way.

In Klick's system, once a project manager has set the budget for the resources allocated to a project, they would often lock it to ensure that they didn't go over time or budget. However, locking it prevented those working on it from accurately logging their time, because only the project manager could extend resources. The resulting friction meant that people just didn't log their time properly, skewing the data that Klick needed to make appropriate decisions.

Once the issue had been verbalized, the conversation turned to generating solutions. A consensus had been reached in the discussion thread within a few hours about the best way to proceed, and Aaron's team made the necessary coding changes to the platform to remove this obstacle. Because the Klick team was empowered to give honest and rapid feedback, they had identified and solved a company issue within hours of Aaron's original post.

Small stories like this one add up over time. Faced as it is with large, bureaucratic competitors that move at a much slower pace, Klick's agility is a key asset. Having a culture that fosters it is not a luxury but a strategic necessity.

 ## Decoded Metrics

Managers no longer have to rely on snapshot data but can look into their organizations and see what is happening in real time. This allows us to measure things that we never could before. These talent-centric metrics help empower our people and improve our companywide performance. You'll see this section in several of the other chapters, where we'll introduce a new metric that is suited for the Decoded Company.

## Metric: The Anxiety-Boredom Continuum

As we mentioned earlier, we should set goals that are challenging enough to keep employees motivated but not so hard to achieve that they get discouraged. How can data help talent and management to better calibrate their goals?

Ask a game developer. Back in the days of coin-op arcades, ego and pride propelled some hard-core users to feed buckets of quarters into the machines. It was all about skills: how quickly you responded to stimuli, your ability to memorize action sequences, and your powers of concentration translated into high scores. But developers soon learned that making a game too difficult was a turnoff for most players. Exacerbating this was the fact that the games' levels of difficulty were preset, either by a switch (at the beginning of the game the player could choose beginner, intermediate, or advanced) or by an algorithm, in which the game started off easy and then progressed to higher levels of difficulty on a predetermined curve.

The trick was to create and sustain a high enough level of challenge to keep a player interested without crossing the threshold that would make them stop trying altogether. James Slavet, a partner at the venture capital firm Greylock Ventures, calls this the ideal spot on the "anxiety-boredom continuum." It's important to understand this spectrum if you want to maximize your best people's performances. He wrote:

> Star performers can get bored easily, and often function best when they're expected to rise to great challenges. You want expectations to be high, but not completely overwhelming. With this in mind, check in with your employees periodically about where they are on this continuum, while also keeping an eye out for signs of where they stand. If they have low energy, or are showing up late and leaving early, they may be bored. If they're responding to small setbacks with anger or frustration, or getting sick a lot, they may be pushing too hard.[40]

Game developers have a tool that allows them to use a player's data to customize an environment that is optimized for his or her skills. It's called dynamic difficulty adjustment (DDA). It analyzes the way a player moves through the game, the amount of time it takes to complete a level, the difficulty they are having with a particular element, and even their in-game interactions. Then it uses that information to ensure that the player is adequately challenged by the demands of the game and entertained by the narrative of the story. The video game *Left 4 Dead*, which was released in 2008, introduced something called the AI director. It's an artificial intelligence software that monitors and analyzes each player's performance and generates a unique number of enemies and level bosses to defeat based on that information. The director evaluates a player's current situation, status, skill, location, and health to determine where the player will encounter enemy forces or find valuable health packs, ammo, weapons, or other useful tools. Each player will experience a level in a unique way depending on their own set of circumstances.

In the workplace, ambient data can help employers in a similar fashion: Collected data will show an employee's progression as they become more familiar with certain aspects of their job. As their rate of completion and the quality of their work increases, algorithms can alert managers that they require additional challenges. In the same way that our informed intuition helps us minimize risks by highlighting potential issues in projects before they happen, this type of information can alert us to the risk that an employee might be bored or underchallenged, signaling us to address their needs before they start looking for another job.

 **Try this now!** Games are a great way to experience the anxiety-boredom continuum. *Left 4 Dead* is a great game that was created by Valve, a Decoded Company we'll introduce you to in the next few chapters.

## CHAPTER SUMMARY: ALL-SIZES-FIT-NONE

When organizations can better understand the practical knowledge an individual has about a specific type of work, they can dynamically shape processes to reflect it. GeneSequencer enables us to help a colleague at Klick when they execute a type of project for the first time through the dialing up of certain processes, including training interventions or the use of a buddy for extra support. When executing the same type of work in the future, the process can be relaxed and a higher level of autonomy allowed. Like process, we believe policy can be personalized around an individual; likewise can the opportunities be for rewards and recognition.

## DECODED TOOLBOX

### Dashboard

A dashboard can give a team a powerful, dynamic, and agile way to stay focused on the right priorities in a fast-paced world. When building a dashboard, you must first have a clear understanding of what exactly you want to measure. Most organizations and managers track things such as results instead of things that are predictive. Successfully executing on a goal requires the ability to identify potential issues while still having the time to make changes. That means we need to think about the indicators that can influence the result you want to measure. Instead of measuring profit, examine the things that drive profit: It could be utilization rates or the number of signed work orders. For a sales team, it would be more useful to look at the number of leads or scheduled meetings instead of final sales numbers. A dashboard should generate numbers about things that exist within the sphere of influence of your team; that is to say, things that it has the power to act on.

Dashboards can vary in scale and complexity. They can be as simple as an Excel spreadsheet or as complex as an analytics solution implemented by your IT department. They can be used to measure anything from personal fitness levels to companywide performance; that's the beauty of this customizable tool—the sky is the limit!

Here are two ways to get started:

**1) Make your own: Use a spreadsheet.**

Each row should be the name of something you want to track, and each column should reflect the time period (days, weeks, months). Go to decodedbook.com/dashboard and check out some of our templates if you need some inspiration!

**2) There are many services that you can use which provide customizable dashboards.**

- Google Analytics has a great dashboard feature that enables users to analyze the details of their site traffic.

- Services such as HootSuite or Postling offer social media dashboards to help you track your activities across various social networks.

- Lifetick and Joe's Goals are two services that provide dashboards for keeping track of personal goals, such as fitness, health, or education.

- For key business metrics, look at subscription-based services such as Chartio, Geckoboard, or Unilytics. These companies all offer a free trial period, so try a couple, until you get a better sense of which features are important to you.

Given the printed nature of this book, it's possible that some of these tools might no longer exist by the time you read this. For an updated list of tools, go to decodedbook.com/tech-as-a-coach.

## One-on-One Weekly Meeting

Scheduling a twenty-minute weekly meeting with your team to evaluate goals, check in on progress, and provide consistent feedback can replace the dreaded annual review with fifty-two opportunities to make sure your team is happy, motivated, and productive.

One of the main components of a Decoded Company is its ability to react to patterns and not exceptions. Everyone has bad weeks and good weeks; weekly one-on-one meetings create a fair system that addresses the real issues identified over time instead of the perceived issues created by recency bias. Having some type of quantified feedback helps participants reduce emotion and focus instead on performance. The weekly meetings are a perfect opportunity to review goals managed with dashboards. Remember, the purpose of these meetings is to check in and provide feedback, but also to identify moments for coaching and inspiration. While we are not the first to suggest one-on-one weekly meetings (a 2005 academic paper by Hortzman and Auzenne called one-on-one meetings "the single most effective management tool"), the decoded advantage emphasizes tracking and measuring data that can provide a better context for the discussions at hand.[41]

1. Set a time frame during which you experiment with weekly one-on-ones with your team. We recommend a minimum of at least two months.

2. Schedule a twenty-minute meeting with each team member.

There are several different approaches and templates you can use to help you structure the meetings:

- The O3 (one-on-one) template provided by Manager -Tools.com offers guidelines for a thirty-minute meeting. The basic breakdown is: ten minutes for you; ten minutes for them; and ten minutes for developments. The Web site offers many resources that can be found online to give you an idea.[42]

- Remember to try and link this to quantitative numbers. Some examples of recurring agenda items can include:
  - **A review of last week's tasks.** This can be a percentage of tasks completed. A steady decrease in this number from week to week can indicate a potential issue.
  - **Positive/negative highlights from the week.** Ask them to rate their week on a scale of one to ten.
  - **What was accomplished and what will be accomplished in the upcoming weeks.** This can be broken down into percent completed or a simple binary yes/ no on completion.
  - **A review of time lines and budgets to make sure everything is on track.** You can use a red/yellow/ green system to flag issues that need review.

This way you are combining a structured session with captured data that you can track from week to week. It gives you a great at-a-glance view of how your team member is doing and ensures that you understand the big picture, in case they have a bad week or make a mistake. As you become more confident, you can even play around with assigning a specific weight to each goal to help further hone your coaching abilities. Check out decodedbook .com/tech-as-a-coach for some templates to get you started.

At the end of the experiment, take a look at your team's overall performance. What do you notice? Has happiness improved? Productivity? What are the trends that you can see? Was it a helpful experience? We would love to hear about your experiences, so let us know at experiments@decodedbook.com.

## Concierge

The concierge is a new role for the Decoded Company that takes into account the real-life implications of living in a hyperpersonalized world. The concierge's responsibility is to help maintain morale while continuously striving to deliver personalized services to each staff member.

The idea of a concierge can be implemented within a company at various levels.

- If you are a CEO/C-suite, consider hiring someone for this position on a trial contract for six months. This will let you experiment without the commitment of changing your organizational structure, although we think you'll want to afterward! Here is a sample job description, based on one we used at Klick:

We're looking for a talent management specialist/ concierge to join our Engagement and Culture Team. This role will use some of the traditional HR tactics (management training, career counseling, metrics, performance review, and learning) to really drive engagement and culture but without the constraints, rules, and regulations typically associated with HR. What we want is for you to create a bespoke solution for each team member that's going to create an environment where they can perform and where they'll grow as fast as we're growing. Your job will be to encourage employee engagement in all the ways you know how and to figure out a few that you don't. You should have three to five years of experience with at least three of the following: training and development, management, career counseling, metrics/ key performance indicators, performance review, corporate communication. Bonus points for events, corporate social responsibility, PR, and video.

- Hire an intern and ask them to come in from 12:00 P.M. to 8:00 P.M. instead of the traditional 9:00 to 5:00. Have them walk around every day at 7:00 P.M., and if they see anyone still working at their desk have them see if there is anything they can do to help: buy them dinner; arrange for dry cleaning; run out and grab some groceries; send flowers to their spouse; pick up a toy for their child—anything reasonable that will bring a smile to their face.

- If you can't hire an intern, consider offering your team access to concierge-like services:

- Services such as TaskRabbit.com offer microoutsourcing for everything from picking up groceries to cleaning out closets. TaskRabbit's price varies per task, so you might want to set a budget on how much you want to spend each month.
- FancyHands.com offers virtual-assistant services that can be used to help make reservations, schedule appointments, book travel, and even do research. Fancyhands.com is a subscription-based service, and for $65 a month you can get up to twenty-five requests to be shared among your team.

A final note—Many of these experiments are just ways to apply the spirit of the Decoded model in your own organization. You'll find plenty of experiments that require nothing more than a spreadsheet! This is just a temporary solution to help familiarize yourself with some of the concepts. As you'll see in subsequent chapters, the real magic happens when we implement sophisticated, ambient-data-driven systems that can help decode your entire organization or department through one integrated platform.

 ## DECODED EXPERIMENTS

As always, there are practical tools and experiments that you can put into place today to start turning your technology into kick-ass coaches. Join us and the rest of the Decoded movement online where we are sharing experiments, tips, and resources to help unleash an army of coaches dedicated to getting you and your organization into the best shape possible.

# ADAPTIVE LEARNING AND TASK MANAGEMENT

There are a few different ways to experiment with adaptive learning systems and dynamic processes that help you reshuffle priorities quickly and easily. We use Genome tools like GeneSequencer, but there are many other options.

Personal Software and Applications

- *Omnifocus* is a context-based task-management software for iOS that takes into account your location and your changing priorities to generate a list of what you should be working on.

  *Remember the Milk* is a similar Web-based application that also has Android and Windows clients.

- *Any.do* is also a task-management system that learns from your entries and starts to make helpful suggestions once it has learned some of your patterns.

Gamifying Processes

- Pick one of your internal processes. Create a list of tasks for completing this process from beginning to end.

- Create three different levels: Beginner, Intermediate, Expert.

- Take your list of tasks for each of these levels and add or remove items as needed. Your beginner task list should be the most robust, and your expert list should be the most streamlined.

- Determine the number of times someone would have to complete the process perfectly at each level before being allowed to move up. For example, you can say that a beginner needs to complete it five times perfectly and an intermediate another three times with no errors before that person is considered an expert. This helps people advance at their own speed and makes it okay for someone to take their time, since the emphasis is on a process with no mistakes instead of an arbitrary deadline.

- Make sure you include reviews by the appropriate people as a part of the checklist, to ensure that tasks are being followed correctly.

- Track your team's progress.

This experiment will give you a few key pieces of information. First, it will give you a very good sense of what your team's capabilities are and will enable you to plan training accordingly (we'll get into this in the next chapter). Second, it will help you create a process that will minimize mistakes by ensuring that everyone is going through the same consistent process while enabling those who learn faster to jump ahead, ensuring their engagement remains high.

 ## INDUSTRY EXAMPLES

Below you'll find some examples of how using technology as a coach can be applied within specific industries.

- **Real Estate:** For real estate agents, having technology as a coach that can alert them to important information, like leasing properties that are about to expire in the next six months, can be a valuable prioritization tool, ensuring that they have enough lead time to secure new tenants. In the long run, this can help ensure that properties don't sit empty unnecessarily, helping to improve profitability and efficiency. Other pieces of information can include any access card issues or maintenance requests submitted by the tenant, to help them stay connected and aware of the situation, which will lead to better client service.

- **HR/Recruiting:** Lots of companies have applicant tracking systems (ATS) in place already, most of which have some form of dashboard for reporting on the applicant pipeline. This is your standard form of "pull" dashboard that requires you to go to it for a report. Imagine taking that same data and transforming it into a "push" e-mail that gets sent to all hiring managers within the company, showing them their particular view of the pipeline.

  For any organization focused on growth, the ability to hire into a leadership pipeline that constantly develops future leaders is critical, so the need to keep the pipe full at the top should be a primary concern. A system like this coaches all relevant people throughout the organization, ensuring that they are reviewing enough applicants, conducting enough interviews, and making smarter hiring choices.

Over time that system can become more robust, especially when tied to workload measures for given teams to highlight when that team's manager should be in active hiring mode. Factor in predictive workload information based on presales data and the window moves even farther out. Data about project types and activities can further enhance the manager's awareness by enabling them to cross-reference it with the experience and specialties of team members, so they can highlight emerging gaps that may need to be filled (e.g., a software team may do an excellent job of developing large-scale Web apps but emerging client work in mobile could trigger a flag as the demand builds). You can add social pressure to the system by exposing interview volumes to teams so that they hold their managers accountable if they feel that their workload exceeds the current effort to hire.

- **Software or Hardware Sales:** Consider a sales engineer for a software or hardware company. By hooking into your travel system, you could identify the customer the engineer is visiting and provide pertinent information before they board their flight. You could design a tool that pushes a synthesized summary of Customer Relationship Management (CRM) customer information, support or maintenance issues, and up-sell opportunities. For example, the engineer can receive a pushed e-mail that captures their most recent customer service interaction, current configurations with relevant promotions, the marketing department's road map for future iterations of the products it already has, support calls it's made, and any other system's relevant data that is linked directly or indirectly with this customer's record and configuration. (We've done something similar with Genome, which we'll show you in an upcoming chapter.)

# CHAPTER 3: TECHNOLOGY AS A TRAINER

- How did US Airways speed up the training of their call center staff? How can you do the same and cut Malcolm Gladwell's ten-thousand-hour rule in half?

- How does Sprint's Compass system use teachable moments to put out fires in real time?

## YOU CAN GO HOME AGAIN

The alarm clock example from the previous chapter shows the importance of data-driven personalization in increasing productivity, but it doesn't explain how technology can be used to better train your teams. Training is a critical factor in talent performance, and it has a significant impact on your bottom line, both positive, by driving higher performance, and negative, by costing a lot of money.

In this chapter we'll show how technology can evolve into a trainer who learns from your whole organization's base of experiences and applies those insights to training, development, recruiting, and even project management processes. We'll also focus on talent-specific metrics and explore how to evolve Human Resources within a Decoded organization. Let's start by taking a look at a very big, very messy example of a troubled training program that was ultimately fixed by using what we call Technology as a Trainer.

In 2011, US Airways decided to bring all of its overseas call center work back to the United States. The company announced that three new call centers would be opened in Nevada, Arizona, and North Carolina, creating new job opportunities for hundreds of Americans.

At the time that it made this decision, US Airways had 32,000 thousand employees responsible for about 20,500 flights a day to 190 countries, serving some 80 million passengers each year. Familiarizing new hires in those new centers with US Airways quality standards meant one thing: a lot of training. New hires ran the gamut from customer service representative master ninjas to complete beginners. All of them needed to be brought up to speed quickly, so that they could provide a level of service consistent with US Airways's vision for delivering quality customer experiences.

Although it might have called it something different, US Airways wanted to tap into its data as a sixth sense from the very beginning of the new project (see the next chapter for a detailed description of Data as a Sixth Sense). It set out to create a system that would display information from its various call centers that it could use to guide training, but it ran into several problems. First, the system it had was difficult to use, which meant that managers spent more time fiddling with features and searching for the data they needed than they did coaching their colleagues.

Second, it required the manual input of a lot of self-reported, possibly biased qualitative information, including coaching session notes, feedback, and recommendations, making it difficult to objectively assess whether an employee was improving or not. This also meant that agents couldn't track their daily improvements because their metrics were based on a supervisor's active participation in inputting them.

"It was difficult and time consuming for managers to tie coaching to specific agents' performances, so it wasn't done as often as it should have been," admits Melody Niese, director of reservations planning and analysis for US Airways.[1] "Agents had to wait to speak with their supervisors to find out how they were doing, and that generally happened only when there was a red flag." That's a classic example of hindsight management, which is focused on reviewing past problems rather than avoiding future ones.

Something had to change, and it had to change quickly. US Airways needed its new call center staff to hit the ground running. It needed a technology that could predict or anticipate when the agent would need support instead of waiting until after a mistake had occurred.

Using the philosophy of technology as a trainer builds on the foundation outlined in the previous chapter by using data and systems to watch blind spots, identify teachable moments, and proactively intervene with just-in-time training interventions. Utilizing technology as a trainer applies the same philosophy to training programs that technology as a coach does to traditional enterprise systems. It rejects the concept of monolithic training programs in favor of deeply personalized experiences delivered only when they're needed. Technology as a trainer allows your organization to radically accelerate the awarding of tenure to new employees without putting any brakes or limits on more experienced and proficient members of your team. Decoded organizations use technology as a trainer (and coach) to guide their people in a proactive, transparent, and accountable way, watching their blind spots and stepping in before someone gets in trouble. US Airways needed to leverage this approach and customize it to each employee instead of having a referee yelling "offside!" when it was too late. We'll get back to them later.

## FINDING TEACHABLE MOMENTS

There's an old saying that's often attributed to Benjamin Franklin: "When you want something done, ask the busiest person you know to do it." We figured that some of the busiest people we know are entrepreneurs, so if anyone could show us how to get real, practical training done it would be one of them. When Rahaf asked Dan Martell, Clarity.fm's CEO and founder, about traditional workplace training, he laughed out loud. "Is that those boring things they send you to for skills that you might never need to use?" That's a pretty good definition.

He continued:

If you really want to understand real-time learning, just look at entrepreneurs. Every entrepreneur starts a company to do something they've never done before. The skill set that great entrepreneurs have is, they know how to be resourceful and they know how to identify what they need to learn at the moment they need to learn it.

He should know. Martell is a serial entrepreneur who has already made two successful exits. He started his first company in 2004, at the age of twenty-four, a social enterprise consulting and application company called Spheric Technologies.[2] By the time he sold it four years later the business had grown to thirty people, enjoyed a 152 percent year-on-year growth, and won a slew of business awards. His second venture was a social marketing application called Flowtown, which raised venture funding and was acquired by Demandforce.com in 2011.[3]

When Martell needs to find a solution or acquire a new skill, he scrambles, motivated by necessity and pressured by deadlines. It was this need for flexible and customized advice that was the catalyst for creating Clarity. Clarity's users sign up to access an impressive database of entrepreneurs and experts. When they need advice on something or are stuck and need some coaching, they use the database to find a relevant expert, and they schedule a call. The experts charge by the minute (though most donate their fees to a charity of their choice) and provide teaching at the exact moment it's required. Imagine, for example, that you're planning for a one-on-one meeting with one of your reports that's going to require a tough conversation. You might use Clarity to find an expert who can coach you through how to deliver your message in a way that will have the most impact.

"Clarity allows you to custom-make advice and source personalized best practices," Martell explains. "It's an efficient, highly valuable way to get information to someone right when they need it. It's that teachable moment opportunity."

The Clarity model just makes sense. How many times have we needed a new skill and immediately turned to YouTube or Google for the solution? From troubleshooting computer software to configuring a new phone, we only hunt for the information at the precise moment that we need it. It sounds so obvious, and yet the approach to traditional training inside corporations couldn't be more different.

## TEACHABLE MOMENTS

It's ironic that we collectively know so much about the psychology of learning, through generations of studying schools and natural learning, and yet we're still delivering ineffective, one-size-fits-all training programs.

Three critical factors influence a training program's effectiveness:

- **Context** is the recognition that training materials are more likely to be retained when they contain relevant information to your task at the time that you need to do it. Knowing that you have to do something you don't know how to do focuses the mind; urgency and necessity are what make you pay attention. Being trained on something that lacks context—a task that you don't need to do right now—is much less successful and results in lower information retainment.

- **Practice** is the ability to apply what you've learned immediately, in your day-to-day job.

- **Feedback** is the necessary fine-tuning that helps identify opportunities for improved performance.

These three factors come together to make the silver bullet: a program that is insanely personalized to the individual experiences, strengths, and desire states of your people. Recognized by real-time data analysis, a teachable moment is what we call the exact instant when an employee should receive training, which is then delivered in a customized way that caters to that employee's exact needs. By identifying teachable moments, technology as a trainer substitutes foresight for hindsight and replaces the bulky, boring, and arbitrarily scheduled training programs that teach your people skills that they might never use.

Sprint is perhaps not a company that many would identify as a forward-looking leader in technology as a trainer and informed intuition. Back in 2008, the American telecom was struggling with declining profits and had one of the worst reputations for customer service in an industry not exactly known for customer service.[4] Among other complaints, a Sprint customer spent an average of nearly eight minutes on hold while the rest of the industry averaged wait times of under a minute. Those customers got so frustrated that 35 percent of them hung up, pushing them one step closer to the competition. It's often said that things have to get worse before they get better, and Sprint certainly put that adage to the test. Its stock plummeted by 50 percent that year as the company announced a string of retail store closings, four thousand layoffs, and a write-down on goodwill of $29.7 billion.[5] Once you factor in the global economic slowdown and increased competition from companies like Skype, you have all the ingredients for one epic stress bomb.

Sprint decided it needed to refocus on customer service, and turned to the data it had been collecting to pinpoint how best to address the issue. It quickly realized that a lack of data wasn't the issue. It was, in fact, the opposite. It had too much information, and none of it was helping it use its informed intuition. There was a big gap between the data it was collecting, the metrics it was measuring, and its vision for the company's future. As we'll explore in further detail in the next chapter, Sprint worked with NICE, a big data vendor, to implement an internal system called Compass that automated the collection of relevant data, including detailed information on calls, volume, and the behaviors that impacted consumer satisfaction.

At one point Compass flagged a troubling statistic in one of the company's forty-five call centers. The handle time in that center (how long a CSR spends on the phone with a client) was nearly four times longer than the companywide average. Quicker resolution rates lead not only to higher customer satisfaction but to more revenue for the company, so this was a serious concern. Metrics had previously been tracked in spreadsheets with manual inputs and high levels of self-reporting that resulted in missing, unreliable, or biased data. Without Compass there was a high chance that this critical information would have been overlooked.

Thanks to their informed intuition, managers were able to track down and identify the problem: a group of recently hired agents were unfamiliar with certain features on a newly released device. Therein lies a teachable moment. Sprint was able to identify the agents who needed training at the precise moment when they really needed it. They were able to intervene with real-time training, and the handle-time metric that had flashed warningly just a few hours before dropped back to its normal parameters.[6] "Call centers are used to working with large amounts of data and managing people with data," said Jason Pointelin, the manager of analytics and performance management systems at Sprint. "By integrating analytics with performance management and coaching, you have actionable information."[7]

Since that terrible, horrible, no good, very bad year in 2008, Sprint has claimed first place among carriers in the American Customer Satisfaction Index and reduced the budget for its call centers by half. Customer satisfaction has increased by more than 30 percent.[8]

Sprint is on the right path to becoming Decoded, but there is

still so much more that can be done. Delivering just-in-time training is a good beginning, but the real value comes in customizing it
to meet the learner's unique needs.

# GOOGLEEDU

Even companies as advanced and cutting-edge as Google have
struggled with outdated training practices. Google decided it was
ready for a change in 2012, and so it gave GoogleEDU, its two-
year-old learning and development program, a Decoded-style
makeover, instituting a new philosophy that focused on delivering
data-driven, personalized insights to its thirty-three-thousand-
plus employees.

Rather than relying on one-size-fits-all learning programs,
Google aimed to identify the right teachable moments to deliver
highly relevant information based on an understanding of each individual's needs. It turned to the data it collects internally to shed
some light, starting with performance reviews, to identify areas of
learning where people could use improvements. Being one of the
biggest ambient-data collectors of our time, Google also had various statistics to look at to pinpoint when in a person's career tra-
jectory it makes the most sense to take a particular course or
training program. For example, a new manager won't be trained
on how to evaluate employees until right before the review period,
ensuring that they get the information they need exactly when they
need to use it. Google also identified that periods of transition—
such as after joining a new team or relocating to a new office—are
times when Googlers can benefit the most from coaching.

Karen May, Google's vice president for leadership and talent, spoke recently about the importance of catering to an individual's needs. "More individualized, customized recommendations are part of how we grow," she said. "We're trying to individualize and personalize the learning experience."[9]

Employee expectations are changing, and meeting individual needs through customized delivery creates happier employees. "We do see in our overall satisfaction scores that it does make a difference when we invest in people," says May. We would obviously agree.

##  KLICK ACADEMY AND KLICK TALKS

Like Google, Klick uses the technology as a trainer philosophy to embed data-driven training into its culture and everyday operations. Genome helps Klick identify when someone needs to learn a particular skill. That triggers an automated process that takes the team member's unique profile into account.

One of the ways that we seamlessly integrate intelligent training into our system is through an initiative called Klick Academy that delivers a personalized training experience tailored for each individual's experience and performance. Additional elective courses, resource libraries, and lunch-and-learns are available to talent as well.

The Klick Academy was created in 2004 and is managed internally by Klick's Concierge team. The underlying philosophy is that there are no such things as generic, role-specific requirements. There are only prerequisite experiences triggered by actual work. Part of the Klick Learning Solutions group's mandate is to ensure that employees are learning constantly, by strategically designing its various learning vehicles, such as Klick's course catalog and Klick Talks.

At the Academy's core is a group of short online courses that are a part of the process of bringing new employees onboard. They include an overview of the company's culture, an introduction to Genome, and a primer on the health industry (Klick's primary target market). After many years of overseeing hiring into Klick, Leerom has observed a real need to help new employees understand how different our environment is quickly. His real goal for the core courses is to deprogram new employees of what they learned in the unhealthy environments they're coming from. It's a tangible way for them to understand how we see the world, what we stand for, and how we behave.

In addition to the core courses, there is a wide variety of elective courses (generally five to thirty minutes long) designed to help employees continuously learn and refine their skill sets. The courses are not mandatory, but a manager who sees a gap in a team member's capabilities might recommend that they complete a specific one.

The courses cover a wide array of subjects, from introducing an employee to a specific client to industry regulations, technical tutorials, and even an introduction to statistics. Anyone can suggest and build a course by working with the Learning Solutions group to deliver high-quality content that follows adult learning practices. The general rule of thumb is that you should create a course if you find yourself teaching or explaining a subject regularly, because there is demand for that information.

Klick Talks are much simpler and basic than courses. If you

have a question about absolutely anything—from procedures such as filing expenses all the way through to the company's vision and mission—you can submit it through Genome (as a ticket, of course), and you're guaranteed to receive a video answer from someone within twenty-four hours. Klick Talks are limited to two minutes in length and are indexed and archived in Genome, and they provide a rich and organically grown repository of content. Instead of imposing a top-down, hierarchical structure on the material, every course and every Klick Talk is tagged with keywords that make it easy for our talent to search for and find them.

Now here's where the power of data in delivering training becomes obvious. If you recall, Genome's vast database contains information about every project and task that an individual undertakes for the entire duration of their time at Klick. Thanks to this vast historical data, we know the skills that are needed to complete a type of project or to fill a role. Rather than using static role descriptions created by someone in HR, these capabilities are tagged and clustered together to create personas that define the ideal hire. Every member of the Klick team also has a detailed persona within Genome, comprising their work history, kudos, system interactions, work role, metrics, etc. Managers can compare the skill set required of the ideal persona with that of their team members and immediately spot knowledge gaps. Then they can search Klick Academy for the required materials and easily deliver a customized training program to address them. A manager could look at the commonalities in skill sets associated with the most successful projects in the company, and then make sure that her team gets the right training to help them succeed.

In returning to our earlier Klick Labs product manager example (see the previous chapter), we see that the initial persona defined by Jay was based on his past experiences in software companies and in performing the role during the launch of our iCONNECT product. That early draft persona was essential for our Concierge Team to recruit for the role, and it was then adapted within Genome as we learned more about the backgrounds and skills of the people we hired. Those new team members started forming their unique Genome personas on their first day at Klick, beginning to build a rich history comprising digital footprints and body language as they completed coming onboard, closed their first tickets, and began work on their first projects. Each weekly one-on-one and quarterly review contributed more information to the ideal persona, as well as providing opportunities for Jay to identify gaps in his team's knowledge and skills. Using a combination of Klick Academy and our goal-driven dashboards, Jay can quickly curate a customized mix of courses, lunch-and-learns, and mentors for his product managers, so as to keep them engaged and challenged, and constantly learning.

Once again, the principle of Technology as a Trainer plays a big part here, since the programs are delivered online. Each person progresses at his or her own pace; it's not embarrassing if you have to ask a question or redo a module. Unlike an instructor, a machine never gets annoyed with you if you need to be shown something over and over again. It will keep coaching you and testing you until you finally get it right.

## US AIRWAYS' NICE SOLUTION

If you remember back to the beginning of this chapter, US Airways wanted to use technology to help them train their CSRs but the system it had was clunky, it relied on too many manual inputs, and, worse still, it didn't allow the representatives to use it themselves. The automated data system US Airways ultimately installed in collaboration with NICE helped employees develop a clear and objective picture of what was expected of them. Its dashboards enabled individual agents to take ownership of their performance and to identify areas where they are falling behind, prompting them to take steps to modify their behavior to bring those numbers back into an optimal range.

This transparency has had a huge impact on the processes that are used to bring new employees onboard. "Having visibility allows us to get our new agents up to speed much faster. When we put together our new hiring plan, we estimated it would take about nine months for agents to get up to full productivity," said Melody Niese. "Thanks to the insight we have into the process now, agents are actually taking only five months to get to this point. We attribute this to having better visibility into performance and a more informed coaching process."[10]

Clearer expectations have had a positive impact on agent morale, driven in part by a data-focused approach for rewarding and recognizing employee contributions. "[Agents] are better prepared for meetings with their supervisors, since they know how they are performing in advance," said Niese. "Seeing this information numerically gives them the ability to correct their behavior and drive toward better performance."

The managers who are responsible for delivering the training are also reaping the rewards of using technology as a trainer. The automated system means they no longer have to spend their time searching for the data they need to provide meaningful and relevant feedback. The data gives them a clear picture of what the agent needs in order to improve, allowing them to make more effective suggestions that are targeted to their individual needs. "We have the data to coach and the time to coach, so it can be more efficient, helpful, and targeted. We can focus on getting the best out of agents," said Niese.

# TECHNOLOGY AS A PERSONAL DEVELOPMENT COACH

US Airways' old, predecoded performance process is very common in businesses all over the world. We all know that these outdated management approaches don't work, and yet a serious case of corporate inertia prevents many of us from changing.

There's a particularly vicious cycle in the interplay between traditional performance reviews and employee development. The need to manage performance is owned by the HR Department, which is tasked with identifying and closing gaps. Their mandate is to create fairness through the application of consistent, "fair" policies to all employees. The nearly ubiquitous approach is to start with a companywide annual performance review, conducted at a staggering cost in lost productivity, which is then analyzed in order to identify and prioritize training expenditures. The universal disdain with which we all complete those reviews should call their accuracy as a data source into question. Any decisions made on the basis of that data are equally suspect. The learning and training investments will almost certainly prove inadequate to address the gaps that were likely misidentified in the first place, with the inevitable result that real gaps never get addressed.

The above methodology embodies the traditional HR approach of centralized talent development. Not surprisingly, we're not big fans of that model. We think development should be the responsibility of every leader within the organization. After all, what could be more important for every member of your management team than to be focused on increasing their team's engagement and skill set?

Let's drill a little deeper into the way personal development is handled by most companies. Someone (often in HR) looks at an open role, identifies the needed competencies to fill it, hires someone who matches them, then builds a curriculum around the major required skill set and delivers it in a massive dose. Future development plans for talent advancement are similarly based on the skill sets deemed required for the role. Predefined time lines are established for when training is delivered. Although the training programs may use the best adult learning principles in their design (a fairly rare occurrence), their inflexible schedules and high costs of delivery mean that there can be little customization and retention. All of this adds up to an unsurprisingly low ROI: The average instructor-led corporate class delivers a lower than 58 percent retention rate, which means that nearly half of the knowledge imparted in your live training is completely forgotten over time.[11]

Most training programs value in-class (or live) training over its eLearning and mLearning equivalents. Knowledge retention rates often increase during in-class sessions, which also foster camaraderie and forge interpersonal connections. This has led to a persistent belief that live training is the best way to deliver much of the hands-on skills training that employees need to be successful. As a result, we send new recruits through extensive programs conducted deep within a corporate training facility. We fly our people to conferences, so that they can take workshops and seminars.

The annual amount spent on learning and training—U.S. companies spent $13.6 billion on leadership development alone in 2012—is nothing short of staggering when you consider the mounting evidence that this is a very ineffective approach.[12]

The Decoded approach, engineered as it is to equip creative thinkers and knowledge workers with just-in-time, deeply customized learning, is the obvious alternative.

 ## Decoded Metrics

### *Compound Weekly Learning Rate*

Our accounting systems were largely designed to report on the performance of companies that made real-world things and shipped them off to customers. In keeping with their bias toward things, they treat people as costs and facilities and equipment as assets. Naturally, they devalue training as money spent rather than invested.

We use the language of accounting and financial reporting to share and compare information about the performances of corporations, even though it lacks a sufficient vocabulary to talk about them in modern terms. Most companies, large and small, have developed an internal set of management metrics that are quite different from the ones that they report externally, requiring their CFOs and accountants to expend hundreds of hours translating between the two.

The idea that training is an expense and not an investment within the larger talent ecosystem is just one of many indications of how outdated current accounting processes are and how wide the gap is between their antiquated perspectives and the cultures found within Decoded Companies. We believe that an organization's ability to teach an employee new skills is an investment that has a direct and measurable impact on the bottom line.

A person's ability to learn is like "compounding interest on an investment: after two or three years, a relentless learner stands head and shoulders above his peers," as James Slavet wrote. "So try asking your team this question: how did you get 1% better this week? Did you learn something valuable from our customers, or make a change to our product that drove better results?" Being aware and measuring each team's learning progression can be a powerful tool. "As your team gets into a learning rhythm, you can review this as a group." He adds that "1% per week adds up."[13]

## Meeting Promoter Score

According to a 2011 Harris Interactive survey conducted for Clarizen, 70 percent of knowledge workers surveyed felt that company status meetings don't contribute to work productivity, with 40 percent declaring the meetings a waste of time.[14] Of the 2,373 adults surveyed, 67 percent said they spent between one and four hours preparing for those unproductive meetings. In addition, 57 percent of respondents indicated that they multitasked during meetings. This isn't breaking news. Much like gremlins fed after midnight, we all know that meetings are monsters that endlessly duplicate themselves, devouring our precious time and depleting the mental reserves that we should be using to complete our actual tasks.

James Slavet shares this distaste for meetings. "Most meetings suck," he writes. "People who don't have the authority to buy paperclips are allowed to call meetings everyday that cost far more than that. Nobody tracks whether meetings are useful or how they could get better."

He recommends asking meeting attendees to rate the meeting's usefulness on a scale of one to ten, and to ask for one suggestion on how meetings can be improved in the future. Given the proliferation of networked mobile devices and calendars, this can be relatively easily implemented with a little bit of clever scripting. A quick e-mail sent to attendees as a meeting ends can prompt them to reply with a rating and a suggestion, closing the loop when the meeting is still fresh in their minds and providing real-time feedback to the organizer. Aggregating those responses provides organizationwide data that can help identify bad meetings, and significantly reduce meeting overhead.

## CHAPTER SUMMARY: JUST-IN-TIME JUST-ENOUGH TRAINING

The single advantage of technology as a trainer is its ability to recognize exactly what type of training someone needs and to pinpoint exactly when they should receive it. But technology as a coach and trainer can impact every part of your business, from recruiting to project management. Having the ability to embrace the diversity and unique experiences of your talent gives your Decoded organization a big competitive advantage—not just in attracting top performers but in helping to improve your organization's revenue and worker satisfaction.

Both Sprint and US Airways saw quantifiable results after implementing technology as a trainer systems that enabled them to provide higher quality services to their customers. Whether you're a large company like Google, a midsize one like Klick, or a start-up like Gengo or Clarity, having a data-focused system can only add a positive net benefit to your strategic goals.

In the next chapter, we'll dig deep into Data as a Sixth Sense and look at how our data can give our people superpowers.

# DECODED TOOLBOX

## Teachable Moment

When a teachable moment is recognized by real-time data analysis, it becomes the exact instant an employee should receive training, which is then delivered in a customized way that caters to that employee's exact needs. Teachable moments must take into account context, practice, and feedback.

## Klick Academy

Klick Academy delivers a personalized training experience tailored for each individual's experience and performance. Additional elective courses, resource libraries, and lunch-and-learns are available to talent as well.

## Klick Talks

An internal library of two-minute videos that answer questions asked by Klick staff. Each question must get a response within twenty-four hours. The library is tagged to optimize an organic informational hierarchy.

## Compound Weekly Learning Rate

The compounding value of the training, development, and improvement of your team.

 ## DECODED EXPERIMENTS

As always, there are practical tools and experiments that you can put into place today to start turning your technology into kick-ass coaches. Join us and the rest of the Decoded movement online, where we are sharing experiments, tips, and resources to help unleash an army of coaches dedicated to getting you and your organization into the best shape possible.

## TEACHABLE MOMENTS

Teachable moments are all about identifying the trigger that identifies the opportunity for a relevant training intervention. While it is very difficult to simulate Genome's teachable moments algorithm, you can do the following experiment to practice identifying where these learning opportunities exist in your current processes and experiment with using some manual triggers—your own people!

- Take the process chart that you made for GeneSequencer from the last chapter.

- Identify any high-risk spots where errors are most likely to occur. These are prime opportunities for teachable moments!

- Identify a trigger, especially for beginners, that can alert you when someone is approaching this risky spot. This can be as simple as adding a checklist item for alerting a specific team member. This person can be the manual trigger, who can then offer a purposeful training intervention. ("Oh, you're filling out the estimate sheet? Here are a few tips to help you out!")

- Make sure that the intermediate level includes several opportunities to practice what they have learned previously, as well as the chance to give some personalized feedback.

## KLICK ACADEMY

Klick Academy was born from the desire to create a lightweight, shared learning system.

If you're using any form of internal social tool that supports tagging, try introducing a new tag, like #StealThisIdea. We use this at Klick when people post great client work, development approaches, or creative examples on Chatter. Searching for #StealThisIdea gives you an awesome library of resources with no real additional cost or overhead. Things like this tend to get adopted pretty quickly by people who find them useful, though remember that you may need to seed them with a few of your own posts at the start to get the adoption curve started.

You can also look at online platforms such as Udemy.com that enable people to create private courses. Members of your team can create short courses guided by tools and a template that will only be shared internally. Additionally, Udemy has a public list of courses that might be useful.

# KLICK TALKS

Before starting a system like Klick Talks, it might be useful to do a mapping exercise of the types of questions that your team has that it hasn't been able to find answers for easily. The mapping is easy to do!

- You can use Google Forms (as part of Google apps), a shared spreadsheet (Web-based or even on an Excel doc on a shared drive), or even just a new Gmail address (for example, ihaveaquestion@gmail.com). For the next month, ask your team to add any questions for which they can't immediately find answers.

  You can answer the questions directly or in a shared forum, and use weekly team meetings to highlight the best of them. At the end of the month you'll have a solid understanding of the need for this type of system, at which time you can invest in a video-based approach (see http://decodedbook.com/tools/video for an updated list).

- If you're eager to jump in, you can use a video-sharing site like Vimeo to create a password-protected channel where you can upload and view your videos. You can film answers with a camera on a smartphone or a laptop, or a regular video camera. They don't have to be perfect; they just have to answer the question.

## COMPOUND WEEKLY LEARNING RATE

The goal of this metric is to track, measure, and evaluate the learning that's taking place, in order to gauge your team's engagement and performance.

- Set aside some time with your team. It can be as simple as a fifteen-minute weekly stand-up meeting, a weekly lunch, or a Friday afternoon happy hour. Inform your team about the weekly compound learning rate and tell them to come prepared to talk about how they got at least 1 percent better that week.

- Set up a spreadsheet for tracking the ideas over time, which can provide an excellent experience for new hires as they can learn the best practices of their peers.

- Consider establishing a reward for the week's best idea, to drive participation and creativity (and give public kudos with a tag like #1percent, so they're easy to find if you're using a social system that supports it). You can even include this as a metric that you review in your weekly one-on-one.

## MEETING PROMOTER SCORE

Understanding the efficiency of your meetings can be one of the most important pieces of data you measure. Nothing kills morale faster than long, boring, tedious meetings that feel like a waste of time.

- Check out our Decoded Meeting Promoter app at decodedbook.com/tools/meetings to start tracking how valuable your people find your meetings.

# INDUSTRY EXAMPLES

- **Retail:** Retail is an interesting industry to consider for technology as a trainer simply because the teachable moment occurs at the end of the shift; otherwise you would be interrupting employees as they were interacting with the client on the sales floor. We can apply the tech trainer methodology using a dashboard that contains data points such as: sales information; goals set with the manager; and how they compare with other top performers, with an automated e-mail at the end of each shift and a reminder before the start of the next one.

- **Telecommunications:** Consider a mobile field-service-technology representative who has to troubleshoot client equipment and deliver a high level of customer service. We can use technology to geolocate the representative as they arrive on-site to interact with a customer. The tech trainer can identify the equipment that the customer has, cross-reference this with the representative's previous experience and training, and then push real-time learning snippets for anything the rep might not be familiar with.

- **Financial Services:** Sometimes a teachable moment isn't an individual event but rather a team or company-wide one. Consider, for example, a financial services company that has to follow a recently updated federal regulation. There is an immediate and pressing need for everyone in the company to be updated on what the changes mean for their business in order to ensure compliance. In this case, you might use a home-page take-over on the intranet to interrupt their day with a very short video alerting everyone about the issue. You could then deliver a training intervention that provides just-in-time education about the change and a quiz to validate retention. Employees who don't pass the quiz can get placed into a longer training program to provide additional education, while those who do have lost no more than an hour of their day. The need to deliver such rapid training does open the risk that the training fails to address all possible customer scenarios. In that case, tying this into a Klick Talks–like tool allows employees to capture and post real-time inquiries from the field, which are quickly answered and archived to form an organically growing knowledge base on the topic.

- **Biotechnology:** Consider the case of a midsize biotech company with a meeting problem. Working within the world's most highly regulated environment requires a lot of people to sign off on every step of every process. Most companies in the life-science industry struggle with balancing the need for that oversight with calendars filled with constant meetings. Those meetings aren't always efficiently run, the goals aren't defined, people don't come prepared, and the outcome isn't great (sound familiar?), but they are required. Many companies end up launching a training program around meetings as well as plastering their meeting rooms with motivational posters that employ some cheesy acronym to define best practices for meetings, which are ignored almost as quickly as they are posted. That approach might be effective for a few weeks, and then everyone will revert to their bad habits. Instead, take the outputs from Slavet's "rate my meeting" exercise, which turn into perfect inputs for a teachable moment around meetings. Booking a meeting triggers the teachable moment, which could launch as a wizard to walk the booking creator through a better process. By pulling in your past feedback and meeting score for this meeting type, as well as any data about attendees and their backgrounds and experiences, the wizard becomes personalized to teach and coach you. An automatic "rate my meeting" after one meeting feeds back into your next meeting, and could even trigger a reward if your score improves.

## DECODED SCORE: TECHNOLOGY AS A COACH AND TRAINER

Answer the following yes or no questions below and fill out your score. Give yourself 1 point for each yes and 0 points for each no, for a best possible score of 4. At the end of the book you'll be able to use your score as part of a detailed Decoded assessment so you can get even more insights into how to embrace the Decoded philosophy.

1. Do you personalize your policies for each member of your team (rather than the traditional one-size-fits-all approach)?

2. Is your training delivered in just-in-time just-enough interventions around teachable moments (rather than a monolithic, far in advance approach)?

3. Do your systems use historical data and pattern matching to coach and make recommendations (rather than a referee yelling "offside!")?

4. Are your reviews done on a weekly basis and driven through goal-oriented dashboards and automated agendas (rather than the much despised annual performance reviews)?

Technology as a Coach and Trainer score : _____/4

# CHAPTER 4: DATA AS A SIXTH SENSE

- Why is everything you remember about your own life probably wrong? How does acknowledging your faulty memory make you much more productive?

- How did Google build the world's best spelling corrector without teaching it anything about spelling?

- What drove the SEC to label everyone employed by Whole Foods as "insiders" for stock trading purposes?

- How can an institutionalized "Spidey sense" save your organization millions of dollars and help you retain your best people?

- Why did a pile of wide-eyed cuddly toys drive Starbucks CEO Howard Schultz crazy? What can it teach you about focus?

- What can a Hungarian psychologist and an American venture capitalist teach you about productivity?

- Check how smart your intuition is: If a loved one has a heart attack, what's even more likely to save them than an ER doctor?

# WHAT IS DATA AS A SIXTH SENSE?

Comparing the dashboard of a World War I–era Fokker DR-1, the plane flown by the Red Baron, with the dash of an F-22 Raptor, the most advanced fighter jet in the world, is a good way to understand the idea of data as a sixth sense.

World War I pilots were almost literally flying by the seat of their pants. They had very few instruments to gather data and no computer to analyze it with. Their decisions were based entirely on training and gut feel. This is like managing your team entirely with traditional management approaches based on the simplest data gathered largely through direct observation.

Now fast-forward to today. The F-22 has a plethora of sensors and instruments to gather data and a computer to make sense of all that info. One of the most important is the heads-up display, or HUD. The HUD displays all of the pertinent info the pilot needs in one central place, so he or she doesn't have to spend time trying to make sense of all the data the instruments are collecting.

The pilot still has the final say in what their plane does, but those decisions are much more informed than their 1918 counterpart. Think of the instruments as ambient-data capture, the computer as analytics, and the HUD as a dash. Making use of the info in the dash to aid in decisions is using your *data as a sixth sense*.

# PENNY FOR YOUR THOUGHTS

We were chatting with Peter Arvai, the cofounder and CEO of Prezi.com, which has produced a cloud-based presentation software that enables users to create compelling visual presentations.

"I love the idea of data superpowers," he said. "Gut feels, instincts, and experience can all drive your informed intuition, but what about adding ideas to that list?"[1]

It was a good question, and it led to an hour-long conversation. "We are seeing a boom in the idea economy, where businesses are placing a premium on ideas that matter and will have a big impact," he shared. "There has been a lot of talk about the consumerization of the enterprise, but the next phase is even more significant: the creativization of the enterprise—where ideas are king."

It's this belief in the transformative power of good ideas that has defined Arvai's vision for Prezi.com. The start-up, which was launched in 2009, currently boasts over eight million users whose presentations have been viewed more than 250 million times.[2] It's the dominant theme on its corporate blog. "At Prezi, we believe that the free exchange of ideas can change the world," it says. "It's in our DNA, it's a modus operandi that guides our development. We are constantly striving to help people share their stories to promote greater understanding."

For Arvai, idea streams are an extremely valuable source of information, one that he hopes analytics will help him better understand. "What can data tell you about something as abstract as ideas?" he asked during our chat. "What kinds of informed decisions will you make with that knowledge at your fingertips?"

Combining idea generation with analytics? We were already salivating at the idea of a new tool that we could add to our sixth sense arsenal. We'll share what Arvai told us a little later on in the chapter. But first a little background.

The big data movement and the explosion in analytics and decision sciences has put an unprecedented amount of data in the hands of companies and allowed them to use it to make better decisions. We're not the first people to have noticed this trend. Consider this: According to a recent report by Harvard Business Review Analytics Services, what differentiates companies that are using data correctly from the ones that aren't is a massive impact "measured by improved financial performance, increased productivity, reduced risks and costs, and faster decision making. Survey respondents who qualify as analytics leaders reported that their organizations are achieving these benefits at a much higher rate than other organizations."[3] We think we've made a pretty strong case for this ourselves.

In this chapter we'll take a closer look at the kinds of data that Decoded Companies collect, and at some of the pros and cons of various data collection methods, such as self-reporting versus collecting ambient data. We'll demonstrate how data can act as an early detection system and help minimize risk by flagging any deviations from the norm. We'll also look at how data can help create forward-looking processes. We'll tackle the issue of metrics and look at what Decoded Companies should be tracking. Last, but certainly not least, we'll show you how companies such as UPS, Target, Facebook, Whole Foods, Klick, Gengo, Prezi, Sprint, and Starbucks are using analytics to instrument their organizations in order to develop their superpowers—their data as a sixth sense—to reverse flagging sales, improve performance, and prevent the repetition of mistakes.

## DATA-DRIVEN DECISIONS

For most of us, our days are filled with decisions. From the CEOs of multinational firms who are determined to bring their visions to life to customer service representatives fielding phone calls from clients, all are constantly making decisions driven by a mix of organizational culture, process, and, often, gut feel. Over the past several years, analytics has been added to the mix, helping us to make ever better decisions, to know things and see things that wouldn't have been possible without the data-driven systems in place.

At the click of a button, a CEO can see which sales team has reached its quota, track the project status of a VIP client, and make sure her South American office is keeping its operational costs in line with the rest of the organization. She might even use a predictive model to help decide which product to release next year. In other words, Mr. Davenport would surely approve of the way in which she's using analytics to compete.

The customer service representative can see the average time he spends on a customer call, the number of calls he answers each shift, and the customer feedback ratings he gets evaluating his performance, analytics that have become standard in his industry.

We live in a data-abundant economy, and companies are reaping the rewards. Organizations that excel at harnessing the data around them to make better informed decisions are already halfway to becoming Decoded. They've already bought into the value of data but are only applying it to the external, customer-facing side of their business (and possibly in a very siloed way internally, still a long way from the ideal).

The breadth of information available to both the customer service representative and the CEO speaks to the abundance of information that data science has allowed us to capture, track, and measure. Additionally, not only are we surrounded by data, but we are each actively creating it, adding our own digital footprint to the information ecosystem of the Web. Just how much information are we putting out there?

## THE AGE OF DATA ABUNDANCE

Every minute of every day sees over 100,000 tweets sent, 3,600 new Instagram photos posted, over 200 million e-mails delivered, and over 47,000 apps downloaded in the iTunes App Store.[4] It's astounding to believe that it's just a fraction of all the data that we produce: GPS signals, social media status updates, geolocation check-ins, digital photos and videos, our purchasing history, our browsing history, our mouse cursor movements, our search engine history, our cell phone records, our medical records, our banking records, and our taxes are just some of the ways we continuously produce data. Businesses have been poring over the trail of data left behind by consumers for years—from credit card transactions, RFID, and GPS data to online browsing history and Facebook likes—hoping to use it to better understand their target audiences.

Every two days now we create as much information as we did from the dawn of civilization up until 2003.

—Eric Schmidt, chairman, Google

## DATA AS A SIXTH SENSE: EVIDENCE-BASED DECISION MAKING

"Advanced analytics should be one of the top priorities for CIOs," says UPS's Jack Levis, director of process management. "Beyond knowledge is wisdom, and beyond that is clairvoyance." In chapter 2 we saw how UPS used its informed intuition to shave miles off daily routes and save gallons of gas (not to mention a few polar bears).

*Data as a Sixth Sense* is our ability to pair analytics with instincts to gain a perspective that's grounded in data but tempered by experience, giving us an unprecedented amount of information to assess a situation. It allows us to do two important things: leverage our existing experience and strip out our personal biases. Developing data as a sixth sense is the second principle of becoming a Decoded Company. In this chapter we're going to focus on the mechanics of how this is done by taking a closer look at actual systems that companies have put in place to minimize risks and increase performance.

There are really two sides to the sixth sense coin: what happens leading up to a decision point and what happens during it.

In the lead-up to making a call, your sixth sense functions as a sort of organization proprioceptor, operating similarly to your body's sense of the relative position of neighboring limbs and the strength of effort employed in moving them. A Decoded Company with the right systems in place can collect all of the required data to provide organizational proprioception to your people, giving them that background sense of what neighboring departments and groups are doing, as well as that of the efforts of their team members. We think of this as eliminating blind spots.

When one of your people reaches a decision point, their intuition may tell them that the facts they're seeing don't agree with their gut instinct. We'll share an example of that in a Klick story a little later (see "A Harry Decision" in this chapter), but the key is the behavior change that lets them recognize that feeling and equips them with the tools to handle it.

Data as a Sixth Sense can augment and support our instincts, but it is not intended to replace them. We all know the value of a gut feel—that inkling that alerts us that a project is headed toward a delay or identifies which pitch a client will love. Data can complement our good instincts and save us from our bad ones. Presenting it in just-in-time, easy-to-read formats enhances managers' decision making while still respecting their years of experience. In fact, as you'll see later on in this chapter, some of the tools take their experiences and gut feels and literally codify them—turning them into lines of computer code to develop smarter algorithms.

The better we become at collecting, interpreting, and displaying the information that we have around us, the fewer blind spots we'll have—and the more forward looking we can be. Much as when we're driving a car: With better visibility we can spot risks and adjust our behavior before it's too late. Our brains are incredibly adept at teasing patterns out of random noise—far more so than the best computers have been—but they are incredibly susceptible to the influence of personal biases, too, whose presence we are almost always unable to even recognize. Technology has now created specialized pattern matchers that are able to query vast histories of data in real time, assemble thousands of data points into trends that our mortal brains couldn't possibly see, and apply that new understanding to future situations in ways that far exceed our capacity to model. Humans are really good at hindsight—it's always twenty-twenty—but the use of these new data-rich systems can give us equally good foresight.

One example is what UPS calls "preventative maintenance." Its importance is probably one of the lessons that your dad taught you when you got your first car. The difference here is that it has historically been practiced in a blind way, based on what the manufacturer says is the average life span of a given part. By analyzing the data that it collects from its army of trucks, UPS is able to predict more precisely when a part is about to give out, so it can replace it only when it absolutely has to. Getting a few extra miles out of the shocks in your car isn't a huge cost savings, but doing it across a massive fleet translates into big money.

# KNOW YOUR COMPANY

The path of a company from a few founders in a garage (real or virtual) to ten people in a room to thirty people in an office is pretty consistent regardless of industry. The challenges those early founders face turn out to be pretty much the same ones their peers in other verticals are going to have to surmount. Few know that better than Jason Fried, cofounder and CEO of 37signals. Most people who know his company have probably used its immensely popular Basecamp project management and collaboration tool or read its bestselling books, *Getting Real*, *Rework*, and *Remote*. Jason has a fairly unique vantage point of the life of small companies as both the leader of a forty-person team and a vendor who supplies infrastructure software to hundreds of thousands of organizations, so we really sat up and took notice when 37signals launched Know Your Company in mid-2013.

As with most things 37signals does, it chooses to take a very different approach to launching a new product. Rather than a big, splashy media push, Jason posted a very sincere letter addressed: "Dear business owner with growing pains."[5] The letter outlines how he had just hired his thirty-eighth employee, and it had become much harder for him to stay current on how his team felt about their company, the vision, the direction, the work, the culture, etc. Being in the software business, he decided to solve it by building a system, and that system was working so well that he began offering it to other business owners. One of the statements in that letter—"if you don't know your people, you don't know your company"—really resonated for us, and so we sat down with Jason for a chat about the importance of data.[6]

"I own this place, and it's my responsibility, but I don't know the people as well as I used to," he explained. Osmosis had worked really well as a management tool until he hit about thirty people—a common break point for that approach—but closing in on forty had triggered real pain and a self-reflection moment. He ultimately realized that there were three core outcomes that he wanted to accomplish on a weekly basis:

- To learn something new about how his team felt about the business, their work, and their culture

- To know what everyone else was working on and for the team to share in that information

- To help the team connect over nonwork-related social topics to help them bond

He also wanted all of the information captured, cataloged, and plotted over time, so that he could look back on it and analyze it for trends. 37signals had tried various approaches to accomplishing this over the years, like asking people to write down their status, but they never stuck. Annual, or even quarterly, surveys didn't feel frequent enough, and their tendency toward including multiple questions and barraging employees felt like an interrupting burden. As is well documented in *Remote*, its staff is spread all over the globe (twenty-five of the thirty-eight people work in twenty-five different places), so the need for social connections outside work are especially important when you can't all sit at the same lunch table.

The system he came up with has been running internally since March 2013. The team gets e-mailed a question three times per week, and they click through to a Web page to provide their answer. They can't see one another's input until a few days later, so everyone answers without the bias of groupthink. Jason has access to a Web portal to view the historical answers, input new questions, and track notes for each team member. In classic 37signals fashion, the product is simple, elegant, and smart and takes advantage of people's existing behaviors rather than trying to force new ones. "E-mail might be one of the greatest communication technologies ever invented," Jason told us. "Almost everyone in the world with a computer has an e-mail address, and many of them now access it from a phone in their pocket. It's the most ubiquitous software interface on the planet." The Monday questions focus on what people are working on, Wednesdays are for company questions (e.g., What's one thing you would like to know about our company?), and Fridays are for social connections (e.g., What was the first job you held?). All of the answers to the Monday and Friday questions get distributed back out to the whole company, and everyone has the choice of whether their Wednesday answers are shared.

Jason shared an example from their use of the tool that illustrates the power of data. He had a hunch that their very popular and employee-written blog, *Signal versus Noise*, would benefit from the addition of a full-time writer, but he wanted to inform his decision by checking in with the organization's gut feel.[7] He used the Wednesday question to ask if people thought it was a good idea and he got back a strongly consistent "no" response. That was a little surprising, so he dug into the comments. It turned out that people weren't objecting to the idea of a professional writer but rather to the idea that their own voices would be marginalized as a result. His intent was really the opposite, and so their answers helped to inform his intuition and to avoid a potentially bad situation; his team helped him to understand how to communicate his decision if he decided to proceed. It also significantly changed his mental concept of *who* he would hire. The 37 signals team is made up of fairly quiet and focused people, so his instinct was to hire someone in the same vein. The answers helped him see that the exact opposite—a highly social collaborator—was probably a better fit for the role.

This little example shows the value of the right data at the right time in front of the right person. Most leaders make decisions purely on gut feel or on what they think they know. If the decision turns out to be a bad one, most of their reports won't feel comfortable sharing their dislike, which leads to what Jason calls a silent backlash. Those are the worst kinds because they breed resentment, overflow into people's work, and lead to their feeling slighted, even if the slight was very unintentional. Systems like Genome or Know Your Company avoid that by using data to inform the intuition of decision makers at all levels of the organization.

By August 2013, 37signals had signed on more than fifty companies to use Know Your Company with their teams. They're seeing typical response rates in the 50 to 60 percent range, which is considerably higher than comparable systems. Unlike most enterprise tools, and perhaps more impressively, the response rates don't drop off over time as companies use the software. That's partly due to some hard-learned adoption lessons from nine years of selling Basecamp. Companies of twenty-five to seventy people that are interested in using the new product have to work directly with Jason, and they have to make a commitment to formally announcing the tool to the company before it gets switched on. A template announcement is provided by 37signals, which they can customize as long as it clearly communicates what's in it for the employees, what's in it for the leadership team, and how the system works. This high-touch sales approach may limit the product's growth, but it also guarantees that the end result will have much more significant impact.

 ## Big Brother Is Watching

Know Your Company uses entirely self-reported data, which tends not to trigger people's Big Brother reflex (if you don't want to share, don't fill in the form). That is definitely not true for ambient data, although the context of the usage tends to greatly affect the type of reaction. To return to our UPS example, few of their employees would object to the use of ambient-data collection for the purpose of preventative maintenance. The data isn't personal, and it doesn't relate to the individual employee driving the truck, so they feel safe about its being used for decision-science purposes. But that's not at all the case when we think that someone is using data about us to market to us or make decisions about how much compensation we deserve. That sets off all kinds of red flags, especially when the data points to something as intimately personal as being pregnant.

In a 2012 *New York Times Magazine* article entitled "How Companies Learn Your Secrets" (and throughout his excellent book *The Power of Habit*), author Charles Duhigg wrote about a man who was furious that his teenage daughter had been receiving baby-themed coupons in the mail from Target. He confronted a store manager and demanded an explanation. "My daughter got this in the mail. She's still in high school, and you're sending her coupons for baby clothes and cribs?" he asked incredulously. "Are you trying to encourage her to get pregnant?" The store manager apologized profusely, and even followed up with a phone call a few days later. This time the man's reaction was sheepish. "I had a talk with my daughter," he explained. "It turns out there's been some activities in my house I haven't been completely aware of. She's due in August. I owe you an apology." How did Target know that the man's daughter was pregnant before he did?

Even more to the point, what about privacy? Who wants to have Big Brother or The Man watching their every move? (You didn't think we'd write a whole chapter about data and how it informs intuition and not address privacy concerns, did you?) These are common objections that we've heard from new Klick employees, friends, family, and even many of the other companies covered in this book. Their concerns aren't misplaced. Living in as data-rich an environment as we do, it can be scary to think about how much information about us is being collected and analyzed. The problem isn't particularly new, either. Target and many other companies have been using predictive analysis for more than a decade.

Whenever it can, Target assigns its customers guest IDs, unique identifiers that track how and when they engage with Target. This enables them to build comprehensive profiles of Target shoppers. For example, they can see which store they visit and how often, the average amount of money they spend, whether they buy something in a retail store or from the Web site, which coupons they redeem, and which products they buy repeatedly.

To find out which of its customers are pregnant, Target works backward from the point at which expectant mothers voluntarily add themselves to the store's baby registry. Within the first twenty weeks of pregnancy, it found that expectant mothers typically stock up on vitamins and supplements. In their second trimester, they purchase larger than normal quantities of unscented lotion.

Purchases of things like cotton balls, scent-free soaps, washcloths, and hand sanitizers can be indicators that a woman's delivery date is approaching. If you're feeling a little creeped out, it's not surprising. Knowing that a huge corporation uses data to deduce such intimate things about you can't but feel like a violation.

The good news is that Decoded Companies don't use data for evil purposes. The Decoded organization is one that values its people and its culture above all else. And that culture is founded on transparency, trust, and accountability. Using data for evil runs completely contrary to the core beliefs that a Decoded Company holds, and so you should find the idea completely alien to your belief system if you've bought into the concepts of this book. We'll take a look at how data can actually play a part in fostering that type of culture in the engineered ecosystems chapter. Decoded Companies use their data to protect their talent and help them thrive.

We've identified three consistent principles of data capture that are true across all of the companies we've studied:

## Decoded Data Principles

1. **Decoded Companies are open and clear about the data they collect.** No secrets allowed. Decoded employees fully understand what information is being collected and why.

2. **Decoded Companies collect things that are on the corporate public record.** Genome collects all sorts of information but none of it is private: the projects you work on; the clients you're responsible for; the people on your team; your ability to meet deadlines; how much company training you've had; the number of vacation days you've

taken; your budgets; etc. None of these data points are private and they are visible to anyone at Klick at any time. You'd never turn to your boss and say, "Sorry, that client project I'm working on is confidential. I can't tell you who is on my team and how much money we've spent so far." That would be crazy! The power comes from Genome's collecting this data across the whole company, so that trends can be brought to light.

3. **In the absence of the corporate public record, Decoded Companies employ a clearly adhered-to opt-in clause.** While transparency is always essential, there might be some data that you want to collect that does not fall within the corporate public record. In this case, you must offer a clearly stated opt-in policy that offers your employees the choice of whether or not they want to participate in this program. This is an essential part of maintaining an ethical analytical practice. It's imperative to respect the wishes of any employee who does not want to participate in data-collecting practices that deal with matters outside the public corporate record. (We'll get into that later.)

For Target, there is a massive benefit in being able to predict pregnancies that goes way beyond the sale of more diapers even if its use of data doesn't adhere to the three principles. Target knows that there are only a few times in a customer's life when they are likely to switch their loyalty from one primary household goods store to another. Target's data revealed that pregnancy is one of those times. By sending pregnant women strategically timed coupons, it primed them to make Target the default store for *all* their purchases—both at that moment in their pregnancies and for years to come. Predictive analytics has been lucrative for Target. Since the program's implementation in 2002, its revenues have grown from $44 billion to $67 billion.[8] However, Target does not meet the transparency guidelines, because consumers are unaware of exactly what data is being collected and how it is being used. The things that you buy are also not within the scope of the corporate public record—what you choose to buy at a Target store is a private and personal choice. In order to adhere to the third principle, Target would therefore have to offer consumers the opportunity to opt in to these types of programs in order to remain compliant.

 **Reading list:** *The Power of Habit* by Charles Duhigg

The use of data collection and mining for loyalty purposes arguably began with the launch of American Airlines' AAdvantage program in 1981, but the field has changed rapidly along with the rise of Internet use and the proliferation of smart devices.[9] While corporations are able to capture more and richer information than ever before, they have also learned to be careful about how they use it. Target learned that women who hadn't told anyone that they were pregnant were disturbed when they received flyers in the mail that were obviously targeted to expectant mothers. They used that feedback to iterate and change their outreach approach, mixing the specially targeted items into a seemingly normal flyer. Learn from the lessons of history and avoid having to come to the same backward-looking learnings by following the principles from the beginning rather than applying them after the privacy horse has left the proverbial barn.

As we've previously mentioned, to be Decoded is to be in a state of constant experimentation. The Decoding philosophy encourages systematic curiosity; it expects you to challenge your assumptions, your beliefs, and existing systems. But it isn't all data rainbows and unicorns. Like any company with a culture of experimentation, Klick has tried things that seemed like good ideas in theory but turned out to be not so good in practice. Bad decisions do get made, even when you have awesome data superpowers.

 The following is an example of an experiment that we thought about implementing at Klick but ultimately decided not to. It's sometimes easy to get swept away by data and to develop what Leerom describes as an "unhealthy obsession with tracking and measuring everything."

Leerom and Aaron wondered if they could derive the same level of insights from e-mail communications that they get from Genome's sophisticated ticketing system. They decided to experiment by hooking Lexalytics, a sentiment analysis system, up to Klick's e-mail server. Lexalytics scans each e-mail and analyzes it for things such as tone, sentiment keywords, the formality of the correspondence, and the frequency of both sent and received communication. If it could establish what a normal pattern of communication between Klick's people and clients looked like, they hypothesized, then it should be able to create an early detection system that would identify when a client relationship was going south. But, as it turned out, the system wasn't capable of accurately analyzing the subtleties in language and tone that we often use in e-mails. This created many false positives, as the system flagged relationships as being in trouble when the reality was that everything was just fine. It also created tension internally. Staff complained about the new system, and since the value-added benefits were so low, it was a no-brainer to deactivate it.

Beyond that it was something of a cultural gray area. Decoded Companies are open and clear about the data they collect, and they only collect things that are on the corporate public record. Most organizations routinely monitor communication (e-mails, phone calls, texts) that take place on corporate devices, and employees know it. Looking for patterns in corporate e-mail is not so different from analyzing door security swipes to determine who is in the office and when. Genome, in fact, routinely collects door swipe data, and it can be queried to find out which floor of the building someone is on at any given time (which is hugely useful when you're spread across four floors or a big campus). But that information is publicly available to everyone, and the same rules apply to the senior leadership team. Anyone in the company can log in and check to see where Leerom is (a little later on, we'll even show you how we use our door swipe data to help Klick talent make healthier choices!).

 **Privacy:** As we mentioned earlier with door swipe data, the policy adheres to the Decoded Data Principles because it is transparent and a matter of public corporate record.

That's not the case with monitored communications. This kind of data isn't shared openly with the rest of the company but kept secret inside a corporate black box and only brought out for rare exceptions (when company secrets have been leaked through e-mail, for example). The association with negative events and Big Brother tracking does not make for warm fuzzies and helps to fuel fears that the collected information will be used punitively.

Aaron always maintains that, like any tool worth using, data can be used either constructively or destructively. For example, door swipe data itself is neither good nor bad. A manager could use the data to identify employees nearing burnout or where an individual is on the anxiety-boredom continuum. Alternatively, a manager could use the data to reprimand an employee for every minute they were ever late for the previous three months. In reality, taking this data away from the manager in the latter scenario won't make them a better manager; it merely limits the blast radius. In this way, abundant accessible data serves more as an amplifier of the intent and capabilities of our leaders. We do, however, use the data for a bunch of fun things, as we'll see in the engineered ecosystems chapter.

We spoke to Ben Waber, author of *People Analytics* and co-founder of Sociometric Solutions, about some of his thoughts on tracking, the issue of Big Brother, and how tricky establishing the right policies can be.[10] "Some things are socially acceptable, but a slight change in policy can get you very close to that edge," he said. "It's important to really think about the risks and rewards." He compared it to the increasing use of data-heavy applications on our smartphones. As consumers, we are willing to give up some of our privacy in exchange for some very useful rewards, such as personalized recommendations, knowing where our friends are, and being able to benefit from geolocation-based reviews, directions, and more.

**Reading list:**

*People Analytics* by Ben Waber

*The Naked Corporation* by Don Tapscott and David Ticoll

We are rapidly gaining the capabilities to track a staggering amount of ambient data, things that go beyond mere security badge swipes. "The next generation of company ID badges is going to have some sophisticated technology embedded inside them. Things like real-time voice analysis to look at who you speak to, and how you address that person, will be used to predict your happiness and performance," Waber explained. "Within the next five years, every ID badge will have these types of sensors in them and will cost the same amount as a regular RFID card." Insights into these types of metrics will be hugely valuable to managers for understanding what drives and motivates their talent.

While transparency into what is being collected and why is essential, these types of information streams can often fall outside the scope of the corporate public record. In this case, the key factor is to get opt-ins from employees, especially if you are going to measure things like phone calls and conversations. Without their buy-in, you'll lose the trust of your talent and the company's culture—and performance—will suffer.

We asked him for an example that showed some potential risks and rewards. Waber told us the story of how Bank of America used this approach to discover a startling insight that directly impacted its management policies. "At a Bank of America call center, they already have data for every minute of the day of what each person is doing. Management was focused on the employee as a single, individual unit," he said. That individual-based focus translated into a policy in which employees were asked to make sure that their breaks were never at the same time as anyone else's. "Your job is to have people call you up to yell at you about things that aren't your fault," Waber said. "That translates into a turnover rate of about 40 percent per year in U.S. call centers." Recognizing the stressful nature of the role, Bank of America noticed that performance metrics differed within certain call centers, and it realized that the culture of each specific center had a direct impact on how effective it was. "Using some of these advanced badges, they measured collaboration between people. They found out that the biggest predictor for performance was looking at who you talked to among your colleagues. That single metric was six times more predictive than any other metric that was being measured," Waber said. As with all Sociometrics projects, the participants had the option to opt in and controlled who had visibility into their personally identifiable data. The findings showed that people with the most cohesive face-to-face at-work networks completed calls in half the time. Management was curious as to when and where this interaction was taking place, since the break policy ensured that no one was taking a break at the same time by design. "They realized that people were overlapping lunch breaks by fifteen minutes, and that's where 80 percent of interactions were taking place," he said. In true Decoded style, Bank of America launched an experiment in which they took half the teams and let them take their breaks at the same time. Three months later they looked at the results and discovered that cohesion was up by 18 percent, and people were completing calls 23 percent faster—a $15 million reward for Bank of America generated simply by changing one corporate policy.

## NOT-SO-BIG DATA

Every company collects data. Your organization probably has a data center in which it keeps everything from copies of client files and records to e-mail server backups (given broad industry trends, there's a sharply increased likelihood that it's located somewhere in the cloud—probably in a Google data center—regardless of your company's size). Information from operations, finance, and HR are usually housed in databases and are often siloed, sometimes due to regulatory or privacy concerns.

Data literacy—your ability to find, evaluate, understand, and use data—is quickly becoming one of the most important skills and determinants of business success. Although the data itself is binary, data literacy is not. We measure data literacy on a spectrum, with every person and organization falling somewhere along a line that takes into account their own experiences and knowledge. From a small business that has neither the plans nor the ability to integrate data into a broader strategic objective, to a fully versed corporation that uses predictive analysis to make decisions, data exists at every step of the way along the path to becoming a Decoded Company. The ultimate goal is to strategically apply data principles to unleash new insights, increase efficiency, and empower talent. In order to be able to act upon the insights from data, organizations need to make sure they are well instrumented to capture the various data streams that exist inside their walls.

Much of that data qualifies as part of the much hyped so-called Big Data movement. Big Data has all kinds of expensive and complex connotations, from massive server farms to massive databases with crazy indexing technologies.

Luckily for us, the data we're talking about in this book doesn't fit into the definition of "big." We're going to be looking at data sets that are a little more manageable, like the ones that are already available within your organization, no matter what its size. We're also going to show you how you can start using that information right away to help you run your business. Since we're not talking about Big Data, for our purposes we'll define data as follows: *any information that can be measured, captured, or visualized about any activity or decision that is happening within an organization. It can be quantitative (numbers, surveys, log files, sensor data) or qualitative (texts, videos, pictures).*

## QUANTIFIED SELF

It's not just corporations that can benefit from this new data abundance. Individuals can gain new insights into their own behaviors, too. Tim Ferriss, the bestselling author of *The 4-Hour Workweek, The 4-Hour Body*, and *The 4-Hour Chef*, is fanatical about collecting data, especially when it comes to his own health. He's the data nut who sometimes gets his blood tested every two weeks. On his blog he wrote:

> I've recorded almost every workout I've done since age 18. I've had more than 1,000 blood tests performed since 2004, sometimes as often as every two weeks, tracking everything from complete lipid panels, insulin, and hemoglobin A1c, to IGF-1 and free testosterone. Just as some people have avant-garde furniture or artwork to decorate their homes, I have pulse oximeters, ultrasound machines, and medical devices for measuring everything from galvanic skin response to REM sleep.[11]

*The 4-Hour Body* is the product of his obsession. The book compiles his own findings and those of hundreds of other people to create a customized fitness and nutrition regimen that accounts for a user's unique body chemistry, genetics, and habits.

Data is powerful because it helps us see and understand things that we otherwise would have missed. For Ferriss, data is his sixth sense, because it allows him to isolate, on a chemical level, exactly what worked and didn't work in helping him attain his fitness goals. Using this information he was able to gain thirty-four pounds of muscle in twenty-eight days without steroids and with only a total of four hours in the gym.[12] It sounds crazy, but Ferriss has the hard data to prove it.

 **Reading list:** *The 4-Hour Body* by Tim Ferriss

While Ferriss might be an extreme case, the emergence of new Web applications has made it possible for us to gain new understandings of our own minds and bodies without the need for expensive ultrasound machines or bimonthly blood tests (phew!). All you need is a computer and an Internet connection. Remember Buster Benson, who was part of the crack Bezos's Personal Programmers team at Amazon in the early 2000s? Buster went on to become one of the Web's foremost experts on the Quantified Self. He's dedicated to finding correlations between the things that are objectively measurable and the subjective (happiness, meaning, etc.). For him, the Quantified Self movement is about using data to unpack the baggage we all carry around, particularly about topics like happiness. He maintains a spreadsheet of the ten or twelve things he's currently tracking at any time, which, at the time we spoke, included whether he had a coffee in the morning, how much quality time he had spent each day with his wife and son, and whether he had gone for a run. These data points all go into a statistical correlation calculation to try to figure out which factors lead to his feeling like a more fulfilled human being at the end of the day. You can see more of Buster's data obsession on his Web site at busterbenson.com.

Did you know that you can also easily track and measure the effects that such things as coffee, meditation, or skipping breakfast can have on your overall mental skills? Quantified Mind is a site that allows you to track how your cognitive skills vary from day to day. The site features short and easy tests that are grounded in academic research but have been modified for the Web. And that's just one example of how the data we produce can be applied on an individual level. Quantified Self is the Web community for members of the analytics-driven movement that strives for "self knowledge through numbers." Members document how recording their moods, sleep patterns (remember the high-tech alarm clock in chapter 2?), eating habits, and more helped them gain new insights and, in some cases, tackle problematic issues such as their weight and depression.[13] In the cases of the Quantified Mind and the Quantified Self, data can take the guesswork out of what we think works for us and what actually does, and helps make us healthier, happier, and more productive.

## INTERNET OF THINGS

Data is also allowing us to interact with the everyday objects that surround us in new ways. We are living at the dawn of the age of the Internet of things, a convergence of sensors, computing, and interactivity in which the intelligence of our smart devices is being extended to our entire household.

The Nest learning thermostat, for example, uses algorithms to do a better job of controlling the temperature in your house than you could ever do on your own. Users manually adjust the temperature for the first few days after installation. Nest learns from these inputs what temperatures make you comfortable and what your schedule is, and it automates your system accordingly. Nest is also designed to save energy and reduce monthly bills. The service also delivers a monthly e-mail, the Nest Energy Report, which is filled with personalized tips and information. Jay has a Nest in his house. His February 2013 energy report included:

- the full number of kilowatt hours saved by all Nest users since October 2011 (630,788,513 kWh);

- how his house did compared with the month prior (-11 hours of energy use in February compared to January);

- a tip on earning more Nest Leafs, the green icon shown on the thermostat when your house is ecofriendly (while you can always turn the temp down until the leaf appears, here's a hint: Setting the temperature to 60°F will almost always get a leaf; try lowering your away temp to 60°F or turning the heat down at night);

- interesting facts comparing the number of Nest Leafs he's earned compared with everyone in his area (35 percent more), his state (50 percent more), and Nesters overall (40 percent more);

- a look at the Nest Leafs he earned in February (nineteen total, four more than January), how his month compared with all Nesters (in the top 45 percent), and his Leafs earned all year (thirty-four).

Thanks to the Internet, it's also possible to access and adjust Nest's settings from a smart device, a tablet, or a computer, where users can also analyze and track their own behavior.

# BUSINESS ANALYST < DATA SCIENTIST < MASTER ORCHESTRATOR

Taking advantage of all of this data requires everyone in your organization to possess some degree of data literacy. But specialists are required as well. As documented in chapter 1, roles whose descriptions include the words "data science" are very much on the rise. *Fortune* magazine declared the data scientist "the hottest gig of 2022" because of the billions of new devices that are coming in the next decade that will be creating and sharing information.[14] The role is described as "one part mathematician, one part product-development guru and one part detective." Companies have already started creating those types of roles as they search for people who can dive into the data pool.

We believe that the true value of data can't be realized by those who only know which analytics to run on which particular data set. The real opportunities are for those who understand the strategic questions that need to be asked before a company can improve its competitive advantage. Having such a strategic vision goes beyond the job descriptions of a business analyst or a data scientist. There is a need for master orchestrators: people who can draw meaning from large data sets, link them to a plan of action, orchestrate the completion of the plan, and then cycle back to the beginning to measure and optimize for next time.

These are people who have the business savvy to ask the questions and the data chops to find the answers; at the same time, their instincts are skeptical—they can be relied upon to constantly question the business logic of whichever algorithms are being implemented. This analytics-focused mind-set will be bubbling up to the highest ranks of organizations as leaders develop the necessary skill sets and perspectives to guide their businesses into this new data age. At the same time, we all need to remember that data is just a tool. We shouldn't become overly reliant on technology, nor should we become complacent and simply trust whatever the data says. Master orchestrators must provide the critical human element.

## MACYS.COM AND THE MASTER ORCHESTRATOR

From frontline UPS truck drivers to hospital administrators, analytical skills are becoming a regular part of the job. As more and more people grasp the advantage that comes from having informed intuition, traditional roles are evolving to keep up with this new analytics-focused trend.

At Macys.com, the move to data visualization was initiated and championed by executives rather than the IT department. "Everything is top-down, driven by the executive level," said Kerem Tomak, vice president of marketing analytics. "The highest levels at the company started requesting and creating the needed data-driven decisions rather than relying on gut feel for day-to-day decisions."

For example, if a Macys.com executive wanted to understand the impact that shipping delays were having on a particular market, he or she could just look at the international shipment dashboard, which displays sales data by country and generates a heat map that highlights potential issues such as delays. Transforming the collected data into a visual output, like a map, reveals trends in a powerful way. It makes it easier to get to a decision-making point by eliminating the need to read and digest a long report or analyze reams of data. The computer does that automatically, allowing users to interact with the data in a more intuitive way.

While the specific tools are being developed by technical and analytical departments, many executives are becoming adept at manipulating the data themselves in order to unlock their sixth sense and make better informed decisions. Tomak believes this helps Macys.com executives understand the whole picture and the multitude of forces that can drive and impact a business unit. "They can visualize the source of the data and get an easier grasp of the connections that are creating different trends," he said. "They can make faster decisions that way."[15]

And speed is nothing to shrug at—it's a survival imperative at Macys.com. The online retailer has just seven seconds to entice a customer into making a purchase before it loses them to a competitor. "We need a laser focus on how we deliver products and services the minute the customer comes to the site," Tomak added.[16]

## THE RIGHT TYPE OF DATA: SELF-REPORTED VERSUS AMBIENT

Two of the most critical issues for Decoded Companies are knowing which kinds of data are the most important to collect and measure and having the technical ability to collect and measure it. We could, for example, track the times that an employee clocks in or out, but that wouldn't help us measure their happiness or how much they contribute to the organization. Traits such as happiness or engagement have traditionally been considered the softer side of metrics—qualitative versus quantitative—and are measured with fallible mechanisms such as surveys—when they're measured at all. The systems and scale that were required to track them reliably were impossible to achieve with existing technology, but now there are tools that can do this that are readily available for implementation. The best of them rely on ambient data.

There are two types of data: self-reported and ambient. Self-reported data requires a user's manual input in order to measure it. Filling out time sheets, surveys, performance evaluations, and expense reports are all examples of this type of data. Ambient data is information about a behavior that is automatically collected without the user's having to actively enter each data point. Swiping into work with an active RFID badge, sending e-mails, making calls, and even adding events to an electronic calendar are all examples of ambient data.

We've all been in this classic self-reported versus ambient scenario. Ambient is clearly going to win!

## The Problem with Self-Reported Data

Sir Frederic Bartlett, one of the most influential psychologists to study memory recall, wanted to see how personal and cultural contexts affect our ability to remember details. So he set up an experiment in which he read a Native American folk story called "The War of the Ghosts" to a group of subjects. The story, just a few paragraphs long, tells of two warriors who are invited along to a battle by a war party of ghosts. One decides to go and, after being wounded, returns home to tell his villagers his tale before he dies.

Bartlett asked the participants to recall the plot at various intervals in time, from immediately after hearing it to a year later. What he discovered was that they gradually changed the narrative to better fit in with their existing worldview, which Bartlett called their "schema." Some subjects left out certain plot points from the story, while others rationalized the supernatural elements in a way that made more sense to them. Any self-reported data we introduce into a system suffers from the same schema effect (think back to the recency effect we've covered in annual performance reviews).

Consider, as well, the fallibility of what we do remember. In his seminal 1932 book, *Remembering: A Study in Experimental and Social Psychology*, Bartlett noted the gaps between our memories of events and the events that actually occurred.

Remembering is not a completely independent function, entirely distinct from perceiving, imaging, or even from constructive thinking, but it has intimate relations with them all. One's memory of an event reflects a blend of information contained in specific traces encoded at the time

it occurred, plus inferences based on knowledge, expectations, beliefs, and attitudes derived from other sources.[17]

That is the crux of the issue with self-reported data: It is rife
with biases. Too much of the information being tracked has been
filtered through the interpretations of the people who input it.
They might have distorted it deliberately, much as an employee
might fill in a time sheet to reflect what they think their boss wants
to see rather than how they really spent their time. Or it might happen subconsciously. A self-evaluation can skew more positively or
negatively depending on a person's beliefs about their own behaviors, strengths, and aptitudes.

Bartlett believed that individuals process memories based on
their own unique historical and cultural frameworks, and that they
tailor their recollections to align with them. Our recollections of
our experiences working on projects, or of our interactions with
certain colleagues or clients, are inevitably biased, and not just by
our opinions of ourselves but by the schema through which we organize the world. We will almost always fill in gaps and add and
omit details to make sure our remembered versions of events ac-
cord with our preconceptions.

While there are times and places when self-reported data can be
valuable, in general, Decoded organizations should focus their attention on tracking and analyzing ambient data. There are several
advantages to using ambient instead of self-reported data streams.

- **No behavioral shifts needed:** Ambient data enables companies to track behavior without having to depend upon
  behavioral changes to do it. Ambient data collection is
  hassle-free, both for leaders who want to implement

these policies and for staff who are looking to avoid the extra effort required to adhere to new regulations or processes (though it's important to remember the three principles of Decoded data capture outlined earlier in this chapter).

· **Neutral perspective:** Ambient data provides a level of neutral and objective transparency that isn't influenced by personal bias or varying standards. What one person considers an exceptional performance might be rated only satisfactory by another. Ambient data strips all of that away and looks at the core of what's been measured.

## GOOGLE, FACEBOOK, AND THE CASE FOR AMBIENT DATA

You're no doubt familiar with Google's "Did you mean . . . ?" feature, which suggests spelling fixes for commonly misspelled search terms. What you probably don't know is that it works entirely based on ambient data fed by Google's users into a sophisticated, statistical, machine-learning algorithm. According to Douglas Merrill, Google's former CIO and vice president of engineering, the algorithm looks for a repeated pattern of a search term entered followed very quickly by an almost identical term seconds later.[18] That pattern indicates someone realized the mistake they made the first time and fixed it the second time, teaching the algorithm one way to misspell the correct term. With its steady diet of ambient data from hundreds of millions of users, Google was able to create a spelling correction system without teaching the system anything about spelling.

# DATA AS A SIXTH SENSE

The value to Google is significant. Anything that helps keep its dominance of the search market helps to protect its advertising revenue stream. Correcting spelling helps users perform more accurate searches, which encourages them to continue using Google.

Facebook is another example of an ambient-data powerhouse. It doesn't rely on you to explicitly tell it who your top five closest friends are as you happily reveal that each and every time you log on to the site. Facebook tracks who you communicate with on its site, how often, from where, and through which method (posting on a wall versus sending a Facebook message). All of these actions are monitored, gathered, and analyzed, giving Facebook an intimate look at the relationships in your life and how they manifest online. This understanding is embodied in Facebook's proprietary algorithm, which determines the subset of all possible posts from your friends that actually end up being displayed in your news feed. The average Facebook user has about 190 friends, many of whom post more than one activity or status update per day.[19] It would be overwhelming if all of them ended up in your news feed, so their algorithm helps to balance out that content, ensuring that you see more things that you're interested in and receive less news from people you didn't speak to in high school and still don't really care about (but are strangely friends with on Facebook anyway). Facebook says that its algorithm now weighs more than one hundred thousand factors in determining what you'll see.[20] An earlier version of that calculation, called EdgeRank, was built around three key values that are still important:[21]

- **Affinity:** How strong is your past relationship with the poster? Strength here is measured by the ambient data stream that you've created in interacting with the person or brand in the past. The more frequently you've been to their profile or page, liked or commented on their posts, or messaged them, the higher your affinity.

· **Weight:** How much is this particular post type worth? Commenting takes more effort than liking and so is seen as being more valuable. Generally speaking, the higher the amount of effort that goes into content creation, the higher the value.

· **Time decay:** How long has this post been alive? The newer the post, the more valuable it is. Posts decay over time, ending up with a lower time decay value.

You can see by even this simplistic explanation that its algorithm is highly driven by your past behavior and interaction with Facebook. You don't need to explicitly provide any of those values in order for Facebook to do its magic—and would probably self-report different values filtered through your schema if you did.

Facebook's analytics team is so good at spotting behavior trends that it can predict when a user is about to leave their job—or their spouse! A third of all divorce filings in 2011 contained the word "Facebook," and more than 80 percent of U.S. divorce attorneys say social networking citations are on the rise in divorce proceedings.[22] In an even more predictive fashion, a recent study found that the more that sexually inexperienced teens talked about sex on their Facebook page, the more likely they were to report that they planned to engage in sexual activities (i.e., it reliably functions as a predictor that they will become experienced).[23] Ambient data peels back the layer between what we say and what we actually do, even if that thing we do is poking someone we're not supposed to be poking, according to those pesky wedding vows.

 **Privacy:** Facebook's data policy has been controversial in the past. The company is not transparent with the data that it collects and what it plans to do with that information. Furthermore, many of the actions that it measures are *not* on the corporate public record, making it a huge privacy risk for users.

 **Reading list:** *The Facebook Effect* by David Kirkpatrick

## WHOLE FOODS MARKET: A HEALTHY MIX

Whole Foods Market is a great example of a company that uses a mix of ambient and self-reported data to generate metrics that shape sixth sense–led decisions. The company has been ranked among *Fortune* magazine's "100 Best Companies to Work For" for fifteen consecutive years, since the list's inception. When Whole Foods' first store opened in Austin, Texas, in 1980, there were only nineteen employees. Since then it has grown to over seventy-three thousand employees with more than 310 stores throughout the United Kingdom, Canada, and the United States.[24] The company went public in 1992 and has since become the ninth-largest food and drugstore in the United States, and it has achieved a rank of 284 on the Fortune 500 list. In 2011, the company reported more than $10 billion in sales and currently lists more than twenty-four hundred natural and organic products under its Whole Foods Market, 365 Everyday Value, and Whole Catch brands.

Whole Foods managers post their store's sales data each day and regional sales data each week, and compare the figures with historical information from the previous year and provide year-to-date totals. Once a month each store gets a detailed report that contains an in-depth analysis on profitability, including a breakdown of sales, product costs, salaries, and operating profits for every Whole Foods store. It's worth repeating that point for clarity: It doesn't receive a report only on their own store but rather on the same data points for *every* Whole Foods store. That shared ambient data gives their managers a sixth sense about what's failing and working across the board and can inform their intuition about how they can maximize sales at their own location. The data is an essential resource for decision making, because the individual teams (and not a traditional hierarchy) manage their own spending, ordering, and pricing (we'll talk more about the team unit in the next chapter). According to a 1996 article in *Fast Company,* Whole Foods shares so much information so widely that the SEC designated all sixty-five hundred employees it had at the time as "insiders" for stock-trading purposes.[25]

Ultimately, being a Decoded Company is about experimenting to find the right mix of data, of the information that establishes a direct relationship between an individual's decisions and their impact on the business. Impact can be measured in several different ways. The most obvious is financial. From either revenue or cost-savings perspectives, data allows you to see the full chain of actions that link a person's activities to the dollars coming into or going out of the company. Data can also help an organization measure the impact of an individual on morale, productivity, or happiness (more on that in a later chapter).

The right type of data has to be accurate. The more thoroughly the chain of action is tracked, the better and more reliable the data will be. If there are too many gaps, then you will be forced to supplement the data with assumptions and blind guesses that can lead to mistakes in decision making.

When it uses self-reported data, Whole Foods embraces the Decoded philosophy by extending its data-rich approach to understanding its talent. Every year it conducts a companywide morale survey to gain insight into its employees' states of mind and sentiments. Employees are asked to rate their confidence in their leaders on a team, store, and regional level, to share their fears and frustrations, and to identify any gaps between the company's actions and its core values. The results and findings are shared in the annual shareholder report. Although that self-reported data is subject to the biases of the employees, the scale and scope of the talent base tends to negate any individual schemas and results in essentially ambient data.

This is well worth remembering: You can fill gaps in ambient data with self-reported data as long as it comes from a large enough sample population.

 ## GENOME'S GENESIS

For many companies, becoming a data-focused organization is a survival imperative. But making the necessary changes can be an enormous undertaking; it's normal to feel overwhelmed and unsure of where to start. The good news is that these types of transformations can occur incrementally. You don't have to become fully instrumented right off the bat but can follow a gradual process.

After Aaron took the first step of banning intracompany e-mail for work tasks at Klick, he and Leerom started to look at the tickets for cues to the company's digital body language. They looked at the number of tickets generated per client and the number of tickets per dollar, and gained insights into the way they were running their business and their talent. Some of the patterns came up so frequently that Aaron gave them names. "Ticket tennis" is when we notice, for example, that a ticket is being bounced around without being resolved. It's indicative of a communication breakdown between individuals or teams, and it can pinpoint areas of concern that we might otherwise miss.

The insights and patterns that Leerom and Aaron gleaned had revolutionary implications for the way they would build Klick. This is how companies evolve. We stumble upon insights, in this case the patterns and trends that we could get from ticket data. Once we cracked this we realized that, while we will never be able to run a perfect business, we can drastically minimize surprises. Over time the reduction of mistakes provides a massive competitive advantage.

In Klick's case, the ticketing system was the foundation of what would become Genome, a sophisticated analytics tool that uses data to break free from the limitations of one-size-fits-all management in order to provide its employees with a personalized work experience that has helped it become an industry leader.

## EXCEPTIONS VERSUS PATTERNS (SIGNAL VERSUS NOISE)

While data-centric approaches like Genome will greatly minimize risk and identify blind spots, eliminating mistakes altogether is impossible, and it shouldn't be the goal. Even the most talented employee will make a bad call, anger a client, or deliver a project that's late or over budget. Sometimes factors that are outside an employee's control, such as new regulations, can cause delays or issues on the client side. As we mentioned earlier, ambient data provides a neutral and objective view of an individual's performance over time. This can be very much to the employee's advantage.

## A HARRY DECISION

The amount was $207,942.49. Leerom and Aaron were in total shock; they just couldn't believe it. They were $200,000 over budget on one of Klick's biggest and most challenging projects to date. It was 2003 and the company was only six years old. A fast-growing team meant that it had become harder to keep track of every detail of every project. Though the team was able to deliver to the clients on time, behind the scenes it had been a complete disaster.

Not only had the company overspent on the project, the deadlines were so tight that many team members were working near endless hours, and were exhausted and close to burning out. The person accountable was the project manager, a man named Harry, who had been with Klick for five years. Harry had a lot to answer for: a project that had completely derailed; an overworked team with poor morale; and a budget that had spun completely out of control.[26] Needless to say, Aaron and Leerom were far from impressed.

Should they have fired Harry? Would you have fired him based on the above information?

Emotions run high when projects go wrong, often shrinking a manager's perspective until that failure drowns out any other input. In this case, the facts clearly suggested that Harry wasn't competent and should be fired. Aaron's intuition told a different story, and his finely tuned internal master orchestrator told him to look for more info before blindly following the facts. Data can be a critical asset in identifying the difference between a simple mistake and a more serious underlying performance issue. Luckily for Harry, Genome came to the rescue. When he analyzed Harry's performance Aaron gained a level of objectivity about his overall contributions to the company. While Harry's numbers included the single largest loss that Klick had sustained on a project, they also painted a very clear picture. Over the previous five years, Harry had worked on over $6 million worth of business. Crunching the numbers further revealed that Harry's projects had been over budget by an average of just 0.517 percent, an incredible number that showed how talented he was in properly managing budgets and delivering projects on time. Even with that major loss, Harry was one of Klick's top-performing employees. He still is, and he has been promoted more than four times since that fateful project occurred. Read on to discover why.

The risk of losing good people like Harry goes to the very heart of the company's culture. As Leerom always says, the clients follow the talent. Had he and Aaron not paid attention to the bigger picture provided by the data, they would have deprived themselves of a highly competent and valuable project manager, adversely impacting Klick's ability to attract top-tier clients.

In many companies a mistake like the one Harry made would get you fired. Within a data-centric Decoded organization, however, any one project is merely a single data point among all the others. That long-term, timeline view makes it easy to identify longitudinal patterns, bad and good, that might otherwise be missed. Managers can see whether their reports are consistently delivering projects late and/or over budget, or simply performing at a level below their departmental average. Conversely, it makes it much easier to identify consistently high performers, even when they aren't necessarily in the spotlight. Unfortunately for some of Harry's colleagues, Aaron was also able to use Genome to identify a few project managers who had averages far worse than his, generally between 10 and 15 percent over budget!

Remember, performance on projects is only one information stream. If you'll recall, systems like Genome can also identify if a person is a team player, how quick their responsiveness is, and their efficiency at completing tasks, all of which add up to their tenure— the collective sum of their experiences. The data can provide an objective view that takes into account many more inputs, enabling managers to make better informed decisions that are grounded in fact. This protects both the talent and the organization. Employees know that making one mistake won't jeopardize their job if they are otherwise consistently performing well, and employers can rest easy knowing they have a comprehensive understanding of how their talent are contributing to their overall business objectives. All of this contributes to an environment built on trust and respect, creating a much safer space for risk taking and experimentation.

 **Privacy:** The activities measured were done with transparency, and all activities were on the corporate public record, making this an ethical data-collection policy.

In most businesses there is a lot of unfairness because the noisiest clients or teams get the most airtime. Data can help cut through the noise to the real heart of the issue. Leerom sees this as a way to uncover a pretty intangible measure: luck. Over time, data will show you that some people are incredibly lucky or incredibly unlucky. It's one thing to have an exception or a bad day, but with enough time, you'll be able to see the real pattern of each individual's contribution to various projects and teams. You can separate the exceptions from the rules. Data provides a clearheaded and neutral way to see each team member objectively. This enables you to properly evaluate and manage your most important resource: your people.

If you think about the massive database behind Genome, everything in there represents something that we've learned (sometimes the hard way), but thanks to the data, it has helped us become more efficient and able to make better decisions. Harry's disastrous project provides a case in point. After the dust settled, Leerom and Aaron called a meeting to dissect exactly what had gone wrong. What they heard was troubling. Every attendee of the meeting said the same thing: "I told you this was going to happen."

What they heard was really upsetting. Every department said they had raised an alarm, and we couldn't understand how we could have missed so many warning signs. It was only after the fact that it became apparent that everyone had raised red flags—but to the wrong people. The head of creative had mentioned it to Aaron and the head of client services had mentioned it to Leerom, so they each had a little inkling that it wasn't quite right. No one had talked to each other, so the scale of the issue wasn't apparent until we were looking back at it. As an organization, we didn't know when it was time to pull the handbrake until it was too late to stop.

The costs of this project went deeper than simply being over budget. When you make mistakes like this, you lose great people. We ended up delivering the project on time, but we had our talent working nights and weekends, resulting in burnout and the loss of a valuable team member. One of the things Leerom and Aaron obsess about when we collect a learning experience like this is to understand how we can prevent this battle scar from ever repeating. We tried to find a creative application of technology to institutionalize this learning. Our goal is always to codify our learnings literally into the computer code that runs Genome.

# PROJECT 360: QUANTIFYING GUT FEEL

Aaron and Leerom came up with the idea behind an internal tool called Project 360s, one of Klick's foundational tools that helps team members quickly communicate important project information if they ever feel like a project is coming off the rails. Embracing a people-first philosophy means that you can't let a project that impacts your people run off the rails that badly ever again. Nothing is higher order than the engagement and satisfaction of your team. Losing good people ultimately means losing good clients and customers.

Project 360s are a diagnostic that uses a mix of self-reported and ambient data to evaluate the status of all open projects. The process is simple: Every week Genome looks at all the projects an individual interacts with and asks that person to rate the state of the project as red, yellow, green, or blue for awesome. If they select anything but green or blue, it asks them to give one bullet-point reason as to why they feel there is a risk that this could become a problem (yellow) or that it will have a negative impact if not changed immediately (red). We trust our team implicitly; their experience and tenure is worth much more than its weight in gold, so some of the best comments have been as simple as "My Spidey sense is tingling." The employee is also asked to look at the allocated budgeted hours remaining for that project and say whether they are a realistic estimate of the amount of time needed for the work still to be done. Every person who is working on a particular project, regardless of discipline or rank, answers the same set of questions.

Each week, the project managers and their managers, the program directors, sit down for a quick review of their portfolios. The collected data provides them with very relevant information, capturing the collective health sentiment of a project and flagging problems before they become serious issues. It also makes it harder to avoid talking about issues or to evade them by pretending that everything is okay. Program directors used to have to rely solely on their intuition combined with the project manager's assessment of their own project. While the program directors still rely on their gut feel, their intuition is better informed by using this new, far broader data set; it gives them a sixth sense. Furthermore, the ability to dive deep into complex programs efficiently without investing the time to interact with the broader team allows Klick to leverage tenure more effectively.

This team input enables Genome to quantify the gut feelings and experience of all project participants while communicating a clear cultural mandate of the value of moving quickly and not being bogged down in procedures. In the absence of this tool, a program director only discovers that something is wrong after the fact, when there's an unhappy client on the phone or a deadline has been missed. Project 360s enable directors to look at the big picture generated by the data and Genome and to apply their own tenure to making sure that big missteps are avoided. It's more efficient, as it applies the wisdom of crowds—the collected data—to institutionalize an organization's learning and to rapidly accelerate the tenure of new employees in senior positions by helping them avoid mistakes others have made before.

Part of the automation that we enjoy is thanks to the data that we've already amassed. Genome's ticketing system (described in the previous chapter) has collected massive amounts of historical data on estimates, budgets, hours tracked, projects, clients, and talent. Depending on how we filter that data, we can gain all sorts of insights about our organization. These include everything from broad organizational insights (e.g., Has the introduction of a new policy actually increased efficiencies?) right down to the granular day-to-day level (e.g., measuring a specific project manager's performance and contribution to the business).

Additionally, because Genome contains years' worth of project completion averages, the system is designed to intelligently identify any project that deviates too much from the general historical averages and flag that project to the appropriate person for review.

How cool is it to be able to capture and quantify your entire talent pool's collective power of intuition and then incorporate an easy to use tool for quickly raising the alarm? It's the equivalent of sending a bat signal into the night sky, and every Klick team member knows that they have the power to fire it off at any point in time to call in reinforcements. The technology has also made it easy for people to raise an alarm in a safe environment. Like any company, we have a lot of people who can be shy or introverted. They may not be willing to speak up during a tense meeting or to their manager, but they can be very comfortable expressing their gut feel as objective feedback in Project 360s.

The success of this system has led us to start expanding the concept into the other two pillars of a successful account. Doing good work that makes clients happy and earns money is a fairly obvious recipe for success, but it's also a very accurate description of our business. Project 360s ensure that we do good work on budget, and so we're beginning to introduce Client 360s, which are built on the same framework and logic, to address the last piece. Client 360s use the ambient data in our calendar invites to determine when our people have had a touch point with any of our clients. We feed those into our weekly reviews, asking for a red/yellow/green (with comments) on the relationship and the client. Collecting that self-reported data across lots of touch points gives us a realistic and actionable view of any client at any moment in time based on the people who most recently interacted with them. The next phase will use future calendar entries to prompt an e-mail, designed for mobile devices, to communicate our current view of the client to anyone about to meet with them, providing the ultimate opportunity to address concerns in real time.

## GENGO

Project 360s are a powerful Klick example of how technology can help an organization map its instincts. For another take on how informed intuition can shape companies, let's revisit Gengo, the Japanese translation company.

For CEO Robert Laing, developing an informed intuition is a critical skill. "One of the things we've tried to do with new employees is to teach them how to display data and charts," he said. "I've always been really surprised in my career that so few people can interact with data effectively. Data is about storytelling and about explaining to people what's going on in various aspects of the business in a way that they can immediately grasp."

# DATA AS A SIXTH SENSE

Laing's team has a group chat on Skype in which they do what Laing describes as "data dumps," sharing raw data that employees are free to poke around in. "We get most people to learn SQL, so they can learn to run queries by themselves," he said. "You'll get people who have no programming skills who can now use data to find solutions to problems."

Laing also uses his sixth sense through a data-centric approach that focuses on the most valuable segment of their network: the senior translators who, in addition to translating texts, often coordinate bigger projects among more junior colleagues. "Translation is something that is very subjective, very human," he said. "We wanted to take that process and turn it into something objective that can be measured and scaled."

Gengo uses a scorecard comprising mixed self-reported/ ambient data and a red/yellow/green system to measure five areas of responsibility: the quality of the submitted work; the pickup time (how long it takes a translator to accept a job); the speed of the translation; the capacity of the work produced; and whether or not a translator has gone above and beyond their job description in delivering service to a client. Four of the five metrics are ambient data that Gengo generates automatically by pulling information such as consumer feedback scores to calculate a translator's quality.

The above and beyond score is a self-reported metric added manually by Gengo staff, who use it to provide context beyond what the ambient metrics can convey as to how each translator is contributing to the broader community. Emphasis is placed on mentoring and participating online with other Gengo translators to share best practices and ideas. "This enables us to have a very flexible input point where we can add anything that might not fit into the other four categories," Laing explained. "And it adds a human element to numbers generated by a computer."

The scorecards are updated biweekly in order to provide the most up-to-date information and immediately address any issues that might come up (e.g., a translator who is taking too long or who is getting negative feedback from clients). A senior translator can use the scorecard to flag an issue to Laing's team, such as system bugs or high-volume customers with recurring problems.

"We also have a tool named GoCheck that rates translations based on the number and severity of errors," he said. "When we release a new product version we can compare the quality score to ensure that we're moving in the right direction." By working on his data as a sixth sense, Laing had increased Gengo's quality score by over 11 percent in the six months prior to our conversation, an accomplishment that he and his team are justifiably proud of.

## THE IDEA ECONOMY

Whether it's Klick's Project 360s measuring gut feel or Gengo's scorecards capturing a translator's experience, there are many different ways to build informed intuition into an organization that is becoming Decoded.

Let's go back to Peter Arvai and how he made data as a sixth sense part of the architecture of Prezi. As you'll recall from the beginning of this chapter, Peter believes ideas are among the most valuable and yet intangible resources floating around inside his company. He's hoping that analytics will change that and provide a new perspective. Arvai is experimenting with a new feature for the Prezi platform that will allow the company to track the creation and spread of an idea by both its employees and the external Prezi community. Once the new feature goes live, users will be able to borrow ideas found in other Prezi users' presentations in a way that's easily sourced and tracked. If you love a user's take on the latest Hollywood blockbuster, for example, you can grab it and add it to your own, easily sourcing and giving credit to the person who came up with the idea in the first place.

The collected data will be able to identify two important things: who in your company is coming up with the best ideas and who is facilitating the exchange and spread of those ideas, enabling them to bubble up.

"Using Prezi in this fashion would allow users to be able to measure the evolution of their ideas," said Arvai. "They would be able to create a map to truly see how innovation is flourishing both inside their companies and within their community."

Whether you're a CEO or a manager, you only have so much face time with your people. You might see ideas coming only from the limited number of people you have direct contact with, or you might have someone on your team who excels at pitching ideas that they "borrowed" from someone else. Your ability to identify the real source of innovation within your organization may well be skewed. Perhaps there is a shy IT manager who is constantly coming up with great solutions that are shared and adopted within the organization. This person might get overlooked in favor of someone who is better at vocalizing ideas, especially up the chain. Much as a Project 360 gives an introverted employee the ability to raise alarms, Prezi's system ensures that the people who are actually generating the innovative ideas are getting recognition and being accurately valued.

That sounds pretty awesome, but it's only the beginning. "Once we collect more data, I believe we'll see that there are many different roles in the ecosystems of ideas," Arvai explained. "It's not necessarily the same people who come up with *and* spread ideas, but both are important. Recognizing a shortage or surplus in one or the other can be a very useful thing to know when making decisions."

Being able to use analytics to foster an idea-generating ecosystem is a compelling goal. "We'll have the capacity to really change organizational structure, to flatten hierarchies, and to help good ideas come forward," Arvai concludes.

## STARBUCKS AND SPRINT

In his 2010 book *Onward: How Starbucks Fought for Its Life Without Losing Its Soul*, Starbucks founder Howard Schultz and coauthor Joanne Gordon mention the importance of metrics in measuring success and the dangers of focusing too much on the wrong data. One of his first moves after returning to Starbucks as CEO in 2008 was to stop publicly reporting same-store sales as a key metric. Same-store sales, known as "comps," were used to evaluate the performance of each store, but they didn't tell the complete story. For those of you not familiar with retail, comps usually compare the sales of stores that have been open for at least a year in order to provide a true picture of sales growth that isn't influenced by the opening of new stores (i.e., revenue is up within the same store rather than revenue for the whole company is up because we opened ten thousand new stores). As useful as they are, comps are entirely retail focused and don't take into account the company's other out-of-store revenue streams, such as Starbucks' grocery products or corporate coffee machines. More insidiously, Schultz realized, focusing on this metric was incentivizing the wrong type of action from his staff. "[Comps] were a dangerous enemy in the battle to transform the company," he wrote. Starbucks' management team had grown overly dependent on it as an indicator of organizational health, when it actually created side effects that contributed to the company's problems. We often refer to this as YGWYM (you get what you measure). If you tell your people that their bonuses are based solely on causing their laptop to levitate a few feet over their desks, then you had better be in the antigravity business, because everything else is about to fall by the wayside.

In Starbucks' case, a reliance on comps encouraged managers to expand aggressively and deviate from the customer experience that had catapulted the company to success in the first place. But they proved to be a lagging metric rather than a predictor of future performance. The company made decisions based on positive historical figures, and by the time the numbers started to drop, it was too late to prevent the losses that rolled in. Schultz wrote:

> Maintaining positive comp growth history drove business decisions that veered us away from our core. Once I walked into a store and was appalled by a proliferation of stuffed animals for sale. "What's this?" I asked the store manager in frustration, pointing to a pile of wide-eyed cuddly toys that had nothing to do with coffee. The manager didn't blink: "They're great for incremental sales and have a big gross margin." This was the type of mentality that had become pervasive. And dangerous.[27]

Hindsight is always twenty-twenty. What's happened in the past might prove to be an accurate predictor of future success, but it could also be like reviewing the maintenance logs on the *Titanic* while there's an iceberg looming in the fog up ahead.

This is why analytics needs to evolve hand in hand with management philosophy and strategic thinking. Simply plugging into a few data streams and declaring your intuition informed can be dangerous. Informed intuition only works when the data being collected is the right kind. Otherwise it can lead you horribly astray.

 **Reading list:** *Onward: How Starbucks Fought for Its Life Without Losing Its Soul* by Howard Schultz and Joanne Gordon

Remember the Sprint story from the previous chapter? The first thing they identified was a lack of consistency in how it was evaluating the performance of their call center reps. A new metric would be the focus each month—decreasing wait times, increasing first-call resolutions, total customer satisfaction—and employees would scramble to adjust their behavior accordingly. How could they develop best practices for improved performance when the landscape was constantly shifting under their feet? To make matters worse, the rate of change in the mobile industry means an ever-changing product lineup that made it nearly impossible for employees to deliver consistent results. Stress was high and morale couldn't have been lower.

Much like Starbucks, some of Sprint's metrics rewarded the wrong type of behaviors. Its outsourced call centers' performance metrics, for example, were tied to the volume of calls it handled instead of customer satisfaction. Since there were no incentives to increase the number of first-call resolutions, they were rushing the customers off the phone. We've all felt that pressure when calling into a customer support line, a feeling that only gets magnified with each additional call we have to make to resolve the same issue.

It had no automated systems in place, and the nearly eighty metrics it was tracking had to be input manually into spreadsheets by managers who often had to chase down the information, resulting in missing, unreliable, and often inconsistent data. The managers' self-reports tended to emphasize whatever metrics made their call center numbers look good.

What a mess. How could anyone's sixth sense function in such a data avalanche? It obviously couldn't, and the financial indicators made that abundantly clear. "We were awash with data," recalled Lance Williams, director of customer management. "We needed less but better focused information." The answer was Compass, the system it developed with its partner NICE (which was mentioned in the last chapter).

 ## Decoded Metrics

Starbucks and Sprint, companies from very different industries, were both plagued by rotten metrics; their stories are just two examples of an all too common occurrence. In an editorial at Forbes .com, venture capitalist James Slavet lamented this misplaced focus.

> After years of leading teams and then, at Greylock, watching some of the best start-up CEOs in the world, I've learned that the most important metrics are often ones you never read about on the income statement or in the financial

press. Most managers only measure outputs, not inputs, which is like telling a Little League team to score more runs, rather than actually explaining how to swing a bat and make contact with the ball. Similarly, most companies measure traffic, revenue or earnings without considering how to improve the company at an atomic level: how to make a meeting better, or an engineer more productive.[28]

This is what being Decoded is all about: using available data to discover ways to make teams more efficient and productive—looking at the data to identify behavioral drivers, not just performance outputs. Slavet proposed a new set of metrics that organizations should measure in order to identify areas where they can improve. These are so important, he said, that they should be present in media coverage of companies so that potential investors can better judge their health and overall probability of success. We'll take a look at some of them below.

## Flow State Percentage: Overall Efficiency

Most people in the workforce today are knowledge workers. We aren't sitting in front of an assembly line repeating the same task over and over again. Our jobs require critical thinking, problem-solving skills, and the ability to quickly parse information in order to make decisions. For us to be productive we need to have time to get into a state of concentration in which we are completely and utterly immersed in the task at hand, what athletes call "being in the zone" and what the psychologist Mihaly Csikszentmihalyi calls "flow." "The ego falls away. Time flies. Every action, movement, and thought follows inevitably from the previous one, like playing jazz," he writes in his book *Flow: The Psychology of Optimal Experience.* "Your whole being is involved, and you're using your skills to the utmost."

Keeping flow means avoiding interruptions, and anyone familiar with the average workplace knows that's usually not possible. Between a never-ending barrage of e-mails, phone calls, and meetings, we are always being kicked out of our flow state. Paul Graham, who launched Viaweb, the start-up that would become Yahoo! Stores, and founded the wildly successful Y Combinator start-up fund, referred to this challenge in his very popular 2009 essay "Maker's Schedule, Manager's Schedule."[29] Graham noted that there are two types of schedules: the manager's schedule (traditional appointment book with one-hour blocks) and the maker's schedule (generally organized into half-day blocks). Since most executives and leaders are on the manager's schedule, they structure their organizations the same way. For knowledge workers—especially creatives and developers—the hourly interruptions wreak havoc with their flow. According to Csikszentmihalyi, they need about fifteen minutes to get back to flow, and sometimes even that isn't enough time. This loss of high-output concentration time can have a cost impact, but it isn't something that has been traditionally measured.

James Slavet recommends asking employees to track their flow states during an average day. If you take the number of hours spent in flow and divide it by the number of hours they're in the office, you get a good indication of whether or not your office policies and procedures need to be addressed (like maybe letting go of the need to force your manager's schedule onto all of your makers). "For example, perhaps there's a little paper sign at each person's desk that says 'Go Away, I'm Cranking," he suggests. "Or maybe you have a day where no meetings are allowed.'" Either way, this number is a good indicator of a bigger issue that could be overlooked if you're only looking at output. You could mistake a talented employee for an underperforming one, when the reality is that they are constantly being distracted. Without the benefit of this data you might let that employee go, only to hire someone else who experiences the same issue. A relatively simple data-gathering exercise would have told you that you needed to create an environment that maximizes your talent's ability to be creative.

Tools like RescueTime, a productivity-measuring Web application, enable managers to identify employees who are undertasked, unmotivated, or overworked and to measure the impact of changes in the workplace, such as when a team adds members.[30] It enables a culture of experimentation, because it becomes so much easier to test different ideas and use data to choose the one that best fits the organization's culture and style. These services also empower employees by giving them a higher level of autonomy, allowing them, for example, to have flexible work hours or alternative working arrangements (e.g., working from home) without having to worry about how those actions are perceived by colleagues. You'll read more about RescueTime in the experiments section at the end of the chapter.

 **Try this now!** The next time you're at work, try this little experiment. Grab a paper and a pen. Write down the number of times you think you will be interrupted within a three-hour window. (For example: between 9:00 A.M. and lunch.) Every time someone or something interrupts you, make a note on the pad of paper. Tally your results. Were you interrupted more times than you anticipated? Fewer? What does this tell you about your flow?

## Positive Feedback Ratio: Chatter and Kudos

In the course of our lifetimes we will spend an estimated eighty-six thousand hours working. That's eighty-six thousand hours spent with your colleagues. The quality of workplace relationships has a direct impact on the overall health and vitality of talent, and therefore of businesses themselves. Slavet believes that one of the best ways to establish a positive rapport with colleagues is to always reward positive behaviors. He quotes John Gottman, the author of *Why Marriages Succeed or Fail*, who believes that successful marriages tend to have a vastly higher rate of positive interactions than negative ones. "Catch people doing good things. Never miss a chance to say something nice, even if you feel a little silly," he writes. "Then when you have feedback on areas to improve they'll really listen."

 Building on his experience at Rypple, Jay was a big advocate for adding peer recognition tools to Genome when he joined Klick. The result is Chatter, which coincidentally shares a name with the Salesforce.com product, and acts like an internal Twitter channel, and Kudos, which are brief messages of thanks that team members are encouraged to post whenever they have a positive interaction with a colleague—whether it was someone working late to make sure a project was finished on time or someone who went above and beyond their job description to help another teammate. These acknowledgments help foster a feeling of positivity among teams and have been shown to improve the tone of other internal correspondence. They encourage employees to look for things to reward instead of to criticize, providing a constant stream of goodwill and news.

Another Chatter advantage is the social proprioception it creates within the organization. As mentioned earlier, proprioception is your body's unconscious awareness of where its limbs are. Social proprioception is the awareness we get from scanning an activity feed (Facebook news, Twitter, Chatter, etc.) without having to engage in actual conversation. The Kudos feed fosters an ambient awareness of our peers' accomplishments. Without expending much time or effort, everyone becomes aware of the bright spots in every other group, resulting in a much more cohesive talent pool. We'll talk about this in more detail in a later chapter.

When Peter Flaschner, Klick's vice president of marketing, relaunched Klick's popular digital marketing health blog, he couldn't have done it without Brad Einarsen, director of digital insight and the blog's masterful editor in chief. Brad oversaw the blog's redesign and worked tirelessly to ensure it had a new high-quality post up each day, even if that meant chasing down and harassing internal experts. Once the blog was up and running, Peter used Kudos to share his appreciation with the rest of the company:

> Brad is the heart and soul of the blog. He singlehandedly wrangles a mountain of data each week to find the most relevant stories and offers smart analysis on each. He writes profusely and well on a broad variety of topics, and offers a sound and measured perspective. He's a huge part of the public voice of our brand. Thanks Brad, and here's to some amazing times to come.

The post quickly accumulated more than fifty likes and ten comments from every discipline at Klick. Not only did it serve as a mechanism for praising a colleague, it informed everyone about the launch and ensured that people knew what Brad was working on, motivating them to help if he came asking for content. This post also increased the positive feedback ratio for the entire company.

## Keeping the Human Touch

As a company moves toward a more data-centric approach, it's important to factor in the human element and not get lost in the technology. Remember, your sixth sense uses data to augment your instincts, not replace them. At Klick, program management meetings help support this holistic perspective by making sure that managers from different departments who are working with the same clients regularly have face-to-face contact to discuss projects and progress and flag any issues.

 Aaron optimistically created a template that was to be used for each of these meetings, but he quickly noticed that attendees were skipping over many sections, because they felt they were a waste of time. Aaron realized that Genome had a clearer perspective on the interdependencies of complex project portfolios than anyone—it could see which people were working on which client's project, as well as the various wins, opportunities, risks, concerns, budget overages, upcoming milestones, and upcoming bookings. He decided to let Genome create the agenda.

Genome evaluates who should attend the meeting and generates a list of topics that need to be discussed, based on data from throughout Genome's entire database. The meeting is timed to last no more than twenty minutes, so the agenda is strict and deviations aren't permitted. The result is a highly customized meeting that delivers relevant information to every attendee, resulting in increased participation due to increased perceived value. Having all the team leads meet face-to-face ensures that issues are raised in a public setting, which in turn motivates the team leads to act in the best way possible in order to manage their reputations.

It creates an important feedback loop that enables nonclient-facing teams, such as those that work on technical development and information architecture, to see the impacts of their contributions to the project. This has helped raise the level of accountability and ownership across those disciplines, creating a more collaborative corporate culture.

For staff who do not attend the program management meetings, the agenda process adds value to their time when filling out their Project 360s. Their perspective will ultimately have more influence over the health of the program because it will be discussed by the entire program leadership team rather than mentioned to one of them and disregarded.

## Measure Everything

From gut feel and ideas to key performance indicators and job satisfaction, anything that can be measured can give your informed intuition a boost, sometimes in unexpected ways. As we've discovered, collecting data for one thing can lead to insights about another—the correlations and connections between data are sometimes more valuable than the original data itself. We long ago learned that it's better to measure the whole iceberg even if you're only going to report on the visible tip above the waterline. As an example, here's a story about our Project 360s. The second question they ask ("Does the estimated time remaining to complete this project seem reasonable?") turned out to provide us with the best predictor of new project manager performance.

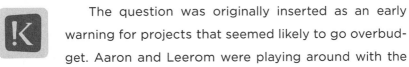

The question was originally inserted as an early warning for projects that seemed likely to go overbudget. Aaron and Leerom were playing around with the data set generated by that question one day, and they discovered something very interesting. When they took all of the yes/no data and grouped it by project manager, they discovered that the PMs with the highest yes rate had been consistently ranked as the best-performing project managers by other metrics and performance reviews. That yes rate turned out to be an amazingly accurate numerical indicator of project management ability, especially when the data was collected over time. It quantifies one of the essential skills needed for being a high-performing PM: the ability to accurately forecast the actual number of hours that each project will take. It has since become the gold standard for measuring PM performance at Klick and is used both as a KPI for existing PMs and as a predictive measure of success for new hires.

Another example of a useful data by-product came from having all of Klick's travel requests go through Genome. Although it was originally intended to reduce travel costs and find efficiencies, the availability of travel data has also revealed a number of useful additional features. Team members who are visiting clients are marked with airplane icons on our dynamic seating map. Our Genome TVs throughout the office will soon show a frequent traveler board. The expense reports tool in Genome knows the dates you were on the road and which clients you were visiting, so it can automatically assign expenses to the right project as soon as you enter the purchase date. These are all neat features, but the most useful productivity and customer experience driver popped up in an unexpected place: e-mail. Since travel requests include the client you're going to visit, Genome can easily use that information to compile an updated and personalized dossier and send it to you half an hour before your takeoff time. Called "In-Flight Reading," the e-mail includes the latest Genome news items you haven't read, as well as a summary of major items, changes, comments, and other client-specific info you might find useful. Your mobile device grabs the e-mail and caches it locally, meaning you have access to it while you're in the air, even without onboard Wi-Fi.

You don't have to overthink this—casting a wide enough analytics net will turn up an amazing array of unexpected insights. Data as a Sixth Sense is a superpower that is well within the reach of every organization, regardless of size or industry. It's just a matter of changing perspectives and seeing what other people can sometimes miss: the wealth of data that surrounds us, just waiting to be unlocked.

## CHAPTER SUMMARY: CODIFYING LEARNINGS

In this chapter, we looked at the mechanics behind developing data as a sixth sense. As we've seen from the examples, being Decoded can mean different things to different organizations. For companies such as UPS, Target, and Facebook, ambient data enables them to make predictive decisions, from when a UPS truck is about to break down to pinpointing when a Facebook user is going to get married. For Google it means providing more valuable search results that deepen loyalty. For Whole Foods and Starbucks the focus is on developing and using the most effective metrics, and then sharing this information within the organization. Klick, Gengo, and Prezi use data to custom-build platforms that map everything from experience and intuition to the creation and spread of ideas.

The ability to track everything from basic patterns of behavior to individual experiences means we can separate the signal from the noise and strip out the biases that might skew our decision-making ability. Our sixth sense can prevent us from repeating the same mistakes. It gives us the power to analyze our battle scars and, as Leerom is fond of saying, "codify those learnings literally with software code."

Of course, it should be used to augment your instincts, not replace them. As Kathryn Dekas, a manager from the Google People Analytics team, recently put it, "You can't have an algorithm for everything. You use data to inform, but you don't rely on the data to make the decision."[31] We couldn't agree more!

# DECODED TOOLBOX

## Master Orchestrator

A new role describing a person who can draw meaning from large data sets, link them to a plan of action, orchestrate the completion of the plan, and then cycle back to the beginning to measure and optimize for next time. These people generally excel at asking the right questions and finding solutions that help support your strategic vision.

## Project 360

Project 360s are a diagnostic tool that uses a mix of self-reported and ambient data to evaluate the status of each open project with a red/yellow/green/awesome approach, combined with comments.

## Chatter

An internal Twitter-like system that enables employees to share microposts.

## Kudos

A Kudo is a brief message of thanks that team members are encouraged to post whenever they have a positive interaction with a colleague.

 **DECODED EXPERIMENTS**

### Master Orchestrator

One of the ways we test for a master orchestrator is by evaluating their strategic-thinking process and their problem-solving skills.

- Go to decodedbook.com/data-as-a-sixth-sense and download the case file.

- You'll have a set time limit to review the information and formulate your approach.

- Once you've completed the test, check back online for the grading sheet to see how you did.

This is a great experiment for your whole team. Have them each complete the test and then discuss the results together to see how you can foster more master orchestrator skills.

## Project 360

Project 360s are a great example of a tool you can quickly, easily, and cheaply implement in your own organization. Although you likely won't have the level of automation and ambient data that Klick enjoys via Genome, you can achieve a similar result through a number of inexpensive tools. Create a weekly process for your teams to indicate how they feel about the health of their projects, using a red/yellow/green/awesome indicator. Review the results during your weekly one-on-ones.

- If your company already uses Google Apps, consider a Web-based form that you can easily create and invite people to complete, with the results automatically flowing into a spreadsheet stored on Google Drive.

- If you're not using Google's tools, consider a Web-based approach using SurveyMonkey, or even an e-mailed Excel spreadsheet.

## Chatter

A Chatter system is like a digital water cooler that your entire company (or team) can get involved with. It's open, inclusive, and informal. The atmosphere should be relaxed and fun—humorous posts, frank conversations, and feedback are encouraged. There are several sites offering these types of platforms that are aimed specifically at businesses of all sizes.

- Services such as Yammer, Huddle, and Jostle.me all offer enterprise social network services with a free trial.

- You can also create private groups on Google, Facebook, and LinkedIn.

## Kudos

Kudos are all about fostering a sense of gratitude and appreciation within your team. It's a deliberate focus on the positive to help maintain a high morale. The main goal of Kudos isn't just to reward and recognize positive contributions, but to broadcast and socialize those events within your team, to establish a solid reference of encouraged behavior. People respond best when they see concrete examples of cultural values being shared. This means it's less about the tools that are being used and more about the sharing and distribution of those stories with a broader audience. So, in addition to the tools listed below, consider how you will incorporate Kudos into your culture, such as at a weekly team meeting or through a monthly team lunch.

- If you are using a tagging-enabled system, incorporating Kudos can be as simple as adding a #kudos hash tag to entries of thanks.

- You can use a private Tumblr or blogging platform, such as WordPress or Blogger, and have people submit their Kudos stories directly.

## Flow State Percentage

Instead of asking employees to track their own flow state, look to ambient data to provide a much clearer and more transparent look at what each person is working on.

- RescueTime, for example, is an ambient-data time tracker that can be used to track flow.[32] It's software that runs in the background on your computer and automatically tracks how you're spending your time. It compiles that information into useful reports that break your day down into a spectrum that runs from *very distracted* to *neutral*, *productive,* and *very productive*. All activities are automatically tracked and recorded (including manual tracking for off-computer tasks, such as phone calls and meetings), ensuring accurate and easy reporting. RescueTime is about $15 per user per month, which is cheap enough for you to try with your team without needing anyone else's approval. If nothing else, it's worth running it yourself to get a sense of how accurately you understand your own time management. (A note about privacy: If you are going to ask your team members to use this, it would be good to get opt-in from them, because the things that RescueTime measures might not fall completely in the corporate public record, so it's best to be transparent and ensure that everyone agrees to this experiment.)

## Positive Feedback Ratio

There are a few ways to measure the positivity levels within your company.

- In your weekly one-on-one spreadsheet, which was discussed in chapter 2, you can simply add a question asking your team how much they are enjoying their job, on a scale from one to ten. Tracking this number over time will give you a good indicator of how each member of your team is feeling and alert you to any changes.

- Web sites such as Glassdoor.com, Vault.com, and Rate MyEmployer.com are all great tools that will give you opportunities to see what people are really thinking. Remember to put your ego aside—some of the things you read might be harsh or critical—but it's okay: Hearing the truth, however painful, is the first step in getting things on track.

 **INDUSTRY EXAMPLES**

- **Health:** Consider Auxogyn, a company that specializes in in vitro fertilization (IVF). In order to select the best viable embryo, the embryologist currently removes the embryos from the incubator once a day for three days in order to gather a handful of data points. The risk to the embryos is too great to do this more often. Auxogyn has created a new system, called Eeva, that can now gather about five hundred data points on the embryos without removing them from the incubator, providing a very thorough look at how they're growing. The algorithm analyzes all of the points and recommends the most viable embryo, which the embryologist can use as input for his or her decision. This is a great example of Data as a Sixth Sense, since the embryologist is using the data to augment his or her own decision-making ability but he or she still makes the final call. This has dramatically reduced false positive rates, from 43 percent to 16 percent.

- **Automotive:** Deciding between a few different designs for a car is a tricky business. You have a few historical data points to go on, but generally you're trying to do something completely new rather than to continue with the same old design. For the executive in charge of the project, tapping outside opinions is risky, because it presents opportunities for the new design to be leaked before you're ready. Instead, consider a system that taps into the organization's internal gut instinct to inform the exec's intuition. A stock market–like system can award all employees a starting balance in their investment account. For each question or problem presented on the exchange, employees have the opportunity to invest in one of the potential answers or solutions. You could start with a wide range of potential choices—say, ten different options— and then proceed with the three that attract the most investment. When you get farther down the project's path, and one turns out to be the winner, the system automatically calculates the return on that investment (ideally by tapping into real-world data about sales, etc.)—either as a gain or a loss—and pays out to that option's investors. Over time this rewards the employees who are best at choosing winners, exposing internal expertise that might have otherwise remained hidden.

As always, if you head on over to our Web site and join the Decoded movement, you'll find plenty of online resources, experiment ideas, and suggestions for instrumenting your informed intuition. What are you waiting for? It's time to claim your rightful superpower.

# DECODED SCORE: DATA AS A SIXTH SENSE

Answer the following yes/no questions and fill out your score. Give yourself 1 point for each yes and 0 points for each no, for a best possible score of 4. At the end of the book you'll be able to use your score as part of a detailed Decoded assessment that will give you even more insights on how to embrace the Decoded philosophy.

1. Do your people make decisions based on data and evidence (rather than purely on emotion and gut feel)?

2. Are your people highly data literate (rather than highly steeped in management philosophies)?

3. Do you collect and analyze ambient data (rather than self-reported data)?

4. Have you found ways to quantify and record organizational gut feels in real time (rather than in historical snapshots and backward-looking postmortems)?

Data as a Sixth Sense score: _____

# CHAPTER 5: ENGINEERED ECOSYSTEMS

- What principles drove Valve's meteoric rise to $1 billion in revenue?

- How did Intuit put more than eighty thousand people out of seasonal work?

- How have today's consumer technologies destroyed our concept of work/life balance while ironically bringing us closer to the people we love?

- What's the best thing managers can spend their pizza lunch money on to dramatically improve their teams? (Hint: It's not pizza!)

- What are the top twelve principles of social workplaces as defined by today's leading business strategists?

- How does Whole Foods' autonomous team structure deliver plenty of managerial edge while staying touchy-feely?

- Why is the military abandoning its classic command-and-control hierarchy in favor of self-synchronized units and network-centric warfare?

## TPS REPORT DEPROGRAMMING

"My observation is that it takes new hires about six months before they fully accept that no one is going to tell them what to do, that no manager is going to give them a review, that there is no such thing as a promotion or a job title or even a fixed role," blogged Michael Abrash, author, game programmer, and employee at Valve.[1]

Valve doesn't believe in job descriptions or managers. Really. Instead it sees its organization as an organically grown collective of bright, self-motivated people who are empowered to "choose their own adventure" in deciding which direction the company should move in. And move it has.

A video game producer and digital distribution company based in Bellevue, Washington, Valve was founded in 1996 by two former Microsoft employees, Gabe Newell and Mike Harrington, and quickly gained popularity for its critically acclaimed *Half-Life* series, a game about a theoretical physicist named Gordon Freeman, who experiments with teleportation technology and unwittingly opens up a portal to a hostile alien invasion. Released in 1998, *Half-Life* (the first of six games in the series) would go on to win more than fifty Game of the Year awards. Its innovative use of single-shooter game play, an approach that has had considerable impact on subsequent games in the genre, has led many industry experts to count the *Half-Life* series among the greatest computer games of all time. Some of the company's other successful game franchises are *Counter-Strike, Left 4 Dead, Day of Defeat,* and the *Team Fortress* series.

Since its inception, Valve has grown to about four hundred employees.[2] It remains privately owned, and while the company is tight-lipped about revenues, its value is estimated at somewhere around $3 billion.

How does it do it? It's embraced the third principle of being a Decoded Company, what we're calling *engineered ecosystems*.

Engineered ecosystems are corporate cultures that are intentionally and deliberately optimized to create a center of gravity for their industry's best talent. They reject established management philosophies and approaches unless they can demonstrate their value empirically. They believe in a people-first approach that puts their talent above their customers and their customers above their profits. They invest in systems to decode their people and understand their wants and needs as well as (or better than) they understand their customers. Engineering our ecosystem allows us to do the single most important thing that every business should be focused on: attracting, retaining, and engaging talent.

Valve uses a data-focused approach to bypass traditional hierarchy in favor of a flexible and agile network that places an incredible amount of trust in the hands of each and every employee. It's just one of a number of organizations that is taking inspiration from the social Web to evolve new ways of working and managing their talent. We'll look at some of them in this chapter.

It's understandable why most companies are balking at these kinds of changes. The emerging norms go against the hierarchical structures that have defined corporate cultures for decades. Historically, companies were ruled by seniority, with people making their way up a preset path, often at predetermined intervals. The new collaborative models that are emerging replace seniority with meritocracy and hierarchies with ecosystems. They have open structures and create data-centric cultures that help motivate and empower talent.

Valve is completely focused on talent; it knows exactly the type of people it wants to hire and what type of environment those people will need in order to thrive. An excerpt from its corporate handbook was posted on the Web in 2012:

> When you're an entertainment company that's spent the last decade going out of its way to recruit the most intelligent, innovative, talented people on Earth, telling them to sit at a desk and do what they're told obliterates 99% of their value. We want innovators, and that means maintaining an environment where they'll flourish. That's why Valve is flat. It's our shorthand way of saying that we don't have any management, and nobody reports to anybody else.[3]

In the Technology as a Coach and Trainer chapter we showed how companies can apply the data they have collected to transform their technology into coaches that deliver customized approaches to learning and development. In the Data as a Sixth Sense chapter we saw how data-driven organizations can be instrumented to make evidence-based decisions and minimize risks. In this chapter, we'll show you how companies like HubSpot, Intuit, Netflix, Whole Foods, Klick, and Valve are deliberately engineering data-driven cultures guided by clearly outlined priorities and vision.

These companies share the common belief that better orchestrated people are better motivated and more able to move to the right place at the right time. And they've reaped the rewards, both talent-based (attraction and retention) and financial.

# YOU KNOW WHAT'S COOLER THAN A MILLION DOLLARS?

Let's review the story so far: Information abundance has enabled companies to develop what we call data-driven superpowers, the ability to leverage information to make better business decisions. Data abundance has also improved companies' understanding of their consumers. The marriage of market segmentation and individual data production has created a huge trend in hyperpersonalization, which is customer segmentation broken all the way down to the individual level; products and services are tailored to match each customer's preferences. This trend of customization, combined with the proliferation of mobile devices and the increasing appetite for Web 2.0 platforms, has shifted expectations in the workplace as well. Decoded Companies use their knowledge about their talent's unique experiences to create hyperpersonalized services for them; they also identify teachable moments for their talent and use their Technology as a Coach and Trainer. Given the looming worldwide talent shortage, companies that aren't adapting to these new needs and capabilities will soon find themselves in a very tight spot.

As of March 2013, the Web contained some 12.77 billion indexed pages of content.[4] Most of them are static reference pages. It wasn't until the widespread adoption of social networking sites by mainstream culture that we really started to see the Web as a social construct, an extension of ourselves into a world in which we could connect with our family and friends effortlessly. Beginning with early sites such as TheGlobe.com, Classmates.com, and Friendster to hi5, MySpace, and Facebook, each successive generation of social networks has helped reshape our world. They've made us more comfortable with the idea of sharing information about ourselves, and many different platforms have emerged to enable us to do so. Content creation has become a big part of engagement in these online spaces. Whether it's by sharing our thoughts on Twitter, snapping a picture of a tasty meal on Foodspotting, capturing an impromptu moment on Instagram, or sharing videos, pictures, and status updates with our Facebook friends, we've all gained the ability to create content and push it out to our networks.

Social networks have provided us with two very important content-sharing tools: speed and amplification. Content shared on social networks is instantaneous and direct; it bypasses traditional media channels to broadcast what we think, see, and feel in real time. This speed superpower has redefined the very concept of breaking news. The list of big news stories broken by social media grows ever longer. From American Airlines Flight 1549's emergency landing in the Hudson River to the death of Osama bin Laden to earthquakes in San Francisco, headlines are often circulated on Twitter long before they are picked up by the mainstream media.

Along with speed comes amplification: the superpower ability to deliver our message to a much broader audience than any individual publisher has before. Every form of media before the Internet kept the power of publishing in the hands of the few. Printing presses were big, expensive, and complicated. Radio stations owned the airwaves. Television required studios. But blogging just needs a beat-up old laptop and a dial-up modem. The content and information we share with our networks are immediately available to the entire world.

The content that is shared the most frequently gets amplified the most. Each share gets recorded and added to a trail of ambient data that creates a measurable, real-time zeitgeist ("the spirit of the times"). Twitter published their version of the zeitgeist in their 2012 Year on Twitter microsite, which identified: the year's Golden Tweets (most retweets); the Pulse of the Planet (biggest conversations of the year, from the Olympics to the U.S. election to the spread of Gangnam style); Only on Twitter (moments shared exclusively on Twitter, from the landing of the *Curiosity* rover on Mars to James Cameron's tweets from the ocean floor); Trends (conversation starters, politics, sports, etc.); and New Voices (high-profile users who joined in 2012).[5]

The benefits of social technologies are by no means limited to the consumer world. In this chapter we'll explain how organizations like Work.com, Berlitz, the U.S. government, and even the Oil Spill Recovery Institute in Cordova, Alaska, are also embracing them.

## DATA-DRIVEN MANAGEMENT: THE ECOSYSTEM ENGINEER

The foundation of any engineering project is data. Mechanical engineers apply the principles of physics and materials science to the analysis, design, manufacture, and maintenance of mechanical systems—an exercise firmly rooted in data. Civil engineers are likewise focused on the design, construction, and maintenance of the physical environment, also heavily reliant on data. We believe there is a role for a new ecosystem engineer, someone who focuses on the analysis, design, implementation, and maintenance of highly experimental corporate cultures that are firmly based on the practices of data-driven management. There's a good chance that person already goes by another title in many organizations—CEO. At Klick, our ecosystem engineer manages all of our concierges. They are responsible for helping to deliberately shape our culture into one that has become a center of gravity for the best talent.

In its *Guide to the Future, Fortune* magazine outlines the challenges that disruptive technology poses to leaders.[6] "The coming changes will be uncomfortable for some," writes Nina Easton, senior editor at large. "Hierarchies may disappear; some teams may function without leaders. The best ideas may come from the most junior person in the company—or from outside the organization all together." This will mean a shift of power toward a more democratized system, one that will herald new opportunities for those willing to embrace this change instead of resisting it.

Companies that have instrumented their organizations to inform their intuition, and that have used data to transform their HR departments into talent-centric Concierge Services, are well on their way toward becoming Decoded. The final piece is when they learn to use data to deliberately engineer a Decoded culture.

As workplaces adapt to being more flexible, meritocratic, and open, data, combined with the ability to share it easily, increasingly becomes the glue that binds everything together. Companies such as HubSpot, InnoCentive, and Netflix are all creating environments that are decentralized without being chaotic, that strive for autonomy instead of bureaucracy, and that maintain market focus while being agile enough to recognize and act upon new opportunities. Most of all, they are creating centers of gravity for talent, using data to maintain happy, healthy, and productive cultures.

As employers adapt to this new landscape, they struggle with the same types of questions. Why are some employees motivated to deliver above and beyond their job requirements while others only contribute a minimal effort? How can we tell if new policies are working and iterate/optimize quickly if they aren't? How can we ensure that autonomy doesn't impact service or product consistency? Most, if not all, business leaders want their workforces to be engaged; many recognize the impact that their happiness has on the productivity and efficiency of their businesses. But they haven't had the kind of data that can help them turn that ideal into a reality.

There is much support for the adage that clients follow the talent (it's certainly been true for Klick). If nothing else, that statement defines the fundamental shift that is driving the decoded movement away from shareholder value and toward talent-centric value. Leaders need to recognize that their roles have changed. In today's economy their greatest challenge is to transform their organizations into centers of gravity for the industry's best talent.

**Reading list:** *The Cluetrain Manifesto*, by Rick Levine, Christopher Locke, Doc Searls, and David Weinberger, offers a set of ninety-five theses for operating a business in these newly connected marketplaces.

Today's CEOs, instead of being solely focused on shareholder value, have the opportunity to deliver it through the cultivation of a talent-centric culture. Vineet Nayar, the author of *Employees First, Customers Second* and vice chairman of HCLT (a global IT outsourcing firm), believes that the core business of any corporation is to create shared value for customers. At most organizations this value is created when employees interface with clients. If this essential function happens at that intersection, shouldn't the role of leaders be to cultivate a culture in which employees feel motivated to create the best possible experiences and value for customers?

Nayar believes he has an answer. "All I am saying is by employees first you can actually deliver your promise of customers first," he said in a 2012 *Forbes* interview. "If you do not put the employee first—if the business of management and managers is not to put employee first—there is no way you can get the customer first."[7]

 **Reading list:** *Employees First, Customers Second*, by Vineet Nayar

Nayar's vision has helped transform HCLT into one of *Business-Week's* 20 Most Influential Companies in the World and given him a whole lot of employees to put first—more than eighty-five thousand of them as of December 31, 2012.[8] The company's consolidated global revenue for 2012 was $4.4 billion, which likewise provides a lot of reasons to believe he's right (4.4 billion of them, to be precise).

 ## THE NEED FOR SPEED

Leerom was in a meeting with several of his mentors a couple of years ago, a group for whom he has the deepest respect. Leerom recalls the story:

> They're all accomplished leaders of organizations whose revenue ranges from hundreds of millions to billions of dollars, and whose personal successes are far greater than mine. It came around to my turn to present, and I used that meeting to show off a couple of new features that we were launching in Genome. Genome is completely custom-developed around our culture, and one of our central te-

nets is radical openness: Genome exposes our leaders' performance just as much as those of our most junior recruits. This group of mentors has always been critical of the degree of transparency in the platform, but on this particular day they were incredibly harsh when I showcased a new social feature called Chatter. Coincidentally, the first post in the feed was from one of our project managers, and he was using the venue to challenge Aaron. As a result, the group began to ridicule me, eventually latching on to a metaphor: You can't give the kids the keys to the Ferrari.

After forty minutes of this, I cut off the conversation and agreed to disagree. I explained that while I've got tremendous respect for their accomplishments and the fact that they all drive Ferraris, they should all consider the implications of not being free to leave the keys on the kitchen counter. I suggested, with all due respect, that they should question their own parenting skills rather than assuming that their kids can't be trusted.

The Chatter post they were looking at was the same one in chapter 2 that enabled Aaron to uncover the causes of the time-tracking issue that had been plaguing Klick's employees. Aaron would never have been able to resolve the issue as quickly as he was without a culture in which people feel comfortable enough to say what's on their mind (even if that means criticizing the company's cofounder in public).

The pace of today's markets dictates a need for agility and speed. The managers of Decoded Companies sometimes achieve it by leaving the Ferrari's keys on the kitchen counter and trusting that the kids are often better drivers than they are.

# THE GLOBAL TALENT WAR

In a 2010 interview with *Business Standard*, Nayar declared that "the most important concern is the war for talent," adding that "there is a vulture movement in talent and we want to forward-invest in it. This is the way in which we want to be in the upper quartile of growth among our peers."[9]

As the search to recruit and retain talent intensifies, employers are realizing that more than financial compensation is required to entice the best people—and most of them know that they could be doing a much better job than they are. The Institute for Corporate Productivity recently conducted a survey of more than four hundred business leaders and reported that only 9 percent of their respondents strongly agreed that their business is doing a good job of recruiting, tracking, and retaining high performers.

The 2010–11 edition of PricewaterhouseCoopers's *Human Capital Effectiveness Report* showed that the rate of voluntary separation (people leaving their jobs either through resignation or retirement) had decreased to 7 percent in 2010, down from 10.4 percent in 2007, in part due to the unfavorable economic climate. However, the opposite is true for those employees categorized as high performers: The turnover rate for this category of talent actually increased, up to 4.3 percent in 2010 from 3.7 percent in 2009.

If the general working population is feeling conservative about holding on to their jobs, the real rock stars know that they have options. They won't hesitate before jumping for a better offer.

## PUTTING PEOPLE FIRST

Howard Schultz, Starbucks' CEO, has credited his employees with much of his company's success. "We built the Starbucks brand first with our people, not with consumers—the opposite approach from that of the crackers-and-cereal companies. Because we believed the best way to meet and exceed the expectations of our customers was to hire and train great people, we invested in employees who were zealous about good coffee," he said.[10]

This talent-centric strategy has helped the company maintain a competitive advantage while selling an essentially commoditized good. "Starbucks knows employees that are treated well will, in turn, treat customers well," said John Moore, author of *Tribal Knowledge: Business Wisdom Brewed from the Grounds of Starbucks Corporate Culture*. Moore, who spent more than eight years working in Starbucks' marketing department, wrote about the commitment that the company has to its employees. "To treat its workforce well, Starbucks offers all full-time and part-time employees the opportunity to receive full health-care benefits, stock options/ discounted stock purchase plans, and other benefits. The company's reputation for being an employer of choice has been recognized countless times."

Thanks to a carefully engineered Decoded ecosystem, Starbucks is the largest coffeehouse company in the world. With nearly twenty-one thousand stores in sixty-two countries, the company has turned its brand into a globally recognized symbol—and a great place for people to work. Putting people first is as much about attracting talent as it is about retaining it.[11] Starbucks' benefits help a considerable amount, creating a work environment that would be difficult to match elsewhere. Unfortunately for the global workforce, few companies are doing the same thing. Jason Jeffay, the human capital global segment leader for talent-management consulting at Mercer, describes the majority of talent recruiting and retention programs currently implemented in most organizations as slow, ineffective, and often focused on the wrong things. Some organizations don't even have any programs in place at all. "To begin with, HR is too often focused on hierarchy instead of critical roles. When HR do identify top talent, they tend to offer more money as an incentive to stay, which rarely works," Jeffay said in a recent interview with *HR Executive* magazine. "They're not proactive enough. They tend to wait too long, by which time the person has his or her foot out the door and HR is left scrambling. It's a needlessly expensive and stressful approach."[12]

The idea of putting people first is not a new one. The family-owned grocery store Wegmans has been focusing on employees as a key to corporate success since 1950, when then-president Robert Wegman began to introduce key benefits, which today include salaries that are higher than the market average, training, academic scholarships, and the opportunity to develop an appreciation for food and wine through company sponsored "knowledge gathering trips." The company was listed number four out of *Fortune*'s 100 Best Places to Work 2012.[13]

The difference between 1950 and 2012 is that today we can apply data to quickly identify the best way to create this type of environment within our own organizations. Thanks to the efforts of experts like Dan Pink and Gary Hamel, we understand what drives people to perform. We know that companies with high morale tend to perform better than those without. We know that workers value autonomy, purpose, and mastery.

We want to expand on this by proposing a shift to a more

talent-focused *and* data-driven workplace, one in which the top strategic priority is maximizing the engagement and retention of top talent. This trend will require a big shift in thinking from how we have traditionally measured value, but we believe this will ultimately drive shareholder value in the long term. After all, the path to being a Decoded Company is building a people-powered analytics bridge between what we believe to be true and what we know to be true.

# PROJECT OXYGEN: THE EVIDENCE-BASED MANAGER

What makes top talent leave an organization? There are many theories, including a lack of passion for the work, a feeling of being unappreciated, unnecessary bureaucracy, poor development programs, and a lack of strategic clarity from management, among many others. Erika Andersen, author of *Leading So People Will Follow*, has spent more than twenty-five years consulting and coaching executives. She says it all actually boils down to one thing: "Top talent leave an organization when they're badly managed, and the organization is confusing and uninspiring."[14] In other words, people don't leave jobs. They leave managers.

In 2009 tech giant Google released the findings of Project Oxygen, an internal initiative designed to identify the most important traits that managers must have in order to be successful at Google.

Google famously tested forty-one shades of blue to determine the optimal link color on one of its toolbars,so its heavy reliance on data-driven management should come as no surprise.[15] The initiative was spearheaded by the People Analytics team led by Laszlo Bock, vice president of Google's People Operations. They looked at a variety of data comprising more than one hundred variables and analyzed everything from award nominations to the words of praise and criticism that appeared in performance reviews and employee surveys. In total, the team gathered more than ten thousand data points and four hundred pages of interview notes. Their analysis confirmed that the biggest factor in talent's performance and job satisfaction was their manager. And it found that there were eight traits or behaviors that had the biggest impact on managers' performances.

## Eight Google Traits[16]

1. **Be a good coach.** Provide specific, constructive feedback that balances the negative and the positive. Have regular one-on-ones in which you present solutions to problems tailored to your employees' specific strengths.

2. **Empower your team, and don't micromanage.** Balance giving freedom to your employees and still being available for advice. Make "stretch" assignments to help the team tackle big problems.

3. **Express interest in team members' success and personal well-being.** Get to know your employees as people who have lives outside of work. Make new members of your team feel welcome, and help ease their transition.

4. **Don't be a sissy: Be productive and results-oriented.** Focus on what employees want the team to achieve and how they can help achieve it. Help the team prioritize work and use seniority to remove roadblocks.

5. **Be a good communicator and listen to your team.** Communication goes two ways: You both listen and share information. Hold all-hands meetings and be straightforward about the messages and goals of the team. Help the team connect the dots. Encourage open dialogue, and listen to the issues and concerns of your employees.

6. **Help your employees with career development.**

7. **Have a clear vision and strategy for the team.** Even in the midst of turmoil, keep the team focused on goals and strategy. Involve the team in setting and evolving its vision and making progress toward it.

8. **Have key technical skills so you can help advise the team.** Roll up your sleeves and conduct work side by side with the team when needed. Understand the specific challenges of the work.

At first glance, the results, derived from intensive analysis and data mining, appeared to be anticlimactic. Don't micromanage? Really? Stop the presses! That's some groundbreaking insight. *Express interest in team members' success and well-being* and *Be productive and results-oriented.* The "impactful behaviors" sounded like a collection of feel-good management mantras that we've all read and heard a million times. It was comical that a data powerhouse like Google had produced something akin to a *Dilbert* cartoon. But, as every Decoded Company knows, it's important to measure everything, because you never know what you're about to stumble on. It wasn't until Bock's team decided to rank the eight traits by their importance that they gained a radical insight into how they should be managing and recruiting their talent.

From the beginning, Google has been primarily an engineer-led company. People who rise to managerial positions have sufficient technical expertise to troubleshoot any issues that might come up within their teams. The underlying cultural belief was that managers needed this technical know-how to be effective leaders. In truth, the data told a different story. Bock's team discovered that the technical skills that had always been perceived as so important were actually ranked last in the list of eight traits.

"In the Google context, we'd always believed that to be a manager, particularly on the engineering side, you need to be as deep or deeper a technical expert than the people who work for you," Bock said in a 2011 interview with the *New York Times*. "It turns out that that's absolutely the least important thing. It's important but pales in comparison. Much more important is just making that connection and being accessible."

Let's take a minute to let that sink in. The data showed Google that its priorities for a manager's skill set were fundamentally opposed to the type of culture it wanted to create. Thanks to this incredible Decoded discovery, Google not only changed its recruiting practices, but provided new guidelines for its existing managers. It was discovered, for example, that one common trend among poorly performing managers was an inconsistency in holding one-on-one meetings with their team (clearly they should be holding weekly reviews and using Technology as a Coach!). Google has now formalized these types of interactions to ensure that each employee is getting the right amount of attention and feedback from their manager. Google implemented coaching programs, too, to cultivate the best behaviors in managers who were falling short. Just one year after these changes were applied, Google reported a significant improvement in 75 percent of its struggling managers. The impact on the business cannot be overstated—think back to James Slavet's quote in chapter 4: "Similarly, most companies measure traffic, revenue, or earnings without considering how to improve the company at an atomic level: how to make a meeting better, or an engineer more productive." Google accomplished both to a staggering degree. In short, the company was able to deliberately engineer a healthier and more productive work ecosystem.

Project Oxygen was an important exercise for Google for several reasons. First, by using its own data, the company was able to create a development program that fit its employees' unique challenges. Instead of simply adopting a particular management philosophy and imposing it, Google identified the company's current pain points, prioritized them, and addressed them strategically through the introduction of customized programs, such as in coaching or training. This is the heart of the Engineered Ecosystem. "We want to understand what works at Google rather than what worked in any other organization," said Prasad Setty, Google's vice president for people analytics and compensation. This is one of the foundational principles of the Decoded Company—the idea that you need to unlock the secrets of your own organization and apply unique solutions, not something off the shelf. What works for Google might not work for you (and vice versa!).

Second, because the project recommendations were based on Google's own data, employees granted them credibility when they were given the tools to evaluate and improve their own performances. The transparency and buy-in that result from involving people in the process and showing them why new practices are needed can help prevent "organ rejection" that can occur when employees refuse to embrace or adopt new policies. As we learned with Data as a Sixth Sense, it's easier to get support for your initiatives when you have the right type of data to make your case. This bias toward empirical data is especially true in organizations with higher data literacy and technical prowess.

Third, the data revealed and debunked several widely held cultural assumptions. Googlers believed that promotions were more likely if they worked at headquarters or if they championed a highly visible project. Both were disproved by the Project Oxygen data. The data did show, however, that one of the most important factors for advancement and promotion was feedback from senior peers within the organization. That hadn't been on most people's radar, but they have recalibrated their behavior since.

## WORK.COM: INFUSING AGILITY INTO PERFORMANCE REVIEWS

Promotions and compensation at most companies are tied to the dreaded annual performance review. Everyone hates them. Even the HR people who roll them out hate annual performance reviews. They cost a fortune to administer, take up tons of time, cause huge frustration, and don't actually result in performance gains. You'd think that something as broken and traditional would fall outside the realm of the engineered ecosystem, but it's actually the opposite—the more hated the policy, the more ripe it is for disruption.

If annual reviews reflected the norms of the social Web they would be more transparent, immediate, and collaborative. They would be fun, and incentives would be in place to motivate employees to act in the best interest of the company while promoting a positive culture. Luckily, some companies have recognized the need for the consumerization of the antiquated review process, and they are stepping in to put an end to one of the most painful parts of working within an organization.

Rypple, acquired by Salesforce.com in 2012 and relaunched as Work.com, is a Web-based social performance management platform that helps companies improve performance through social goals, continuous feedback, and meaningful recognition.[17] According to its Web site, its mission "is to create delightful software that helps people advance their careers, teams achieve their goals faster, and companies retain their top performers." Jay was head of marketing for Rypple before he joined Klick, and he learned a great deal about motivating and managing high-performance teams. One of the most interesting things he learned during his time at Rypple was that a surprising number of managers will pay out of their own pockets for tools that help their teams.

Before the acquisition brought their software into the Sales force.com platform, Rypple was a very inexpensive way to drive performance. "We often compared ourselves to the cost of a team pizza lunch," Jay recalls. "From a cost perspective, we positioned ourselves as the equivalent to bringing in pizzas once a month, because it made it obvious as to which option would result in better team performance." The cost was low enough, in fact, that many managers just paid for it on their personal credit cards and never asked for permission. The bureaucracy involved in getting permission to use and expense Rypple would have been far more work than simply rolling it out to their teams, so they just did it, a key lesson as to why the consumerization of IT is happening.

The Work.com platform enables organizations to create an

internal network on which teams can easily identify and track goals and objectives, get coaching from a trusted network of peers, mentors, and managers, and request anonymous feedback on specific questions such as, What did you think of my presentation? or What's one thing I can improve in order to get promoted? Users can also ask their network to measure their performance using more quantified metrics, so that they have a clear idea of what they need to work on. Work.com balances this self-reported, qualitative data with ambient data around task and goal completion imported from external systems and fed by the results of one-on-one meetings. The combination results in a dynamic system that features lots of fresh, new content while still reflecting a high degree of accuracy.

There is a social gaming aspect to Work.com in which employees are rewarded with digital badges from their colleagues either as a way of saying thanks or for successfully completing certain tasks or challenges that have the added value of promoting cultural values. The badges act as a digital currency, reflecting their accomplishments and serving as a visual representation of their reputation within the company. They can even act as a real-world currency through Work.com's Tangible Rewards program, which rewards employees' hard work with Amazon gift cards.

Work.com's innovative approach relieves some of the pressure on managers by helping employees take ownership of their personal development. Thanks to the data Work.com collects, employees can identify the areas in which they need help and help them manage their coaching and feedback needs. The combination of data-centric measures with social gaming features and the ability to customize feedback adds up to a powerful tool that will allow any company to take the first steps toward becoming Decoded.

## ENGINEERED ECOSYSTEMS IN ACTION: KLICK STORIES

Culture shaping is not something that can be left up to chance but must be purposefully cultivated to align with the organization's best interests. As mentioned previously, the principles of openness, transparency, collaboration, sharing, and merit that we have grown used to on the social Web are essential values of today's workplace.

Klick originally had a formal value system and delivered training in areas such as *client empathy* and *achieving profitability through ingenuity*. We discovered that there was a problem with those approaches: People were having a hard time establishing a link between abstract concepts and their practical applications within their everyday jobs. This disconnect made it harder for us to encourage the kinds of behavior that we wanted to see as a part of our culture.

Taking a different approach, we introduced our Klick Stories feature, an internal online channel for employees to show appreciation or give long-form kudos to colleagues. We intentionally provided no guidelines at the launch beyond encouraging people to thank anyone for anything they felt like.

An interesting thing started happening when Stories launched: People thanked each other for actions that embodied the very values that had been so hard to communicate in an abstract form. Stories became a veritable catalog of concrete examples of how someone could demonstrate traits like empathy and ingenuity—and the circulation of those stories resulted in an increase of those types of behavior. It became a showcase of the values that Klick wanted to promote. The likes and comments provided reinforcement for both the person receiving the accolade and their teammates, socializing best practices and helping to turn them into repeatable behavior. Our leadership team has monitored the types of stories that get told over time, using them as a bellwether of how closely our current culture matches our ideal culture. Identified gaps become organizationwide teachable moments, allowing us to provide small course corrections that reengineer our ecosystem back toward its intended path.

An incentive system was developed to further encourage participation in Stories and Klick Talks: We rewarded the people featured in the three most viewed Klick Talks and the most liked Stories each week. Third-place winners receive a massage at their desk. Second-place winners receive experience certificates that they can redeem for activities such as white-water rafting or flight-simulator training. First-place winners are given the use of the company Porsche Boxster (aka the Klickster) for a week. At the end of the year, the people with the top-rated Klick Talk and Story are invited to join the partners on their annual retreat. Because the winners are decided by their colleagues' votes and not a manager's say-so, these incentives reinforce the importance of merit as opposed to hierarchy: Because everyone can clearly see the data that determined who won, the values of collaboration and transparency are underlined, fostering our efforts to engineer an ecosystem in which everyone is invested in one another's success.

Although some of these rewards represent fairly significant investments by the company, the data shows that they pay back every penny and more in the value they provide our people—which is reflected in both the work product they deliver to our clients and the profits they add to our bottom line.

This isn't a utopian system—there is always the risk of people gaming it. For example, deals can be made between two teams to vote for each other in order to secure prizes. For Leerom, this isn't a big issue. Sometimes even the gaming behaviors are desirable. After all, they had to act like a team and build camaraderie in order to collude, so at the end of the day, it's okay by us.

## ENGINEERED ECOSYSTEMS IN ACTION: "KLICK IT FORWARD"

Corporate social responsibility (CSR) initiatives provide another opportunity to promote cultural values. Typically, CSR programs are seen as a public relations or corporate communications function and are completely separate from the Human Resources department. But if a goal of your company is to become a center of gravity for talent (and it should be!), then CSR is an important way to engage your talent and attract potential hires.

The Klick It Forward program was created in order to forge a connection between Klick's charitable efforts and employee workflow. It's a simple concept: As work gets completed, employees get credits to spend on various causes (Klick has a number of causes it already supports; employees can, if they wish, propose new ones). There is an algorithm that uses several inputs (including project margins, sphere of influence, speed, etc.) to determine the number of credits that are assigned.

Each time he or she makes a contribution, a badge is added to the employee's Genome profile, letting their colleagues know the causes they support. Because Klick it Forward credits are only awarded for delivering high-quality work, the badges also act as social currency—people who have a lot of badges are rock stars within their domains. Each purchase also triggers an automated Chatter post on Genome, adding to the positive side of the companywide feedback ratio. We were very proud to be named the *PR News* 2013 Overall Leader in CSR Practices (for organizations with less than ten thousand employees) for the Klick It Forward program.[18]

# FUN WITH STAIRS

Data can also be used to engineer ecosystems that are playful and fun. Consider the ambient data stream that Genome receives from our company's card swipes. Since there are card swipes next to every door, Genome knows if someone traveling between one of our floors has taken the elevator or if they chose the stairs. That information is included in everyone's internal profile and on our Stair Climber Leaderboard, creating a friendly sense of competition to see who can climb the most stairs in the least amount of time. The results, organized by team and individual, not only provides a fun challenge but also promote healthy habits.

The same badge data is also used for the company's weekly, legendary, and delicious Thai Friday lunches. Everyone on the team can store their favorite menu item in their Genome profile. The system checks to see who's in the office on Friday morning and automatically places an order for everyone with a stored selection. These are just a few of the tactics that Klick uses to engineer an ecosystem that will help attract and retain its talent.

**Privacy:** Everyone is aware of the data that is being collected. The actions collected are also a part of the corporate public record. Opt-out isn't possible because door swipe data is a part of the company's security policy.

# THE TWELVE PRINCIPLES OF THE SOCIAL WORKPLACE

The age of the product-focused company is coming to an end. There was a time when it was enough for a company to have one successful product (like Ford in its heyday), but we believe that tomorrow's true champions will be the companies that are the most agile, diverse, and adaptive. Embracing the tenets of the social workplace and providing tools and a safe and trusting environment for experimentation and risk taking will take a company a long way toward that goal.

Gary Hamel has been researching the social workplace for the past several years. He created an online community called the Management Innovation eXchange (MIX), where business leaders from around the world can share and discuss new ideas. In November 2011, Hamel launched the Management 2.0 Hackathon—essentially, a large-scale brainstorming session—and put one simple yet powerful question on the agenda: *How can we harness the power of the Web—its technologies, approaches, and underlying principles—to reinvent management?* More than nine hundred participants from five continents came together in person and online to explore how "the principles and practical tools of the web might make our organizations as adaptable, innovative, and inspiring as the web itself."[19]

Over the course of the hackathon, twelve principles that embodied the foundations of the social workplace were identified:

1. **Openness:** the willingness to share information and do
   business out in the open

2. **Community:** the ability for people with shared purpose to
   organize and engage

3. **Meritocracy:** an environment where ideas and people
   succeed based on the quality of their ideas and contributions, not on an existing hierarchy

4. **Activism:** tapping into individuals' desires to stand up,
   opt in, and express themselves

5. **Collaboration:** the capability of groups of people to work
   together, divide tasks, and leverage individual strengths

6. **Meaning:** the most powerful motivators come from within

7. **Autonomy:** the freedom to act on one's own, making decisions without direction or approval from higher levels of
   management

8. **Serendipity:** the occurrence of events by chance in a ben-
   eficial way

9. **Decentralization:** the polar opposite of the top-down approach in which activity and decision making are closely
   reserved to small, mostly top-echelon spheres. Decentralization allows them to happen anywhere.

10. **Experimentation:** an environment in which ideas can be
    tested quickly and continually improved

11. **Speed:** the unprecedented pace of change and immediacy of information

12. **Trust:** an acknowledgment that each of us is acting in good faith and that good work will be reciprocated

As the Web continues to enable people to be even more social, more connected, and more collaborative, workplaces are evolving organically to reflect these changes. MIX has identified several ways that teams are applying these new behaviors and perspectives within their workplaces to create environments where:

- coordination happens without centralization;

- contribution matters more than credentials;

- power flows to those who add value;

- the wisdom of many trumps the authority of the few;

- new ideas get amplified rather than crushed;

- performance is judged by peers;

- contribution is opt-in rather than commanded;

- the default is to share information rather than hoard it.

A core challenge for any enterprise is balancing the complexity of people orchestration with the delivery of a consistent level of quality and service. We believe that this equilibrium is unlocked by data.

The big takeaway from MIX's Hackathon is that managers must come to the realization that the siloed, disconnected structure of their teams and workplaces is as vestigial as manual-entry bookkeeping or index card systems for data storage. We have long ago acknowledged that automated data manipulation and management are far superior and permit vastly more scale than any of their analog ancestors, but we continue to manage our organizations with reference to principles that date back to the same era. Every industry is being disrupted by companies that have figured out that the engineered ecosystem is, in fact, the new normal.

It is not a question of whether you should do the same but *when*. "Adapt or die" is a relevant adage in this case.

Your path will not be easy. You will likely find yourself at odds with a deeply entrenched system whose leaders are vested in the status quo. Earlier in this chapter we talked about Valve, the multibillion-dollar game company that has achieved an almost Zen-like state of no hierarchy. Few companies, even Decoded ones, are likely to achieve that nirvana, but it is an entirely worthy goal. When it comes to business organization, there can be little doubt that hierarchies gone wrong are the root of all evil.

## HIERARCHY: ROOT OF ALL EVIL

There's long been a belief that the only way to manage is through a rigid, highly structured, command-and-control–style hierarchy. That might even have been true in the more static business environment of fifty years ago, when being a "lifer" at a company was considered a normal career path. But for today's college graduates, multiple employers—and even multiple careers in more than one industry—are likely to be the norm, according to the Future-workplace research think tank—a proposition that would have been unthinkable even a generation ago.[20] Jay still remembers that his first manager at IBM had been with the company for two years longer than Jay had been alive when he started, a prospect that was actually quite terrifying.

Hierarchies often reward seniority and political savvy over actual merit or leadership abilities. Even when senior management has a clear vision of what needs to be done, broken communication channels can result in delayed or ineffective executions. Hierarchical structures were an outgrowth of the command-and-control philosophy developed by the military over millennia of combat in data-poor environments, and they made sense when the business world was as limited by information poverty as the battlefield. But they no longer apply as knowledge work and data abundance have become the norm.

Today's corporate best practices are an anachronistic vestige of a world that was unable to record real-time data about true performance. Even the military, where discipline can be a matter of life and death, has recognized the need for less rigidity. In a 2007 article for *The International C2 Journal* entitled "Agility, Focus, and Convergence: The Future of Command and Control," David S. Alberts wrote:

> *Command and Control* is an approach that, while it was once very effective in achieving its ends, is no longer the only possible or even the best approach that is available. *Command and Control* is a solution to a problem that has changed. The situations for which *Command and Control* is best adapted have been transformed by the realities of the Information Age. Thus, the assumptions upon which *Command and Control* were based are no longer valid.[21]

Instead, the proposed alternative focuses on autonomous teams that have the ability to make decisions quickly, based on their own unique contexts.

If command and control is no longer right for the modern military, then it is no longer right for the modern corporation. This is an era of incrementalism, of constant small course corrections informed by dynamic evidence gathered in real time, not of grand master plans dictated down by generals behind the lines. Success depends on a rapid response to reality, not on an abstract blueprint. Thanks to data, we can readjust whenever we get relevant information, and the more information we get the better we become at navigating the landscape while maintaining alignment with our strategic objectives.

## WHOLE FOODS: TEAMS AND TRANSPARENCY

During her research, Rahaf was surprised to see Whole Foods emerge as a leader in the charge toward experimental and highly engineered ecosystems. She had read so much about the challenges the supermarket industry was facing, due to competitive markets, high fixed costs, tight margins, and often complex relationships with labor unions. It's not a place one would think to look for an example of a Decoded culture, but Whole Foods Market is a fascinating case study in what *Fast Company* described as "one of the world's most radical experiments in democratic capitalism."

The company, under the guidance of Co-CEO John Mackey, has spent nearly two decades translating its corporate values of teamwork, empowerment, and autonomy into an innovative and effective way to run its business.

**Reading list:** You can read about the thinking behind this twenty-year experiment in John's book *Conscious Capitalism*, cowritten with Rajendra Sisodia, a business professor at Bentley College, with a foreword by Bill George. They maintain an excellent Web site on the movement and the book at: http://consciouscapitalism.org.

Whole Foods eschews traditional hierarchy in favor of an autonomous team approach. Each store is an autonomous profit center, broken down into an average of ten self-managed teams (for example, prepared foods, meat and poultry, produce, etc.), and each team operates autonomously, with its own performance metrics and an elected team leader.[22] Other teams are formed from the superset of those business unit teams (for example, all of the team leaders within a store, all of the store leaders within a region, and all of the regional leaders).

Whole Foods has strongly embraced the decentralized, autonomous, collaborative, and meritocratic nature described in Hamel's social workplace. The business unit team is the most important organizational unit within the organization, and they have a remarkable amount of autonomy. For example, teams have the ability to approve new hires for full-time jobs with no further oversight. Candidates who are recommended by a store leader to fill a specific position on the team not only must complete a thirty-day trial period but also must earn the approval vote of at least two-thirds of the business unit team in order to come onboard. Recognition and bonuses are also linked to team performance.

Each team has its own elected leader and its own metrics; it operates as an independent profit center with responsibility for its own hiring and inventory. The company has engineered a program called gainsharing to reinforce the importance of the team as the central unit; it uses ambient data to measure productivity in the form of the sales per hour each team is able to make. This creates an easily measurable financial consequence to bad decision making. The wrong call on a hiring decision, for example, can cost the whole team in lost sales per hour, so every candidate receives intense scrutiny.

Mackey thinks that the hiring function is an essential part of the team-bonding process, because it enables them to take ownership of their team and the qualities that they feel are important for members to have. Hiring becomes a reflection of the team, so only the best fits for the job are recruited, and candidates are routinely rejected. "Whole Foods is a social system. It's not a hierarchy. We don't have lots of rules handed down from headquarters in Austin," says Mackey. "We have lots of self-examination going on. Peer pressure substitutes for bureaucracy. Peer pressure enlists loyalty in ways that bureaucracy doesn't."

Whole Foods' leadership believes in applying informed intuition and arms its staff with as much information as possible. Its management style is based on the idea of decentralized teamwork, which is only effective when accompanied by trust and autonomy fostered by a certain level of transparency. It believes that staff should have access to financial information, including sensitive information such as salaries. The company has an open policy in which staff can easily look up anyone's salary or bonus figures from the previous year. Co-CEO Mackey says of the policy (which was introduced in 1986): "I kept hearing from people who thought I was making so much money. Finally I just said, 'Here's what I'm making; here's what [cofounder] Craig Weller is making—heck, here's what everybody's making.'" He believes it's important to make this information available in order to have meaningful dialogue about earning and compensation. "I'm challenged on salaries all the time," he says. "How come you are paying this regional president this much and I'm only making this much?' I have to say, 'because that person is more valuable. If you accomplish what this person has accomplished, I'll pay you that too," he says. "It leads to deeper conversations than you'd have otherwise."[23] In addition to salaries, the company shares figures such as team sales, store sales, and profit margins. As noted earlier, so much information was available to store employees that in 1996 the SEC classified all of them as insiders.

While this openness is meant to empower employees, it also serves a strategic purpose: It fuels competition within the company. Regions, stores, and teams all compete with one another to deliver the best results in terms of quality and service metrics. The best performing and most profitable teams are rewarded with promotions and bonuses. Mackey says:

> In most companies, management controls information and therefore controls people. By sharing information we stay aligned to the vision of a shared fate. If you're trying to create a high-trust organization, an organization where people are all-for-one and one-for-all, you can't have secrets.

Engineered cultures adopt a relentless pursuit of the next level: Today's brass ring is tomorrow's baseline. The focus is always on learning and improving upon the experiences from the year before. A constant stream of data provides the necessary inputs for both setting levels and raising bars.

In an effort to ensure that its cultural values don't become diluted as the company grows, Whole Foods makes an effort to ensure that each new store recruits up to 30 percent of its staff from existing stores. Back in 1996, Mackey told *Fast Company:*

> When we went from one store to two, people said, 'It's not going to be the same feeling; you're getting too big.' When we opened the third store, people said that would push us over the edge. Now we're opening store forty-three, and the company is definitely getting too big. But it's not the size of the company that creates the feeling. It's the core values. It's like making yogurt or sourdough bread. You can't dilute it too quickly.[24]

The company is much bigger now, of course, with more than 330 international locations, over $9 billion in annual revenue, and nearly 60,000 employees.

Whole Foods is an intriguing example of a company that has successfully bridged the gap between soft-hearted values and logic-driven business acumen.[25] The company's investment in environmental sustainability, diversity, transparency, and collaboration is balanced by its laser focus on data-driven performance[26] and efficiency.[27] The combination has resulted in a highly motivated workforce with a deep sense of community who value productivity. "There's this notion that you can't be touchy-feely and serious," says John Mackey. "We don't fit the stereotypes. There's plenty of managerial edge in this company—the culture creates it."[28]

# VALVE'S SPHERE OF INFLUENCE

Let's go back to our friends at Valve, the game company with no titles, roles, or managers. Without formal job descriptions and bosses, how do they know if someone's doing their job? Who decides when someone or something isn't working? The answer, of course, is data—especially when used as a sixth sense.

Data enables Valve to deliberately engineer a culture that retains its radical self-management model. Instead of traditional annual performance reviews, the company uses two formalized methods of evaluating performance: peer reviews to help promote growth and learning, and "stack ranking," a data-centric approach to determining compensation. The mix of qualitative and quantitative data provides a rich perspective on each person's individual contribution and allows it to be measured. It also helps to reinforce cultural behaviors that enable the company to thrive with such an unusual yet highly enviable structure.

Formalized peer reviews occur once a year at Valve, although culturally the employees are encouraged to solicit feedback whenever they feel they need it from their peers. The process begins when a group of people are selected to interview each employee about their experiences working with their peers over the previous year. Everyone's feedback is collected and anonymized before being distributed to each individual, ensuring that everyone is continuously focused on self-improvement and growth. This qualitative data-gathering process is very important, since it replaces the top-down feedback mechanisms that most traditional organizations rely on.

Compensation at Valve is linked to the amount of value a person brings to the organization. Unlike Whole Foods Market, where value added was measured at the level of team units, Valve's contribution valuation is done on an individual level. This is the annual process called stack ranking.

Each project or product group is asked to rank its own members based on four metrics. From the Valve handbook:

### 1. Skill Level/Technical Ability

- How difficult and valuable are the kinds of problems you solve?
- How important/critical of a problem can you be given?
- Are you uniquely capable (in the company? industry?) of solving a certain class of problem, delivering a certain type of art asset, contributing to design, writing, or music, etc.?

### 2. Productivity/Output

- How much shippable (not necessarily shipped to outside customers), valuable, finished work did you get done? Working a lot of hours is generally not related to productivity and, after a certain point, indicates inefficiency. It is more valuable if you are able to maintain a sensible work/life balance and use your time in the office efficiently, rather than working around the clock.

### 3. Group Contribution

- How much do you contribute to studio process, hiring, integrating people into the team, improving workflow, amplifying your colleagues, or writing tools used by others? Stepping up and acting in a leadership role can be good for your group contribution score, but being a leader does not impart or guarantee a higher stack rank. It's just a role that people adopt from time to time.

### 4. Product Contribution

- How much do you contribute at a larger scope than your core skill? How much of your work matters to the product?
- How much did you influence correct prioritization of work or resource trade-offs by others?
- Are you good at predicting how customers are going to react to decisions we're making?[29]

Once all the data has been collected, Valve applies a series of algorithms to determine each employee's compensation bracket. Laying out a set of desired cultural behaviors and linking them to performance metrics is a powerful way to engineer an ecosystem. At the same time, the categories are quite broad, allowing each individual a wide scope in which they can customize their roles and the ways that they contribute to the organization.

Valve trusts its talent with the responsibility of making decisions that are in the best interest of the company. This is why strategic hiring is such an essential part of the company's survival imperative. "Any time you interview a potential hire, you need to ask yourself not only if they're talented and collaborative but also if they're capable of literally running this company, because they will be," the company's handbook says.

It's inevitable but also risky that Valve employees would be as involved in hiring as they are, because with its flat structure, any staff member can have a large positive or negative impact on the entire organization. "Usually, it's immediately obvious whether or not we've done a great job in hiring someone," the handbook says. "However, we don't have the usual checks and balances that come with having a manager, so occasionally it can take a while to understand whether a new person is fitting in. This is one downside of the organic design of the company—a poor hiring decision can cause lots of damage, and can sometimes go unchecked for too long." That being said, the company believes that those individuals will eventually be removed.

Valve's hiring strategy is focused on identifying people who are "stronger than ourselves." The company likes to keep its processes flexible and loose to ensure that learnings are incorporated into the hiring practices, but the company does anchor itself with three questions that it asks about any hire:

1. Would I want this person to be my boss?

2. Would I learn a significant amount from him or her?

3. What if this person went to work for our competition?

It's an approach that is very similar to Netflix's "only rock stars" strategy, which will be described in some depth next in this chapter. The company is continuously on the lookout for what it describes as "T-shaped people," individuals who offer the broad perspective of a generalist while having the narrowed expertise of a specialist in certain fields.

Valve is very aware that its model contains some inherent weaknesses. Adapting to such an unconventional organization requires some time, and the company recognizes it could be doing more to support an employee's new transition. Having a flat organizational structure makes it harder to provide development programs and mentorship. Decoded Companies are works in progress by definition, and Valve is no exception.

# NETFLIX: STUNNING COLLEAGUES

When it comes to performance, Netflix CEO Reed Hastings compares the online video rental and streaming company to a professional sports team. In a slide deck from 2009, Hastings says, "Netflix leaders hire, develop, and cut smartly so we have stars in every position." The focus is on great work, not the number of hours that people work or how late they stay at night. "Sustained B-Level performance despite A-Level effort generates a generous severance package, with respect," according to the slide deck. "Sustained A-Level performance, despite minimal effort, is rewarded with more responsibility and great pay."[30] The intervening years since the deck was posted haven't been entirely positive for Hastings and his team, but their overall performance clearly demonstrates the value of their approach. Netflix stock was trading at $22 in late November 2009 and $347 by late November 2013. We believe that their thoughts on culture were seminal in the creation of the move toward engineered ecosystems.

Netflix's engineered ecosystem turns on recruiting and training "stunning colleagues," motivated self-starters who thrive in an environment of autonomy and flexibility. "Our model is to increase employee freedom as we grow rather than limit it, to continue to attract and nourish innovative people, so we have a better chance of sustained success," Hasting notes. With stars in every position, Netflix can get out of the way and let its talent do what needs to be done without weighing them down with unnecessary policies.

As we discussed in the Technology as a Coach chapter, as companies get bigger, operations become more complex, resulting in either more chaos or more bureaucracy (or often both). The traditional response to chaos has been the addition of processes. The problem with processes is that they deliver results in the short term but ultimately slow things down, stifle innovation, and spur frustrated talent to leave. A highly successful process company will have optimized its operations, minimizing mistakes and increasing its efficiency while continuing to scale. But this can only be sustained so long as markets stay the same, which is rarely the case.

The rate and pace of innovation is accelerating, throwing markets into a continuous state of flux. New technologies, business models, or competitors can also throw everything out of sync. Suddenly the same company that had been enjoying the benefits of process is held back by it. The company becomes unable to respond or adapt because employees have lost their agility. According to Netflix, such a company "generally grinds painfully into irrelevance."

Companies are then faced with three common alternatives, none of them that appealing: maintain a small size but have a limited impact; suffer the pain of chaos and inefficiency in order to grow; or implement processes that will ultimately damage the company. Hastings thinks there is a fourth option: "Avoid chaos as you grow with ever more high performance people—not with rules. Then you can continue to mostly run informally with self-discipline without chaos, and running informally is what enables and attracts creativity."

For Hastings, the key is to grow talent density faster than complexity—while maintaining a precarious balance between self-discipline and freedom. Netflix has no specific vacation policy, and employees can take as many days off as they want without limit or tracking. "There is also no clothing policy at Netflix," it jokes on slide 70 of the deck, "but no one comes to work naked." In addition, its travel, expense, and gift policies can be summed up in five little words: Act in Netflix's best interests.

Netflix advocates a rapid recovery model, stating that high performers don't generally make many errors, and that any processes should be there to help them achieve more in their jobs rather than trying to prevent "recoverable mistakes." Think of it as the opposite of the TSA's approach to security, which is to react to each new incident by putting in measures to prevent it from happening again. Someone brings explosive liquids on a plane and they search our toiletries; someone wears a shoe bomb and we remove our shoes; and so on ad infinitum.

Netflix defines its management model as "context, not control," or, providing the right insight and understanding to enable employees to make sound decisions. It all comes back to data and engineering a Decoded culture.

## INTUIT: BUILDING A CULTURE OF INFORMED EXPERIMENTATION

While Netflix was engineering a culture suited for motivated self-starters, Intuit, a company that specializes in simplifying small business management payroll, personal finance, and tax preparation, was focused on creating a culture that values informed experimentation. The company's products, including QuickBooks, Quicken, and TurboTax, help individuals and small- and medium-size businesses manage their financial affairs. Intuit was founded in 1983, went public in 1993, and has served more than forty million customers.

Intuit president and CEO Brad Smith has made it his priority to develop an internal culture of innovation. Around 2005 he began introducing a series of innovation-oriented initiatives that have helped create a workforce that isn't afraid of taking on big industry challenges. There were four main initiatives. The first was the introduction of unstructured time, which allowed employees to spend 10 percent of their work time on a project that they are passionate about, even if it falls outside their normal job descriptions.

A second one was the creation of something called "idea jams": Focused brainstorming sessions are held periodically for employees to develop and present concepts around a strategically relevant area.

The third initiative was an internal software called Intuit Brainstorm tool, which enables employees to submit ideas and receive feedback and ratings on them, as well as to identify team members who are willing to help transform the idea into a testable concept. This enabled employees to connect to colleagues outside their geographic or business areas who share their same interests. Intuit then created a similar externally facing Web site, where customers can review early-stage demos or prototypes.

The final initiative was the introduction of horizon planning for each business unit, which mandates that it allocates research and development resources among Horizon 1, Horizon 2, and Horizon 3 products. Horizon 1 offerings are mature, slower-growing products that yield a high revenue. Horizon 2 are fast-growing new products that have proven themselves in the market. Horizon 3 are funded experiments, tests of potential ideas to see which ones can develop into viable product offerings. Horizon planning ensures that each business unit is constantly investing in improvements of existing products while continuously testing new ideas. The result is a constant churn of innovation.

Intuit's culture is one of experimentation, quick prototyping, and iterative releases—complemented by a mantra of "Bring your whole self to work." The emphasis is on working efficiently and being creative, while also "giving yourself the time to do what matters outside of business hours."

One of the fruits it has borne is SnapTax. Tax return preparation has always sucked, no matter how good you are with a number-two pencil and a calculator. Rather than simply creating a faster horse in the form of yet another Web-based, form-oriented approach, Intuit introduced something completely new. Smith had challenged his team to make mobile devices a priority. When one of his developers asked, "What the hell does mobile have to do with taxes?" Smith replied that he didn't know, but he was sure they would figure it out.[31]

A few months later, the idea behind SnapTax was born: What if you could file your tax return without typing in a single character? Customers can snap a picture of their W-2 form with their smartphone, and the mobile app automatically fills in all the necessary information and files the return for you.

Employee-driven initiatives, an emphasis on R&D, and an openness to experimentation. All of these are components and products of Intuit's deliberately engineered ecosystem.

# HUBSPOT: A PLACE WHERE TALENT CAN THRIVE

"If you are hiring exceptional people who have lots of good options, you should trust them to make good decisions that will improve the enterprise value," said Dharmesh Shah, the cofounder and CTO of HubSpot. We looked at HubSpot's influence map in the Technology as a Coach chapter. Here we'll explore some of its other approaches.

Following in the footsteps of Netflix, Dharmesh published a wonderful slide deck overview of his company's culture in March 2013 in which he shared some of the ideas and philosophies that he has drawn on to engineer HubSpot's ecosystem.

Most of the deck underlines and supports the points we've made throughout this book, particularly as they pertain to the investment Decoded Companies should make in themselves and in understanding their people. The HubSpot Culture Code is particularly noteworthy, so we have reproduced it here in its entirety:

1. We are maniacal about **metrics** as our **mission**.

2. We obsess over **customers**, not competitors.

3. We are radically and uncomfortably **transparent**.

4. We give ourselves the **autonomy** to be awesome.

5. We are unreasonably **selective** about our peers.

6. We invest in individual **mastery** and market value.

7. We defy conventional "wisdom" as it's often unwise.

8. We speak the **truth** and face the facts.

9. We believe in **work+life**, not work vs. life.

10. We are a perpetual **work in progress**.[32]

This should sound very familiar to you. Many of the Klicksters who looked at the deck had the same reaction. Engineered ecosystems inevitably resemble one another because of their focus on the needs and wants of the people who work in them. Here are a few of the ways that HubSpot brings their culture code to life.

# ENGINEERED ECOSYSTEMS

HubSpot has a "no door" policy. All employees (including executives) sit in an open-seating concept office and rotate seats quarterly, so they can get to know one another better. As at Netflix, the company's policies reflect the implicit trust it has in its talent: There are unlimited vacation days, no set dress code, flexible hours, and there is a free beer fridge and game room.

The company demonstrates its core values of transparency and trust in myriad ways. An internal wiki adds a level of what Shah calls "extreme transparency," containing everything from board meeting notes to a weekly post about Shah's thoughts about the future of the company, interesting opportunities, and problems that need to be solved.

In 2011, Shah and cofounder Brian Halligan formalized a program that enabled employees to test their entrepreneurial ideas. Its first seed was planted in 2008, when Pete Caputa, a sales rep, pitched an idea for a reseller channel to supplement HubSpot's direct-to-consumer sales model. Halligan didn't like the idea, but Caputa was so persistent that Halligan finally told him, "If you want to do it so bad, start doing it nights and weekends and show us this will work." Caputa was up to the challenge, and the numbers were so positive that it became his full-time job. Today he has a team of thirty people, and his idea accounts for 20 percent of the company's new business.

HubSpot's program includes a three-step process: Alpha, Beta, and Version One. When an employee has a new idea, they can go directly into Alpha phase and start working on it nights and weekends without approval or permission. In the Beta phase the idea is presented to management, and if it looks financially feasible, receives development and people resources for three months to see if it gains traction. If that phase is successful, the project graduates into Version One and becomes a part of HubSpot's business. As of 2011, six Version One projects had been successfully implemented, and 30 employees out of 260 were working on projects.

Not all the projects are successful. "Frankly, most of them fail," said Halligan. "It's sort of like the success rate of a venture fund. But the employees tend to just go back to their day job, think of something new, and pop up with another idea." Halligan isn't bothered by failure; he wants employees to be constantly learning and trying new things. "We try to attract employees who fight conventional wisdom. Part of creating this environment of innovation is making the organization decentralized and flat," he said. "We want to empower the edges of the organization, and we want to let people who really understand our customers make decisions. Now they can."[33] Since its founding in 2006, HubSpot has grown by 6,000 percent, its customer base increasing from a few hundred to more than five thousand. Its focus on talent-driven performance has much to do with its success.

## INNOCENTIVE: LIKE OIL AND WATER

InnoCentive is another example of a company that is embracing the principles of the social Web. The company has built an open-innovation crowd-sourcing platform on which companies can tap into a network of diverse communities and problem solvers to tackle some of their biggest challenges.

InnoCentive recognized that the notion that all needed knowledge can be found within the walls of the corporation is outdated and inefficient. In today's world, someone somewhere always has the answer, so why not tap into that knowledge network? Inno-Centive built a community of 260,000 individuals from more than two hundred countries who solve problems in various disciplines, including business, chemistry, IT, food and agriculture, life sciences, math and statistics, and physical sciences. Its clients include Procter & Gamble, Dow AgroSciences, the Rockefeller Foundation, and even NASA.

Clients post challenges on an open innovation marketplace and set a prize for the person or team who can offer a solution. Those solutions often come from the unlikeliest of places. Take John Davis, an InnoCentive Solver from the United States who applied his expertise in the concrete industry to come up with a creative solution for the Oil Spill Recovery Institute (OSRI). They had developed a way to freeze oil and water into a viscous mass on oil recovery barges and now needed a way to separate the two substances. Davis had no oil industry experience but recognized that the same tool that uses vibrations to keep cement in liquid form during mass pours could also be used to prevent the oil from freezing, making it easier to extract and separate the materials. "Within the oil spill response industry there are a limited number of people to work on these problems," said Scott Pegau, the research program manager of OSRI. "If this challenge were easily solved by the people within the industry, it would have been solved earlier. I'm fascinated to see that our winning solution uses related technology found in the concrete industry. We would never have found this through our regular RFP process."[34] Davis collected $20,000 for his solution and helped Pegau and his team save potentially hundreds of thousands of dollars in research, not to mention pioneering a solution that will have a positive impact on the environment.

In 2006, InnoCentive partnered with Prize4Life to offer a

$1 million grand challenge for anyone who could find a biomarker to measure the progression of ALS. Five years later the prize was awarded to Dr. Seward Rutkove, who had successfully validated a clinically viable solution. As of 2012, more than $35 million in award money has been posted on the site. InnoCentive is an interesting case, because it enables companies with traditional hierarchies to reap the benefits of informal networks. It acts as a bridge between traditional and nontraditional models, generating solutions for some pretty big challenges along the way. Companies are also embracing this approach to innovate on some of their core technologies—recall the Netflix Prize discussed earlier.

 **Try this now!** Check out Kaggle.com, a Web site that helps organizations run contests to solve any data- or analytics-related challenges.

## BERLITZ: THE TOWER OF BABEL

By leveraging the power of the social Web, large companies can open up new channels of communication and innovation. Founded in 1878 in Providence, Rhode Island, the Berlitz Corporation is now recognized as a global leader in delivering language instruction to businesses, institutions, and individuals in more than seventy-five countries. The organization, which is currently owned by Benesse Corporation, counts more than twelve thousand instructors and employees around the world.

As with all global companies, managing various markets can be a challenge. Berlitz's initial approach had been for each geographic region to have its own separate, internal Web site, but the company soon realized that it had created separate ecosystems that were siloed from one another, preventing the free exchange of information and ideas across regions. The same mistakes were being repeated and time and resources were being wasted as one team tackled an issue that another team had already solved.

Much in the spirit of UPS's ORION and Klick's Genome, Berlitz built a global intranet platform called Smart Place to Accelerate Community of Excellence (SPACE) to develop its analytical sixth sense while empowering its employees to pool expertise and brainpower to tackle some of their strategic challenges. SPACE's features embraced many social Web technologies, including social networking profiles, instant messaging, tagging, wikis, blogs, file-sharing capabilities, and the ability to form self-organized online groups.

Yukako Uchinaga, Berlitz's CEO, was quick to see how the platform could have a tangible impact on the business's performance. "With SPACE, we can collaborate more quickly and more efficiently at a deeper level to foster innovation and see our work in a new light," she said. "Harnessing the collective wisdom of our workforce will be the key to success in business and employee satisfaction."[35]

Berlitz's leadership recognized that connection was essential to both internal and external stakeholder satisfaction; that is to say, to both customers *and* talent. Implementing SPACE has helped the company bring products to market faster, thanks to the faster feedback loops that commenting, tagging, and rating features provide. Troubleshooting occurs faster, because each region now has access to their global network of colleagues, enabling much larger groups of people to collaborate.

With its improved data sixth sense, Berlitz can better identify the products that are the most effective in certain markets. Much of that data is ambient digital body language left behind by activity on SPACE. Those digital footprints—the resources that are most often downloaded, the conversation threads that have the most comments, or the ideas that get the highest ratings—are the quantifiable output of the Berlitz talent pool, in which their experiences and opinions are codified. Much as with Klick's Genome, ambient data gives Berlitz's leadership team incredibly valuable insights that would be too costly and time consuming to collect manually.

SPACE has given Berlitz the capability to be more agile, connected, and global. By embracing the consumerization of IT, the company has empowered its sixth sense, allowing it to release better products and increase its rate of dialogue, collaboration, and problem solving.

## LISTEN, LEARN, AND GET OUT OF THE WAY

The companies we've talked about in this chapter all have two Decoded traits in common: First, they used the collaborative, meritocratic, and flexible nature of the consumer social Web to empower the talent within their own organizations and to creatively solve the challenges that their businesses were facing. HubSpot's transparent wiki makes sure everyone in the company is aligned around the same vision, and its Alpha, Beta, and Version One program gives employees the freedom to try new things without being entangled in corporate bureaucracy. Intuit's formalized innovation platform helped people find colleagues who could support their idea, even if they were in other countries, business units, or had different job descriptions. InnoCentive recognized that the Web is a vibrant ecosystem of ideas just waiting to be tapped. They knew that solutions often come from the unlikeliest and most unrelated of industries. They saw the value in harnessing that creativity, and the results have helped companies implement solutions they would have otherwise missed.

Second, they all place a tremendous value on developing and retaining their talent. HubSpot's unlimited vacation days policy shows staff that the company trusts them to manage their own time. Intuit's 10 percent passion project policy encourages talent to pursue and develop their own interests, resulting in the creation of successful products and initiatives. InnoCentive's mentoring of their solver network ensures that members are constantly learning how to maximize the value of their contributions and negotiate IP agreements that are in their best interests.

As we mentioned in the previous chapter, these things are all reflective of the three main drivers of human motivation as emphasized by Dan Pink: autonomy, mastery, and purpose. When those factors are aligned, the easiest thing for managers to do is to get out of the way and let their talent tell them what's needed.

## SPACE AS CULTURE

Not every ecosystem is engineered because of the technological tools or cultural structure in place. Livefyre is a small but very quickly growing tech start-up headquartered in San Francisco's Union Square neighborhood. It helps companies such as Sony Computer Entertainment's PlayStation division, Condé Nast, Fox, Showtime, the *New York Times*, and the *Wall Street Journal* engage consumers through a combination of real-time conversation, social curation, and social advertising. Its site network powers one billion page views each month from more than fifteen million registered users, which is all the more impressive considering the company had just shy of one hundred employees when we had a chance to sit down and chat with Jordan Kretchmer, its founder and CEO, about how he very carefully engineers its ecosystem.[36]

Jordan is determined to keep out of the way of the culture that his people create every day. Unlike some of the other CEOs we have spoken with, Jordan very intentionally doesn't want to put any kind of tacit, implied, or implicit culture document in front of anyone. "I believe in hiring flexible, transparent, trustworthy, honest, passionate, autonomous people and then letting them do what they do best," he told us. With the notable exception of its meticulously designed office space, Jordan has chosen to engineer his company's ecosystem by doing the exact opposite. "I expect that we'll need to formalize some of our processes and approaches when we get to about 150 people, but I hope that the things we formalize will be the organic ones my team has developed."

The one exception, as noted above, is their physical space. Livefyre started out in a former art gallery that was extremely loud and filled with echoes. Although that made it difficult to work, Jordan loved the feeling of energy it created. When Livefyre outgrew it and had to relocate, he spent a long time looking for the right raw space he could use as a canvas to realize his ultimate vision: space as the template for culture. He found it at One Kearny, a unique building with a particularly unique shape. "I was looking for a space that narrowed at one end, because I really wanted it to be a focal point for all of the company's energy and excitement." The building is like a perfect triangle that has been stretched out on one of the points, with a bank of elevators in the dead center of the floor plan. Jordan saw an opportunity in a layout that others might find challenging, creating a space in which you can stand anywhere and see almost the entire floor and all of the awesome things going on without all of the noise and downside of their former home. "We managed to keep the feeling of excitement and hustle that I loved without the noise and distraction that was driving everyone crazy." The floor narrows to the single kitchen, which has become a very popular hangout spot. "Our office is designed to encourage people to collaborate in person as much as possible," he told us. From the banks of workstations to the low-slung couches to the glass-walled meeting rooms, everything was carefully assembled to encourage in-person contact. Although instant messaging isn't banned, people really do get up and find each other. During our hour-long chat in his office we observed at least six spontaneous huddles, as the team worked through problems.

Space can have a very significant impact on culture. Even the smallest details can become important over time, as can the ways that the space changes after the build-out is complete and the people move in. Jordan had selected a palette of grays and whites for all of the walls and carpet in order to provide a neutral but warm environment. When he questioned whether their chairs should be equally neutral or provide a splash of color, his architect opted for more gray. "The people are the color!" he said, which has stuck for them and become a central part of their belief in hiring, staffing, and growing.

Space as a framework for culture is also a well-known obsession for 37signals. After our conversation with Jason Fried, its co-founder and CEO, covered their new Know Your Company tool (see chapter 4), the topic turned to their now famous office. *Business Insider* published a photo walk-through when the office opened in late 2010, which quickly placed it on top software company office lists around the world.[37] Their own Web site also includes a tour, if you're curious to see what it looks like: http://37signals.com/office. Jason gave us the inside track. "Culture informed the design of the office, not the other way around," he explained. "Our culture is one of quiet, respect, and uninterrupted time to focus. You can't be productive if you're interrupted every twenty minutes, so we designed the office to follow 'library rules.' Everyone tries to behave like they're in a library, respecting that their colleagues are here to learn and are deep in thought. We try to speak in low voices or grab one of our mostly soundproof meeting rooms." Very few companies take the concept of space as culture so seriously that they look into the acoustic profiles of the materials used in their offices. They were also careful to consider the personal space around each team member. "Most companies, especially in tech, pile their people on top of each other. We wanted to make sure that there was lots of space to push your chair back, so everyone has at least ten feet behind them. We also wanted to make sure you wouldn't be distracted by people in your peripheral vision, so the seating is staggered." Jason was quick to point out that the company isn't always about quiet contemplation. Its culture is also very open, in that they blog, write books, and even open-source parts of their code. It wanted to celebrate that openness as part of its culture, so it designed a forty-seat theater into the office in order to be able to host community events and guest speakers to address its team and invited guests.

Since 37signals has been in the space for a few years, we asked if it has had any impact on the culture. Jason's answer was quick: "Our space has helped to sustain our culture, but it hasn't changed it." That sounds like the perfect marriage of engineered physical and cultural ecosystems.

# THE END OF MANAGEMENT 1.0

Almost all of the tools we use in management—workflow design, project management, variance analysis, budgeting, financial reporting, performance appraisals, etc.—reflect yesterday's priorities. As noted in the Livefyre and 37signals examples above, even our approach to designing the spaces we work in is outmoded. In the early years of the twentieth century, Frederick Taylor and other efficiency consultants codified a set of processes that enabled semiskilled employees to do the same thing over and over again, with near perfect replication and ever-increasing productivity. In the 1920s, executives such as GM's Alfred Sloan refined the modern corporate bureaucracy, facilitating greater and greater scales of production and distribution of goods.

Standardizing jobs and establishing lines of accountability through hierarchy have formed the foundation for what Gary Hamel calls Management 1.0, an approach that "has rapidly become a global standard—and remains so to this day."[38] And yet Hamel goes on to describe the widespread frustration faced by senior managers as these practices fail to deliver the results they have been used to, thanks to unprecedented new market shifts.

For executives, the days of managing organizations using one-way conversations are over. "The old system of command and control—using carrots and sticks to exert power over people—is fast being replaced by connect and collaborate—to generate power through people," says Dov Seidman, the CEO of LRN and the author of the book *How*, in a 2011 *New York Times* article. "Now you have to have a two-way conversation that connects deeply with your citizens or customers or employees."

The military may well turn out to have the answer. Alberts's article on command and control recommends moving to a "self-synchronized" model in which soldier units could be formed based on the real-time conditions of the battlefield in order to optimize all available resources at any given moment. The command-and-control structure of these flexible units could be either centralized or decentralized, depending on each group's objectives. Alberts wrote:

> After thinking about what conditions needed to exist in order to make this approach effective (e.g. the establishment of intent, the sharing of intent, the sharing of the information required to assess the situation, and the appropriate delegation of authorities), these ideas coalesced into what we called Network Centric Warfare. Self-synchronization was perhaps the most controversial aspect of this new theory of warfare. Self-synchronization, and the information flows and collaboration needed to make it an effective means to an end, challenged fundamental notions of *Command and Control*.[39]

As we mentioned above, self-synchronization decentralizes the power structure by empowering the members of a unit to make their own decisions. This is much faster than waiting for orders from a hierarchal command that might not grasp the nuances of the situation. These smaller units are still focused on the ultimate objective, but they have more freedom to decide how to achieve it, based on a dynamic and often unpredictable environment.

Organizations are facing the same issue. We have become a culture of process and checks and balances, drowning in an ever-growing sea of standard operating procedures (SOPs). As we've noted time and again in these pages, the traditional approach to risk management has been to identify problems after they've happened, conduct postmortems to determine root causes, and then create new prescriptive checklists and procedures to avoid repeating that same misstep in the future. Today's increased complexity, which requires more frequent check-ins and sign-offs from more and more people, induces sclerosis. Not only will this backward-looking approach fail to predict the new threats that are always emerging in the swiftly changing marketplace, it prevents organizations from moving forward at all.

# RADICAL OPENNESS: THE NAKED TRUTH

The rate of change often outpaces our ability to understand all of the complexities and trade-offs it leaves in its wake. Disrupting the traditional approach to risk management is only a good thing if the new approach achieves faster execution without a significant increase in risk. Although we may all dread airport security lines, few of us would do away with them altogether.

Many of the trends we've looked at throughout this chapter, from the consumerization of IT to the rise of the social workplace, are fundamentally changing the nature of the role of employees, the level of trust we put in them, and the types of risks they open us up to. Employers must, for example, adjust to putting their reputations in the hands of their talent—whether they like it or not. Social media has added a level of transparency to our lives, and that exposure is bleeding into the workplace.

Companies are already more open than they realize: Their organizational charts and hierarchies can be seen on LinkedIn; employee sentiment can be tracked on Twitter; and insiders' views of corporate governance, policies, and hiring practices are posted on sites such as Glassdoor. Social media sites are not just windows but mirrors—and you might not like what you see. As technology futurist Don Tapscott points out, "If you're going to be naked, you better get buff."[40]

Thanks to social media, your talent are your de facto spokespeople. What they say and do—even in their personal time—can have a significant impact on your company.

That was the case for James Andrews, a former vice president at Ketchum Advertising.[41] Back in 2009, Andrews tweeted his distaste for Memphis, Tennessee, saying, "True confession but I'm in one of those towns where I scratch my head and say I would die if I had to live here!" Unfortunately for Ketchum, Memphis was the hometown of one of its biggest clients, FedEx, which knew that Andrews was there to present on (ironically) digital media. A FedEx employee noticed the tweet and forwarded it to FedEx marketing executives, who were none too pleased. Andrews apologized. "Two days ago I made a comment on Twitter that was the emotional response to a run in I had with an intolerant individual," he posted on his blog. "The tweet was aimed at the offense, not the city of Memphis. Everyone knows that at 140 characters Twitter does not allow for context and therefore my comments were misunderstood. If I offended the residents of Memphis, TN, I'm sorry. That was not my intention. I understand that people have tremendous pride in their hometown." Ketchum also issued a corporate apology for Andrews's "lapse of judgment," saying, "We've apologized to our client. We greatly value this long standing client relationship. It is our privilege to work with them." FedEx accepted the apologies, and the gaffe was smoothed over. FedEx spokesperson Jess Bunn said, "Mr. Andrews made a mistake, and he has apologized. We are moving on."

Andrews underestimated the extent of FedEx's online community, the speed of its response, and the passion that would drive it to escalate this issue to the company's senior team. It was the internally driven equivalent of the external channels and platforms that he was supposed to help build between FedEx and its customers. This example highlights just how much the principles of the social Web are already impacting employee behavior. Much like the recalibration of expectations that we outlined previously, employees are savvy about digital tools and won't be shy about blasting your organization for a perceived misstep—both internally and externally.

 ## On the Horizon: Reputational Currency and Internal Free Markets

Reputational risks and buffness (or the lack of it) aside, this is a pretty awesome time to be alive. Our roles as consumers, family members, lovers, and friends have already been radically reshaped. Everything we've talked about so far has the power to do the same for the way we manage, lead, and work.

*The Decoded Company* might have seemed futuristic up till now, but everything we've focused on is already in practice today. As we near the final chapter, we thought we would have a little fun and share some of the visions brewing in our crystal ball. Here's a look out to the horizon, toward where we think this might all be going.

At its most basic level, the goal of any business is to organize its people toward productive means. Thanks to our ability to gather and apply data, we have many more new options for the management of human potential than we've ever had before. Though we're still a ways away from implementing all of their features, engineered ecosystems are already tackling tomorrow's business challenges. Compare the vision below with the traditional hierarchical organization and you'll see how many advantages it brings to the table. We're not quite there yet, but our ability to gather and explore data is only going to increase and with it our ability to creatively apply new ways to maximize productivity and revenues.

Traditional accounting systems made sense when businesses were dominated by factories and assets, but they weren't designed to account for the sale of strategic or creative output or any other form of thinking. When your clients are paying for your people's thoughts, then your most valuable assets become the people who can produce the highest quality work for you. If you're selling people's time, then your top performers' reputations are much more predictive of their future billability than anything an accounting system would track.

Once we acknowledge that we're in the idea business we can begin to design better structures and systems for ourselves. One interesting new system involves the application of a data-powered reputation currency that can add a new layer to basic time billing. If we could use ambient data to understand each team and individual on a granular level, then we would be able to generate a value for their time that would form the basis of an internal free-market economy.

For example, you might have a Team A within your organization that has a reputation for very fast turnarounds that need revisions; Team B, in comparison, is very thorough and steadfast and takes longer but delivers a much cleaner product. Depending on the profile of the client who engages with the company, these two teams are not interchangeable. A situation might call for Team A's speed or Team B's thoroughness. The point is that, now armed with factual data, we can make the right decision about which team to assign to the project, because we understand the distinctive contributions that each makes to the organization as a whole.

If each team or individual worker develops a comprehensive profile that is linked to their internal currency value (which is based on the value of the work they do and not the number of hours it takes them to complete it), then suddenly you have the pieces in place to turn your organization into a free-market economy. When a client project comes in, various teams can compete for it, ensuring the benefits of a diversity of proposals and solutions. Instead of having the client assigned to one specific team, a decision generally driven by organizational structure or availability, we now have the opportunity to match these proposals with the client's specific needs, ensuring a more accurate match.

In the long run you reap the benefit of keeping your rock-star talent engaged and motivated, since they effectively become micro-business owners who have the autonomy to recruit others to their cause, bid for projects, and spend their budget however they see fit. Sticking people into rigid, inflexible teams inevitably produces boredom and restlessness. The internal free market is a hybrid approach that combines the best of both worlds. It's an excellent alternative for those people who enjoy the freedom of managing their own time and projects without having to worry about things like payroll, insurance, and paying the rent. They remain employees with all of the security and benefits that come along with that, but they get to craft their own approach to winning internal business and your company gains the free market economy benefits of true internal competition.

We're already seeing this type of thinking applied online. One such example is eBay. The online retailer has millions of sellers who offer a variety of products. What happens when a buyer sees two sellers offering the same product for the same price? They go and look at buyer reviews. Each seller is graded on a scale of one to five on their accuracy in describing the product, their responsiveness to customer questions, their speed in shipping the product, and the price they charge for shipping and handling. Suddenly the two merchants start to look very different indeed. Their profiles allow customers to prioritize their needs and choose the vendor that best matches them. One buyer, for example, might be more interested in expedited shipping while another really values the time a seller takes to answer their questions. Each of these buyers can now pick the merchant that suits their needs. Although eBay provides the infrastructure, the online storefront, the e-commerce platform, and the reputation management tools, it's each vendor that decides what to sell and for how much. Ultimately their prices are regulated by the market, driven by supply and demand. These same principles can work inside an organization.

As businesses are forced to evolve and adapt, the monolithic models that dominated the corporate landscape for generations will give way to a diversity of approaches. Team units' experiments will increasingly act as a type of generational variance, helping to bring new best practices into the collective through a constantly iterative approach. Think of it as a kind of natural selection. Some teams will be faster and cheaper while others will be conservative and slower. It only takes a very minor difference (or mutation, in evolutionary speak) to help the business grow in a different environment. Over time, the teams that are the most successful will be the ones that can deliver the highest-value work to clients. These teams will create an internal demand for their services, and the organization will grow and adapt accordingly.

This model will provide a strong, natural advantage that will help organizations scale without losing the nimble responses they need to adapt to new technologies or competitors. Instead of simply applying received models from abstract management philosophy, Decoded businesses understand that the answers they need are embedded in their own DNA. The ambient data their talent produces is what allows them to read it.

We're already starting to see this in companies. Valve's totally flat structure is an interesting experiment in this type of internal free market. Valve's talent decides which projects they want to start or join. The company's internal ecosystem ensures that only valuable projects are pursued, since people must convince their colleagues to join them in their efforts. The company becomes an internal economy, with teams and projects vying for resources and support and creating a natural market for defining value. There are specific protocols for choosing which project or task to work on, but the company suggests that employees ask the following questions as they make their choices:

- Of all the projects currently under way, what's the most valuable thing I can be working on?

- Which project will have the highest direct impact on our customers? How much will the work I ship benefit them?

- Is Valve not doing something that it should be doing?

- What's interesting? What's rewarding? What leverages my individual strengths the most?[42]

Newly recruited talent is encouraged to engage with as many different people as possible within the organization in order to gain an understanding of the various projects under way. This dialogue is essential for team building and for ensuring the cohesiveness of the organization as a whole.

"Lots of people at Valve want and need to know what you care about, what you're good at, what you're worried about, what you've got experience with, and so on. And the way to get the word out is to start telling people all of those things," reads the company handbook. "So, while you're getting the lay of the land by learning about projects, you're also broadcasting your own status to a relevant group of people."

Once a project has been proposed, interested parties sign on to work on it. These temporary multidisciplinary project teams are called cabals. Various roles within a cabal, such as team leads, also emerge organically, but the role is more about anchoring the details of the project in one central place rather than managing it. Employees join a cabal by rolling their desk over to it and leave it by simply rolling it away.

The roles that are needed to successfully execute a project vary. It's common for teams to create job descriptions for the life of the project, in order to ensure that everyone involved has clarity and that expectations for deliverables are aligned. Once the project is over, the team's informal structure dissolves, as individuals either join other projects or launch their own. Flexibility is the key, and if a team changes its objectives during a project, team members can easily assume new roles, unhindered by the hierarchical structures that might have otherwise slowed them down.

This flexibility naturally fosters an internal culture that is driven by curiosity and experimentation. "Nobody has ever been fired at Valve for making a mistake. It wouldn't make sense for us to operate that way," reads the handbook. "Providing the freedom to fail is an important trait of the company—we couldn't expect so much of individuals if we penalized people for errors." All mistakes, even those that are costly to the company or that produce a public, consumer-facing failure, are categorized simply as an opportunity to learn by testing out assumptions in the real world. "Never be afraid to run an experiment or to collect more data," the book continues. "If something totally unexpected happens, try to figure out why."

## SELLING CHANGE

Many of the examples in this chapter happened because the leadership team had already bought into the concept. Most of you unfortunately aren't in the position to just cause change to happen without needing to sell someone on the idea first. In the interest of arming you with some approaches that will help convince your managers and leaders, we asked Sunny Grosso of Delivering Happiness at Work about how they help their clients sell change. She shared three specific tips that she would give to one of her clients to sell the idea of happiness and culture:

1. **Start with a real-life case study.** It's hard to do better than Zappos if you're looking for a story about why engineering your ecosystem is so critical. The $2 billion in revenue and $1.2 billion acquisition price tend to get people's attention.

2. **Focus on ROI.** The business world is used to measuring things in terms of their investment. Some of the hard science around happiness has shown that it can lead to some pretty remarkable outcomes, like a 37 percent increase in sales, a 125 percent decrease in turnover, and a 300 percent increase in innovation. There's a Happiness ROI Calculator on the Delivering Happiness at Work site that can give you some idea of your potential ROI.

3. **Finally, appeal to common sense.** We're all human at the end of the day. Once you've introduced the precedence through your case study and painted a vision of the future through your ROI calculations, you can appeal to our shared human nature. Think about how many hours a day you spend at work. Wouldn't you like to be happier?

Sunny also pointed out that there are times when you're just not going to be able to sell your ideas, or when you might want to get a little more established before trying. In those cases, consider a "me or smaller we" approach (as recommended frequently in this book) by starting with personal change or with a smaller team that you directly influence before taking on the whole company.

# CHAPTER SUMMARY: THE DECODED PATH

At the heart of a Decoded Company is the data-powered, talent-centric workplace. Using the wealth of data that surrounds us we are now able to better understand what drives our talent and to create work environments that keep them enthusiastic, engaged, and motivated. It's interesting to note that data, which has traditionally been considered impersonal and cold, in fact provides the key to building a warm and personal workplace. Providing the exact level of training, support, and incentives for each employee, respecting and acknowledging their individuality, and expressing a genuine, quantifiable appreciation of their work build morale, camaraderie, and loyalty like nothing else. From new metrics for measuring learning and challenge to engineering a mechanism that socializes best practices, data is the foundation we use to make some of the most important decisions about how we run our organizations.

Standardization is no longer the correct response for managing complexity. Today's top talent are demanding flexibility, autonomy, and a customized work experience, and they are getting just that in Decoded organizations.

In *Fortune* magazine's *Guide to the Future*, data management is a pivotal role of leadership. "The CEO of 2022 will have to manage a complex business of far-flung inputs," senior editor at large Easton writes. "From customers' and employees' tweets (or the 2022 equivalent) to all kinds of data persistently emitted from billions of phones, sensors, and other connected machines. Companies that can manage and mine all those bits and bytes stand to make a killing."[43] We agree, but with an amendment: The companies that can manage and mine all those bits and use them *internally* to empower and unshackle their talent will do even better.

Data is the key ingredient in the creation of deliberately engi-neered ecosystems that ensure that the right behaviors are re-warded and encouraged with speed, transparency, and precision. Companies that are able to embed the three Decoded principles (Technology as a Coach and Trainer, Data as a Sixth Sense, and Engineered Ecosystems) will be capable of rising to any challenge the market throws at them.

# DECODED TOOLBOX

## Ecosystem Engineer

A new role in the Decoded Company that focuses on the analysis, design, implementation, and maintenance of highly experimental corporate cultures that are firmly based on the practice of data-driven management.

## Klick Stories

An internal online channel for employees to show appreciation or give long-form kudos to colleagues, a sort of internal cultural case study.

## Klick It Forward

A new take on CSR that focuses connecting charitable efforts and employee workflow. Employees who perform well get rewarded with the opportunity of contributing to their favorite cause.

# DECODED EXPERIMENTS

Engineered ecosystems are something that every manager should be obsessed with. Check out decodedbook.com/engineered-ecosystems for more resources.

## Ecosystem Engineer

As we stated in the chapter, the ecosystem engineer should manage your concierges. The main goal of the ecosystem engineer is to actively build the cultural differentiators that will separate you from your competitors. Here is a sample job description based on the one we use at Klick:

- We are looking for someone to champion our culture. We want a champion for our culture. Someone who will ensure that culture grows the right way, that the wheels are greased, and that we're future-proofed for tons of growth. You won't be alone. You'll be leading a team of communications, learning, and talent development concierges to provide bespoke solutions to our entire staff to make sure they're able to grow in all the right ways. Some specifics:
  - Define, deliver, and maintain the Klick philosophy.
  - Ensure that Klick's culture continues to attract the top talent.
  - Ensure that Klick is a place where the best talent can do their best work.
  - Architect and oversee:
    - performance management
    - management philosophy
    - the leadership pipeline (succession planning)

- learning and development
- communications (internal and external) and awards programs

## Klick Stories

Once you have a kudos program going (see the last chapter), taking some of those short messages of thanks and expanding them into a couple of paragraphs is a piece of cake. The idea is to build a repository of stories that capture the best part of your company's culture and talent. Everyone is so busy these days that in many cases some of the greatest stories end up forgotten if they aren't written down and shared.

- Organize and highlight stories using a #stories tag and seed some of the first examples yourself to get the program going.

- Ask one person every week to write up a story to share with the team.

## Klick It Forward

There are many ways that you can reward performance with acts of social good. The easiest way to start is with a monthly process. Determine the criteria that you want to promote, pick the top-five performers (or your top performer, depending on the size of your team), and give them the opportunity to choose a cause.

- Check out charity Web sites such as charitynavigator .org to help identify trustworthy charities to support that are working on the causes you care about.

- Once the causes have been selected, keep track and measure each contribution in order to report on all the accomplishments at the end of the year.

For more great ideas and suggestions as to how you can start cultivating the type of curious, productive, and happy talent required to help your company become Decoded, come on over to decodedbook.com.

# DECODED SCORE: ENGINEERED ECOSYSTEMS

Answer the following yes/no questions below and fill out your score. Give yourself 1 point for each yes and 0 points for each no, for a best possible score of 4. At the end of the book you'll be able to use your score as a part of a detailed decoded assessment to get even more insights on how to embrace the decoded philosophy.

1. Do you understand your own people as well as (or better than!) you do your customers?

2. Do you deliberately and intentionally engineer your company's culture (rather than simply let it happen)?

3. Do you put your people above your customers and your customers above your profit?

4. Have you created a center of gravity for your industry's best talent?

Engineered Ecosystems score: _____

# CHAPTER 6: GETTING STARTED

Congratulations! Finishing this book was the first (and maybe even most) important step on your journey toward being Decoded. Hopefully some of the ideas we've shared have stuck in your head and inspired you to start experimenting and sharing within your organization. Even better, we hope that you've joined us on de codedbook.com and become an active part of the movement.

We've shared our thinking with a lot of people along the way to getting this book published, many of whom have asked how they can apply it within their own companies. There isn't a single answer to that question—every company is different—but we have developed some useful tools to get you started.

## STEP 1: TALK WITH YOUR TEAM

The best way to get started on your decoded journey is to talk to your team about what you've just read. Give them a copy of the book, and use the questions included at the end of each of the chapters to kick-start a conversation about why becoming De-coded is such an essential skill for your organization. This will lead to increased buy-in and more support for the experiment that you're planning on conducting. Check out www.decodedbook .com/getting-started for more resources.

## STEP 2: THE DECODED SCORE ASSESSMENT

Joel Spolsky, a legendary software CEO from New York, wrote an infamous blog post in which he created the equally infamous Joel Test for software quality.[1] The test measures software companies on twelve attributes, ranging from whether they keep their source code in a source control system to whether coders have quiet working conditions. Candidates can use the Joel Test to evaluate whether a company they are considering joining is worth the effort, while prospective clients can use it to assess their vendor options.

In the spirit of the Joel Test, we have developed a superquick Decoded assessment. We recommend that you take this test now and then repeat it in six months, after you've started experimenting, so you can measure your progress. Repeat the test regularly, so you can maintain a sense of your advancement.

If you've been answering the questions at the end of the related chapters, you've already got the numbers in place, just fill them in below and you can start to plot your graph. If you haven't, don't worry; we've included them again, just in case.

The test is simple: Three principles are necessary for building your Decoded Company, and so there are three scores that make up the assessment. Give yourself 1 point for each yes and 0 points for each no, for a best possible score of 4 points per section, or 12 points in total. Plotting the scores on the graph we've provided gives you your shape. A fully Decoded Company would look like this:

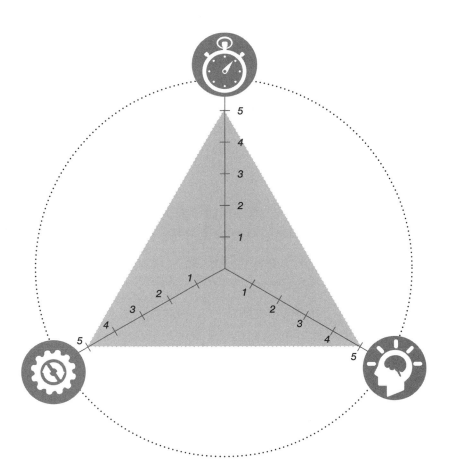

 Technology as a Coach and Trainer

1. Do you personalize your policies to each member of your team (rather than the traditional one-size-fits-all approach)?

2. Is your training delivered in just-in-time, just-enough interventions around teachable moments (rather than a monolithic, far-in-advance approach)?

3. Do your systems use historical data and pattern matching to coach and make recommendations (rather than a referee yelling "offside!")?

4. Are your reviews done on a weekly basis and driven through goal-oriented dashboards and automated agendas (rather than the much despised annual performance review)?

Technology as a Coach and Trainer score: _____

 ## Data as a Sixth Sense

1. Do your people make decisions based on data and evidence (rather than purely on emotion and gut feel)?

2. Are your people highly data literate (rather than highly steeped in management philosophies)?

3. Do you collect and analyze ambient data (rather than self-reported data)?

4. Have you found ways to quantify and record organizational gut feels in real time (rather than in historical snapshots and backward-looking postmortems)?

Data as a Sixth Sense score: _____

 ## Engineered Ecosystems

1. Do you understand your own people as well as (or better than!) you do your customers?

2. Do you deliberately and intentionally engineer your company's culture (rather than simply letting it happen)?

3. Do you put your people above your customers and your customers above your profit?

4. Have you created a center of gravity for your industry's best talent?

Engineered Ecosystems score: _____

Here's a blank graph to plot your new score on.

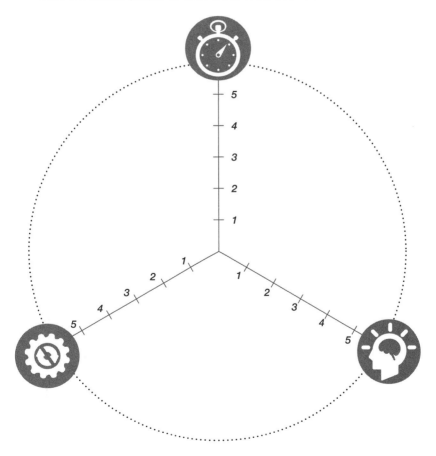

Repeat this test frequently as you start to make changes, and plot your scores over time to keep a record of your journey. It may be very informative to survey your colleagues as well. Don't forget the impact of personal biases on self-reported data!

# STEP 3: UNDERSTAND THE NOW

This book provides a path forward but you need to know where you're starting from. Understanding "the Now" is a prerequisite for forming experiments and making changes. This section provides a starter set of questions for you to answer that will provide clarity about your current state. If you're working through this with a team, we recommend that you use a collaboration platform, such as Google Docs, so that you can all work on the answers together.

*The Decoded Company* is fundamentally a book about talent, so we start with people.

- **Map out the roles within your group.** For each of those roles:
  - Map out the major activities that they are responsible for and identify those that need to be reconsidered (challenge everything—don't blindly accept that the way it has been is the way it should be).
  - Map out the systems that they touch and when they touch them.
  - Analyze the impact, frequency, effort, and time for each of the touch points.
  - Evaluate how they get visibility into what's downstream.
  - Evaluate how they spend their time (as percentages).

- Evaluate how they prioritize their work and how their manager would prioritize it.
- Evaluate the framework they have (if any) for making important decisions.

- **Map out all of your available data sources.** Remember to look for self-reported and ambient data, but give preference to ambient data.
  - Refer back to the systems identified in the previous step and look for any outputs they might offer.
  - Consider this as an aspirational rather than a current-state question. In that case, what data could you get access to?

- **Establish a Decoded lab.** Committees sit around tables and discuss things. Labs experiment and get shit done. Pull people from different groups who will need to be part of the transformation. If you're a really small company, it might just be you. If you're a massive company, it might be better to focus on your own group at first. There are almost always some people who feel passionately enough about this that they're willing to do it on their own time. Buy them lunch every few weeks and you'll have your lab.
  - Have all of your lab members take the Decoded assessment and compare your answers.
  - Define your goals: Are you striving to be a perfect 12 or are there specific areas you're particularly interested in improving?
  - As a starting point, use all of the inputs from the previous questions to create your dream-state dashboards.

- What would they look like if technology and implementation were no obstacle?
- How would they differ per role?
- How would you personalize them per individual/ manager?

## STEP 4: INSTRUMENT EVERYTHING

You need to instrument as much of your organization as you can, with a view toward collecting ambient data. Most of the systems you have in place are already doing this, but you may need to gain access to the logs or databases they create. Some of them won't have logging, so you may need to find other ways to instrument them. Start with your aspirational list of data sources above, and work through it until you have as many completed as possible.

It may be useful to start designing experiments at this early point, as we find that that often teases out missing sources of data or creates prerequisite self-reported data exercises that you need to complete (e.g., a survey of all employees to create a baseline).

A lot of our most useful ambient data comes from two areas of Genome: our ticket tracking system and Chatter, our social channel. If you have the ability to add similar features to your intranet, then you should do so as early as possible.

 **Try this now!** You may not have the ability to institute changes within your intranet (or you may not yet have one). If you're looking for a lighter-weight solution, even as a proof of concept, try some of the third-party providers of ticket systems and social tools. Using a third-party tool won't necessarily get you the customizability or data export you need, but it will be a fast(er) and cheap(er) way to get started.

The reigning social systems are Yammer (now owned by Microsoft) and Chatter (from Salesforce.com). A number of collaboration platforms, such as Jive, provide social tools but may represent too large a shift if you aren't already using them.

Check decodedbook.com/tools/tickets and decodedbook.com/tools/social for some lists.

# STEP 5: ESTABLISH EVIDENCE-BASED LEADERSHIP

Regardless of what level you occupy in the hierarchy—from big cheese right down to the mailroom—you're going to have to convince people that becoming a Decoded Company is a good idea. We've found this is best done through case studies, which is why we've included so many in this book. You might find ours useful, but in all likelihood you're going to need some internal cases of your own before you can get anyone to really believe that change is worthwhile.

Start by working with your lab to figure out some easy experiments that require little or no external buy-in and have quantifiable success metrics. It helps if you have a whole bunch of historical data about how those processes are working now, so that you can analyze it and establish historical metrics. Put your experiment in place, measure carefully, and report on the outcome.

Once you get past those naysayers and have everyone on-board, you're going to need to provide some training. Think of it this way: You're the pioneer leading a brave wagon train into the Wild West. You've convinced a bunch of folks to join you, and now it's up to you to keep them safe, so they don't catch dysentery or get bitten by snakes.

You don't have to teach them to be masters of the outdoors—they'll get there on their own in about ten thousand hours—but you need to help them through the early phases of your journey. Training and guidance are your best bet, at least until you have Technology as a Coach and Trainer up and running (you might have to be the coach for a while).

## STEP 6: HIRE TECHNOLOGY AS A COACH AND TRAINER

The legendary coach John Wooden unfortunately passed away in 2010. He left behind an incredible legacy of coaching advice that you can benefit from, even if you aren't managing a basketball team. Once you hire your technology, give it its Woodenized marching orders.

### Personalized Goals and KPIs

You won't find many people objecting to a replacement for the annual performance review, provided that you can prove your new system raises that very, very low bar. The first step is to replace your current goal-setting process (even if it's just with the people who report to you directly) with an approach that's driven by data and hooked into a dashboard they see every day. We've built this right into Genome because it's so critical to our ongoing success, and we highly recommend you do the same with your intranet homepage, if you can.

 **Try this now!** Again, you may not have the ability to institute changes within your intranet (or you may not yet have one). There are a whole bunch of third-party vendors that make dashboard software, which you may be able to use as a goal display system with your team. Check out decodedbook.com/tools/dashboards for a list of good, Web-based alternatives. If you're a very iPad-friendly organization, take a look at the Roambi app, which does a beautiful job of displaying and interacting with data and can be connected to a wide variety of data sources, including most enterprise Business Intelligence (BI) systems.

## Personalized News and Notifications

Next up is a look at your communication channels. How do you get "official" information into the hands of your people? Look for places where you can apply personalization in order to deliver only relevant content (e.g., news that affects your department, group, team, role, clients, geography, etc.), like we do with our In-Flight Reading dossiers that are automatically generated by Genome before a Klickster boards a plane (see chapter 4 for a recap).

Notifications are also a key part of this personalization. Is there a place where your people go to see important messages? Do they have outstanding tasks they need to complete? Has your coach identified a pattern it needs to draw their attention to?

We recommend your intranet homepage as a prime candidate for these feeds, so that your people will be sure to see them every morning when they log in.

## Teachable Moments

Coaching starts with identifying the teachable moments within your company. Work with your lab to review each of the activities you identified. Pull them apart into a series of steps and look for any that could have a training intervention applied. We provided a few suggested interventions in chapter 2 (buddy system, additional documentation and checklists, etc.), which you can supplement with ideas and tools relevant to your culture.

Adoption of your new coach will be accelerated if you can tie compliance or key training credentials into the system. It's sometimes useful to look for the regular official training sessions that people have to go through in order to earn certification or be recertified and then use your lab time to explore ways to change them from traditional, monolithic training into a series of interventions.

## Make It Beautiful

It's no accident that infographics have become one of the favored and highly viral forms of online content. Human beings respond very well to visual stimulation and can more easily understand complex concepts if they are well illustrated. Now that you have a number of data feeds and dashboards in place, start experimenting with their presentation. Your Decoded culture of experimentation shouldn't be limited to just your processes and activities—the visual output of your experiments can become experiments in and of themselves. You can get fairly far into this with some sketches and low-fidelity prototypes (even HubSpot-style on a whiteboard that everyone can see), but at some point you'll want to make the investment into working with an infographics designer who can work magic with your data.

## STEP 7: ENGINEER YOUR CONNECTED ENTERPRISE

We're assuming that you're a fairly avid use of the consumer social Web (at least of Facebook and LinkedIn), given your interest in this book. It's time to start using all the knowledge you've acquired to make your systems way more social. Look for opportunities to add profile pages, photos, etc. Work with your lab team to figure out what drives your use of social Web properties, and then look for ways to introduce the same elements within your company.

It's particularly valuable to focus on the aspects of your culture that you want to engineer. In Klick's case, for example, we put a lot of emphasis on our corporate social responsibility programs and giving back to our community. Our people put a high value on the meaningful work we do with debilitating diseases because it adds considerable purpose to their lives. We work hard to make sure that we quantify and communicate every aspect of those programs so that we can measure their effectiveness and continuously optimize their performance.

Use your experiments as an opportunity to increase your positive feedback ratio by implementing mechanisms that socialize and recognize innovations, great ideas, and individual or team contributions. This can be as simple as a weekly e-mail to staff or as sophisticated as an activity stream and rewards mechanism like we have with kudos and Klick Stories.

## STEP 8: FUTURE-PROOF

Because of their experimental cultures, Decoded Companies are resilient and adapt easily to change. There are a number of steps that you can take to make sure that your organization is as future-proof as possible, including:

· **Roll out a data warehouse and encourage your team to use it as a lab and playground.** We believe in fairly radical transparency, so our data warehouse contains every data point available to the company except salary information. You'll be amazed at the patterns that your people are able to identify when they have access to the data and the right tools.

· **Expand your data collection efforts to the offline.** You'll be able to achieve a considerable amount by focusing on systems that are already online, but you'll eventually run out of data sources to incorporate. Look for ways to measure and report on offline activities, like we have suggested with the meeting promoter score (see chapter 4).

· **Increase your team's data literacy and coding skills.** Provide your people with opportunities to increase their comfort and savvy with data. Offer some courses or other training in basic coding and scripting, especially for your data warehouse or predictive modeling/analytics, and encourage them to run their own experiments.

· **Deputize evangelists throughout your organization.** Find the people most excited by the Decoded principles and provide them with the tools and channels they need to spread the message. Reinforce it through continuous learning and make sure that their evangelism is a key consideration for promotions and awards.

## Share and Collaborate

The Decoded community is waiting for your questions and contributions! Ask for help and guidance, share the results of your experiments, and help drive the movement forward. Join us on decodedbook.com. Thanks for reading!

# ACKNOWLEDGMENTS

There are many, many people without whom this book would never have happened.

A very special thank you to the rest of the Klick senior leadership team without whom this—and Klick itself—would be impossible: Peter Cordy, Brian O'Donnell, Steve Willer, Lori Grant, Alec Melkonian, Mark Hadfield, Glen Webster, Glenn Zujew, and Steve Wagman.

A very hearty thank you to Adrian Morris, whose thoughtful and beautiful illustrations accompany the text. A very gracious thank you to Peter Flaschner, whose marketing insight has helped to get this book into your hands, and to Chris Winsor, who helped us figure out how to explain the thoughts in our heads. A carefully edited thank you to Arthur Goldwag, who carefully edited a draft of the manuscript. A very appreciative thank you to Jim Levine and the team at Levine Greenberg, who are the best agents a group of authors could ever hope for. And a very relieved thank you to Niki Papadopoulos, Kary Perez, Adrian Zackheim, and the team at Penguin Random House, who made this super easy. A very appreciative thank you to Willo O'Brien, who generously made some key introductions.

# ACKNOWLEDGMENTS

## LEEROM SEGAL WISHES TO THANK:

My loving sister and mother; my other family, the Klick team, which inspires daily in the relentless pursuit of awesome. Our incredible clients, for enabling this opportunity with their progressive thinking and confidence in our team.

A deep thank you to Ron Cohen, whose early read and excellent advice shaped this book immeasurably. An inspiring thanks to Kevin Kruse, Josh Linkner, and David Chilton, who shared their experiences as authors. An additional thank you to Michael Cooper, for providing us with the opportunity to apply some of these ideas at scale in the DREAM family of companies.

A special thank you to Glen Webster for suggesting the start of this project, as well as my closest friends Glenn Zujew, Ben Mulroney, and Zark Fatah, for being so understanding throughout the insanely busy last few years in completing this project.

Lastly, none of this would be possible without the hard work and dedication of D'Arcy Rittich, Benji Nadler, Andrew Woronowitz, and the rest of our development team, who collectively blow my mind on a regular basis. Thank you!

## AARON GOLDSTEIN WISHES TO THANK:

My loving wife, Christina, and my two kids, Sarah and Duncan. My close friend and partner, Peter Cordy. Rahaf—you know why. I would also like to acknowledge my friend, partner, and CTO, Steve Willer. Steve initiated this journey for all of us by introducing the ticketing system to Klick. His objective approach to problem solving has inspired so many of the ideas that have made us successful. None of this could have happened without you, Steve. Thank you!

## JAY GOLDMAN WISHES TO THANK:

My ever wonderful Bianca, whose love and support make everything I do possible (and Inna for giving me Bianca!). My precious Sophie, for being the reason I do everything I do. My dad, whose own thinking about the intelligent enterprise twenty years ago shaped mine beyond measure, and my mom, whose love of creativity has been equally impactful. I am perpetually grateful for being the sum of you both. My sisterling, Nikki, whose drive and successes inspire my own. Jason and Athena, for being sounding boards and keeping us sane. Leerom, Aaron, and Peter for giving me a true home at Klick and treating me as a partner from day one. And Rahaf, for being my Banterful.com companion. My parts of this book would never have happened without all of you.

## RAHAF HARFOUSH WISHES TO THANK:

The following people were essential parts of my creative process: My husband, Jesse, who puts up with living with a crazy writer. The irreplaceable Antoinette Schatz, who kept me sane, organized, and productive. My nephews Hani and Rami, for always making me smile. My family, Nabil, Hanan, and Rania, for letting me ramble endlessly about big data. My sister, Riwa, who punched my writing

# ACKNOWLEDGMENTS

block in the face. My lovely Twinsies: John, Niamh, Kalsoom, Kane, and Tara, who kept me company during my endless pursuit of research rabbit holes. And finally, much love to Jay, Leerom, and Aaron, who provided a constant supply of laughter, banter, and general mischief making.

# A VERY SPECIAL THANK YOU

Thank you to everyone at Klick for being such willing participants in this grand experiment.

Aaron Koeslag, Adam Bradovka, Adina Schwartz, Adina Zaiontz, Adrian Chang, Adrian Morris, Ainsley Sommer, Akhil Kohli, Albert Yi, Alec Melkonian, Alex Chesser, Alex Lai, Alexandra Schultheis, Alexey Davydov, Alexis Torreno, Alfred Oo, Alfred Whitehead, Alireza Ghorbani, Amin Teimoortagh, Amy Duong, Amyn Merchant, Andre Gaulin, Andrew Cain, Andrew Carreiro, Andrew Middlemas, Andrew Woronowicz, Angela Choo, Anthony Giorgi, Anthony Wong, Anuj Rastogi, Ari Baum, Ari Schaefer, Ariana Zhukova, Ariel Goldblatt, Armando Narvaez, Arsenia Aidemirska, Ashley Eng, Audra Paul, Audrey Simard, Baris Akyurek, Barry McKelvey, Benjamin Nadler, Beverly Marciano, Binoy Das, Birgit Cole, Blair Kelly, Brad Einarsen, Brian O'Donnell, Cam Bedford, Can Zhang, Caroline Fu, Caroline Trahair, Catherine Fish, Chad Buchner, Chad Davidson, Che Fehrenbach, Chelsea MacDonald, Chris Oliphant, Chrissy Kindle, Claudia Saikali, Colin Ballantyne, Colin O'Driscoll, Colin O'Young, Craig Wattie, Curt Basher, Cynthia Dahl, Damian De Shane-Gill, Daniela Kirilova, Danielle Anisef, Danielle

# A VERY SPECIAL THANK YOU

Silva, Danny Neiman, D'Arcy Rittich, Darko Antic, Darlene Doubert, Darrell deBoer, David Granatstein, David Maw, David Ng, David Pell, Deirdre Celotto, Derek Hockley, Derick D'Costa, Diane Au, Difei Dong, Dmitry Belopolsky, Dori Cappola, Doug Gavin, Drew Thompson, Ean Bowman, Edward Ntiri, Edwin Lee, Elias Plagiannakos, Elizabeth (Betty) Davis, Elliott Smith, Eric Yu, Erica Yao, Erick Dimistracopulos, Erin Bankes, Erwin Tumangday, Esther Supijono, Eugine Chandrasekara, External Traveler, Fabien Maronnaud, Fatim Sylla, Fiona McIlraith, Franklyn Pereira, Franz McNeill-Buettner, Gabriela Rank, Gail Cheung, Geoff Wyatt, Gerald O'Grady, Ghaith Chukfeh, Giuliano Caracciolo, Glen Reeves, Glen Webster, Glenn Zujew, Gourav Shastri, Greg Ragland, Greg Rice, Harshan Abeyagoonasekera, Heeyol Lee, Heidi Forman, Hilary Krupa, Hoshil Desai, Ian Engson, Igor Tarasov, Irfan Khan, Isli Gedeshi, Jacob Harasimo, Jacob Vintr, Jagdeep Singh, James Chong, James Fehrenbach, Jan Genoch, Jane Forbes, Jane Motz Hayes, Jason Cantor, Jason McGuire, Jason Miller, Jay Ignacio, Jeff Sun, Jeff Vogan, Jeffrey Postles, Jennifer Kim, Jennifer Wilde, Jenny Lynch, Jessica Horvath, Jessica Kot, Jevgenijus Popovas, Jillian Mojeski, Jim Davis, Joanna Fuke, Joanna Goldberg, Joanna Lancaster, Joanna Rainbow, Joe Dee, Johanna Maulawin, John Kent, Jonathan Day-Reiner, Jonathan Lee, Jordan Bedi, Joseph Chan, Juan Carlos Bejarano, Julian Lising, Juliana Miranda, Julie Batten, Jully Kim, Justin Patoka, Justyna Bochanysz, Kaitlyn Labow, Kamal Syan, Karen Lui, Karl Oanes, Karla Zamora, Kate Robinson, Keith Liu, Kelly Tanko, Kelly Yewer, Ken Bernardo, Ken George, Kevin Chong, Kevin Kelner, Kezia Payne, Kimberley Eng, Kimberly Amaral, Kristen Polito, Kristina Trompke, Lauren Kinnear, Lawrence Li, Lawrence Tepperman, Lena Filonovych, Leo Horie, Lester Sy, Lisa Louie, Lisette Viola, Lori Grant, Lucas Sokolowski, Luis Aguila, Marc Genesee, Marc LaPierre,

# A VERY SPECIAL THANK YOU

Marcel Bradea, Marcin Bogobowicz, Maria Taishidler, Marissa Scannura, Mark Ando, Mark Donaldson, Mark Hadfield, Mark Makuch, Mark Tiainen, Mark Vigna, Matt Geneau, Matt Hogan, Matthew Newelski, Matthew Woodruff, Max Gerlach, Maya Chendke, Meagan Hardy, Megan Yamamura, Mehwish Hussain, Mic Gillam, Michael Flenov, Michael Hambor, Michael Lee, Michael Melnick, Michele Perras, Mike Caron, Mike Kotevich, Mike Ott, Mikko Ertolahti, Ming-Li Kuo, Monica Bellini, Monica Chu, Montana McTiernan, Nancy Cantele, Narissa Russell, Natalie Sweet, Nate Haidle, Nelson Mark, Nick Avallone, Nick Morris, Nick Randazzo, Nick Seisl, Nicole Scannell, Oswald Mendonca, Pamela Kerr, Patricia MacPherson, Patrick Ryan, Pau Torres, Paul Chabot, Peter Cheung, Peter Cordy, Peter Flaschner, Peter Ho, Peter Pham, Phil Speed, Philip Rayos, PJ Stephen, Priya Rosario, Rachael Harrison, Rajaie AlKorani, Raquel Malaga, Rennie Renelt, Revision Control, Rey Crisostomo, Rhoda Dinardo, Rob Brander, Rodrigo Alvarado, Rommel Dizon, Ron Zahoruk, Ronak Desai, Sachiko Otohata, Sanjiv Sen, Sankar Uthayasankaran, Sarah Selgas, Scott Carpenter, Sean Feeney, Shahid Yaqoob, Sharmila Sivasankaran, Sharon Virtue, Shawn Yuan, Shelley Mohamed, Sheri MacIntosh, Shirelle Segal, Shivam Kalra, Shu Ito, Simon Greer, Simon Smith, Simon Withers, Stacy Auer, Stacy D'mello, Stephen Miller, Steve Costa, Steve Wagman, Steve Willer, Stewart Stevenson, Sultan Khan, Susie Choi, Tali Hasanov, Terri Tu, Theo Wardhaugh, Thomas Palm, Tim Lewis, Tim Plavac, Timur Adigamov, Tom Andersen, Tom Hrubes, Tricia Thomson, Tulika Prasad, Tyler Howe, Tyrone Murphy, Valeria Marques, Victoria Sherriff-Scott, Vincent Chen, Vincent Kozma, Vivek Nankissoor, Yhen Cheng, Zachary Schwartz, Zahid Dhanani.

Thank you to everyone who has joined our family since this book was published.

# NOTES

## Chapter 1: The Decoded Company

1. http://www.fourhourworkweek.com/blog
2. http://radar.oreilly.com/2011/09/building-data-science -teams.html
3. http://www.linkedin.com/skills/skill/Data_Science
4. http://www.managementexchange.com/video/gary-hamel -reinventing-technology-human-accomplishment
5. http://blog.prettylittlestatemachine.com/blog/2013/02/20/ what-your-culture-really-says
6. http://www.cio.com/article/730457/Data_Driven_Compa nies_Outperform_Competitors_Financially

## Chapter 2: Technology as a Coach

1. http://www.thehistorychannelclub.com/articles/articletype/ articleview/articleid/180/rise-and-shine
2. http://uk.news.yahoo.com/lack-sleep-impacts-gene-activity -054328491.html

# NOTES

3.    http://www.realclearscience.com/journal_club/2012/10/30/
      sleep_duration_associated_with_telomere_length_106393
      .html

4.    http://espn.go.com/page2/s/list/topcoaches/010518.html

5.    http://www.amazon.com/Coach-Woodens-Pyramid
      -Success-Playbook/dp/0830737936/ref=pd_bxgy_b_text_y

6.    http://www.facebook.com/statistics

7.    http://www.twitter.com/about

8.    http://www.linked.com/about

9.    http://www.youtube.com/yt/press/statistics.html

10.   http://store.nike.com/us/en_us/product/air-max-2013-id-run
      ning-shoe/?piid=29883&pbid=407978542#?pbid=407978542

11.   http://www.ecreamery.com/info.html

12.   http://www.chocomize.com

13.   http://techcrunch.com/2011/02/11/pandora
      -files-to-go-public

14.   http://www.knewton.com/blog/knewton/from-jose/2013/
      07/18/big-data-in-education

15.   http://bits.blogs.nytimes.com/2009/09/21/netflix-awards
      -1-million-prize-and-starts-a-new-contest/?ref=technolog

16.   http://www.eharmony.com/press-release/31

17.   Interview with Buster Benson (February 15, 2013)

18.   http://newsroom.accenture.com/news/rising-use-of-con
      sumer-technology-in-the-workplace-forcing-it-departments
      -to-respond-accenture-research-finds.htm

19.   http://techcrunch.com/2010/09/01/google-making
      -extraordinary-counteroffers-to-stop-flow-of-employees-to
      -facebook

20.   http://www.manpower.us/campaigns/talent-shortage-2013

21.   http://www.ted.com/talks/dan_pink_on_motivation.html

# NOTES

22. Interview with Dan Martell (May 2013)

23. Interview with Robert Laing (February 2013)

24. http://blog.gengo.com/why-your-startup-needs-a-visual
    -dashboard-2

25. http://data-informed.com/how-ups-trains-front-line-workers
    -to-use-predictive-analytics

26. http://www.fastcompany.com/3004319/brown-down-ups
    -drivers-vs-ups-algorithm

27. http://data-informed.com/how-ups-trains-front-line
    -workers-to-use-predictive-analytics

28. http://www.fastcompany.com/3004319/brown-down-ups
    -drivers-vs-ups-algorithm

29. http://www.bloomberg.com/news/2012-09-20/ups-makes-no
    -left-turns-in-quest-to-deliver-sustainability-q-a.html

30. http://iveybusinessjournal.com/topics/strategy/hr
    -strategies-that-can-take-the-sting-out-of-downsizing-
    related-layoffs

31. http://blog.kissmetrics.com/zappos-art-of-culture

32. Interview with Sunny Grosso (July 31, 2013)

33. Interviews with Brian Halligan (December 2012) and Andrew
    Quinn (January 2013)

34. Interview and e-mails with Glen Webster (November 20,
    2012)

35. http://online.wsj.com/article/SB10001424052970203721704
    577156704148493394.html

36. http://www.technologyreview.com/news/427790/ibm-faces
    -the-perils-of-bring-your-own-device

37. http://newsroom.accenture.com/news/rising-use-of
    -consumer-technology-in-the-workplace-forcing-it
    -departments-to-respond-accenture-research-finds.htm

38. Malcolm Gladwell, *Outliers: The Story of Success* (New York: Penguin, 2008).

39. Charles Duhigg, *The Power of Habit*: *Why We Do What We Do in Life and Business* (New York: Random House, 2012).

40. http://www.forbes.com/sites/bruceupbin/2011/12/13/five-new-management-metrics-you-need-to-know

41. http://www.sans.edu/research/management-laboratory/article/oneonone-meetings

42. https://www.manager-tools.com/docs/Manager-Tools_One_on_One_Basics.pdf.insert fig6

# Chapter 3: Technology as a Trainer

1. http://www.nice.com/sites/default/files/us-airways.pdf

2. http://www.crunchbase.com/company/spheric-technologies

3. http://techcrunch.com/2011/10/13/marketing-startup-flowtown-gets-swooped-up-by-demandforce

4. http://www.nice.com/sites/default/files/sprint_case_study_convert.pdf

5. Carl Hoffmann, Eric L. Lesser, and Tim Ringo, *Calculating Success: How the New Workplace Analytics Will Revitalize Your Organization* (Boston: Harvard Business Review Press, 2012), p. 105.

6. http://data-informed.com/analytics-converting-call-centers-into-insight-centers

7. http://data-informed.com/sprint-uses-call-center-analytics-to-troubleshoot-spike-in-service-times

8. http://www.theacsi.org/acsi-results/acsi-benchmarks-may

9.   http://online.wsj.com/article/SB10001424052702303410404
     577466852658514144.html

10.  http://www.nice.com/ja/sites/default/files/us-airways.pdf

11.  Keith Bachman, *Corporate e-Learning: Exploring a New Fron-
     tier* (San Francisco: WR Hambrecht +Co, 2000). Available at
     http://www.internettime.com/Learning/articles/hambrecht
     .pdf.pdf

12.  Bersin and Associates, http://www.bersin.com/News/Con
     tent.aspx?id=15596

13.  http://www.forbes.com/sites/bruceupbin/2011/12/13/five
     -new-management-metrics-you-need-to-know

14.  http://www.marketwire.com/press-release/clarizen-survey
     -finds-status-meetings-dont-help-work-get-done-1535250
     .htm

## Chapter 4: Data as a Sixth Sense

1.   Interview with Peter Arvai (June 2013)

2.   http://prezi.com

3.   Harvard Business Review Analytics Services, *The Evolution
     of Decision Making: How Leading Organizations Are Adopt-
     ing a Data-Driven Culture* (Boston: Harvard Business School
     Publishing, 2012).

4.   http://www.iacpsocialmedia.org/Resources/FunFacts.aspx

5.   http://knowyourcompany.com

6.   Interview with Jason Freid (August 2013)

7.   http://37signals.com/svn

8.   The increase can obviously not be attributted solely to pre-
     dictive analytics.

9.  David M. Rowell, *A History of US Airline Deregulation Part 4: 1979–2010: The Effects of Deregulation—Lower Fares, More Travel, Frequent Flier Programs* (The Travel Insider, 2010). http://www.thetravelinsider.info/airlinemismanagement/air linederegulation2.htm

10. Interview with Ben Waber (May 2013)

11. http://fourhourbody.com/contents

12. http://fourhourbody.com

13. http://quantifiedself.com/topics/personal-projects

14. http://tech.fortune.cnn.com/tag/data-scientists

15. HBRAS, "The Evolution of Decision Making."

16. http://www.sas.com/resources/whitepaper/wp_50769.pdf

17. Frederic C. Bartlett, *Remembering: A Study in Experimental and Social Psychology* (Cambridge University Press, 1932).

18. Explanation from this *Search 101* video posted by Google, starting at the 22m 03s mark: http://www.youtube.com/watch?v=syKY8CrHkck#t=22m03s

19. http://www.facebook.com/notes/facebook-data-team/anat omy-of-facebook/10150388519243859

20. http://marketingland.com/edgerank-is-dead-facebooks-news -feed-algorithm-now-has-close-to-100k-weight-factors-55908

21. http://www.whatisedgerank.com.

22. http://abcnews.go.com/Technology/facebook-relationship -status/story?id=16406245

23. http://www.sciencedaily.com/releases/2010/05/1005010 13411.htm.

24. http://media.wholefoodsmarket.com/fast-facts

25. http://www.fastcompany.com/26671/whole-foods-all-teams

26. Names have been changed to protect the reputation of cur- rent employees.

27. Howard Schultz, and Joanne Gordon, *Onward: How Starbucks Fought for Its Life Without Losing Its Soul* (New York: Hyperion, 1997).

28. http://www.forbes.com/sites/bruceupbin/2011/12/13/five -new-management-metrics-you-need-to-know

29. http://www.paulgraham.com/makersschedule.html

30. http://www.rescuetime.com

31. http://venturebeat.com/2011/09/20/people-analytics -google-hr

32. https://www.rescuetime.com

## Chapter 5: Engineered Ecosystems

1. http://blogs.valvesoftware.com/abrash/valve-how-i-got -here-what-its-like-and-what-im-doing-2

2. http://blogs.valvesoftware.com/economics/why-valve-or -what-do-we-need-corporations-for-and-how-does-valves -management-structure-fit-into-todays-corporate-world

3. http://www.valvesoftware.com/company/Valve_Handbook_ LowRes.pdf

4. http://www.worldwidewebsize.com

5. https://2012.twitter.com

6. http://tech.fortune.cnn.com/2012/01/03/future-guide-intro

7. http://www.forbes.com/sites/karlmoore/2012/05/14/ employees-first-customers-second-why-it-really-works-in -the-market.

8. http://www.hcltech.com/investors/fast-facts

9. http://www.business-standard.com/article/technology/ q-a-vineet-nayar-ceo-hcl-technologies-110073100086_1 .html

# NOTES

10. Howard Schultz and Dori Jones Yang, *Pour Your Heart into It: How Starbucks Built a Company One Cup at a Time* (New York: Hyperion, 1997).

11. http://www.loxcel.com/sbux-faq.html

12. http://www.hreonline.com/HRE/print.jhtml?id=533341164

13. http://money.cnn.com/magazines/fortune/best-companies/2012/snapshots/4.html

14. http://www.forbes.com/sites/erikaandersen/2012/01/18/why-top-talent-leaves-top-10-reasons-boiled-down-to-1

15. http://www.nytimes.com/2009/03/01/business/01marissa.html

16. http://www.businessinsider.com/8-habits-of-highly-effective-google-managers-2011-3

17. "Work.com—Sales Performance Management from Sales-force.com," October 16, 2013, Work.com. http://work.com

18. http://www.prnewsonline.com/CSRawardswinners2013

19. http://www.managementexchange.com/sites/default/files/media/posts/wysiwyg/mix_management_2_0hackathon_report.pdf

20. http://futureworkplace.com

21. http://www.dodccrp.org/files/IC2J_v1n1_01_Alberts.pdf

22. http://www.fastcompany.com/26671/whole-foods-all-teams

23. International Center for Outperformance, *Beyond Budgeting Case Study Whole Foods Market*, Dec 2008. http://www.slideshare.net/beyondbudgetingnet/beyond-budgeting-case-study-whole-foods-market-presentation

24. http://www.fastcompany.com/26671/whole-foods-all-teams

25. http://www.aabri.com/manuscripts/09288.pdf

# NOTES

26.  http://www.fastcompany.com/1779611/how-whole-foods
     -primes-you-shop
27.  http://www.hospitalitynet.org/news/4059396.html
28.  http://www.fastcompany.com/26671/whole-foods-all-teams
29.  www.valvesoftware.com/company/Valve_Handbook_
     LowRes.pdf
30.  http://www.slideshare.net/reed2001/culture-1798664
31.  http://www.psfk.com/2013/03/innovation-creativity-in
     -business.html
32.  http://www.slideshare.net/HubSpot/the-hubspot-culture
     -code-creating-a-company-we-love
33.  http://www.inc.com/magazine/201109/inc-500-brian
     -halligan-hubspot.html
34.  http://www.innocentive.com/innocentive-solver-develops
     -solution-help-clean-remaining-oil-1989-exxon-valdez
     -disaster
35.  http://www-01.ibm.com/software/success/cssdb.nsf/CS/
     CCLE-8E63C2?OpenDocument&Site=lotus
36.  Interview with Jordan Kretchmer (August 2013)
37.  http://www.businessinsider.com/37signals-office-tour
     -2010-11?op=1
38.  http://www.managementexchange.com/about-the-mix/
     manifesto
39.  http://www.dodccrp.org/files/IC2J_v1n1_01_Alberts.pdf
40.  http://www.ted.com/talks/don_tapscott_four_principles_
     for_the_open_world_1.html?quote=1722
41.  http://www.cbsnews.com/8301-505123_162-42740256/
     worst-twitter-post-ever-ketchum-exec-insults-fedex-client
     -on-mini-blog

42. http://www.valvesoftware.com/company/Valve_Handbook_
    LowRes.pdf

43. http://tech.fortune.cnn.com/2012/01/03/future-guide-intro

## Chapter 6: Getting Started

1.  http://www.joelonsoftware.com/articles/fog0000000043
    .html

# INDEX

# INDEX

# INDEX

# INDEX

# ABOUT THE AUTHORS

## LEEROM SEGAL

 Leerom is obsessed with building a culture that at-tracts and engages the industry's leading minds. He is deeply curious about how data can be used to improve the predictability and consistency of the business, while aiding in orchestrating all the moving parts. He is also passionate about health and doing meaningful work. Leerom began his career in health over nineteen years ago.

Since 1997, Klick has continued to grow profitably and be recognized as one of the country's fifty best-managed companies, fifty best employers, and fifty fastest-growing tech companies. Klick is a Branham Top 10 Healthcare IT Company and was named by the World Economic Forum as a Global Growth Company to watch.

Beyond his pursuit of growth for Klick, Leerom is most proud of his devoted family and his commitment to community involvement. Through the Klick Foundation, Leerom fully embraces every opportunity for community service.

## ABOUT THE AUTHORS

In 2004, Leerom was named to *Profit* magazine's Hall of Fame for being the youngest ever CEO of a Profit 100 Company. Leerom is a longtime TEDster and TEDMEDster. He is an active member of the Clinton Global Initiative and the Young Presidents' Organization. He regularly contributes to several publications, chairs various digital marketing boards and conferences, and is a member of the Advisory Board of the Digital Health Coalition.

## AARON GOLDSTEIN

Aaron is a founding partner of Klick, helping to drive the adoption of advanced technologies to increase the effectiveness and sophistication of our solutions. As chief operating officer, he helps orchestrate our multidisciplinary teams across all of our client portfolios and projects and draws on his love of complex systems to efficiently deliver marketing, learning, and operational solutions. He works to ensure we always use data to make evidence-based decisions. He is committed to providing clients with the maximum amount of flexibility so that our solutions can seamlessly integrate with existing technologies.

Aaron also drives our culture of collaboration, overseeing not only the production of the work but also all of the underlying infrastructure and systems that make it possible. He is obsessed with making Genome—our innovative operating system—maximally optimize every aspect of our operation.

# ABOUT THE AUTHORS

## JAY GOLDMAN

Jay has been providing a human side to technology for over ten years, as a technologist, user experience specialist, and visual designer. His career has been focused on the interaction between people and technology, and his insights have helped to greatly improve products on mobile, Web, and desktop platforms, including IBM DB2 and Mozilla Firefox. Prior to Klick, he was head of marketing for Rypple, a venture-backed start-up acquired by Salesforce in 2012. Rypple represents an entirely new approach to performance management, moving from monolithic, deeply hated, and extremely expensive annual reviews to feedback loops and coaching. Rypple powers the people management practice at Facebook, Kobo, Gilt, and Mozilla, among others. Jay is a managing director at Klick, focused on our innovation mandate and on exploring the opportunities in new channels and markets.

Jay has contributed to the *Harvard Business Review* and is the author of the O'Reilly *Facebook Cookbook*, one of the earliest books to explore the power of the Facebook Platform.

## RAHAF HARFOUSH

Rahaf is a digital foresight strategist and author who has a deep passion for exploring how technology is affecting the way we communicate, work, and play. As the cofounder of Red Thread, a consulting agency that provides clients with out-of-the-box thinking to tackle strategic challenges, she leads organizations across industries in understanding emerging technology trends and identifying, articulating, and acting on areas of strategic opportunity.

In 2012, Rahaf was recognized as a World Economic Forum Young Global Shaper. She is also a Global Ambassador for the Sandbox Network, a global community for exceptional entrepreneurs under the age of thirty. Rahaf is on the board of directors for Taking it Global and a member of the advisory boards for One-Leap.To, Enstitute, and Syria Deeply. She is a contributor to the *Mark News*, *The Next Web,* and *Techonomy.*

Formerly, Rahaf was the associate director of the Technology Pioneers program at the World Economic Forum, where she identified disruptive start-ups that were improving the state of the world. In 2009, Rahaf published her first book, *Yes We Did: An Insider's Look at How Social Media Built the Obama Brand,* about her experiences as a part of Barack Obama's New Media team during his 2008 presidential election campaign. Rahaf was also the research coordinator for the bestselling *Wikinomics: How Mass Collaboration Changes Everything* by Don Tapscott and worked with him in researching *Grown Up Digital: How the Net Generation Is Changing Your World.*

# LEEROM SEGAL

is the president and CEO of Klick. He has been named Entrepreneur of the Year by the Business Development Bank of Canada, won the Young Entrepreneur of the Year Award from Ernst and Young, been recognized as a Top 40 Under 40 by *The Globe and Mail,* and been named to *Profit* magazine's Hall of Fame as the youngest CEO ever to lead a Profit 100 company.

# AARON GOLDSTEIN

is a founding partner of Klick, helping to drive the adoption of advanced technologies to increase the effectiveness and sophistication of our solutions. As chief operating officer, he helps orchestrate our multidisciplinary teams across all of our client portfolios and projects and draws on his love of complex systems to efficiently deliver marketing, learning, and operational solutions.